"On its colonies the sun never sets,
but the blood never dries"

Ernest Jones, Chartist and socialist, 1851

About the author
John Newsinger is senior lecturer in the School of History and Cultural Studies at Bath Spa University College. His most recent books include *Orwell's Politics* (Macmillan, 2000), *United Irishman* (Merlin, 2001) and *Rebel City: Larkin, Connolly and the Dublin Labour Movement* (Merlin, 2004).

Acknowledgements
Thanks to Lorna Chessum and our sons, Jack and Ed; to Hannah Dee and Mark Thomas at Bookmarks; to Chris Bambery and John Rose for their comments and advice; to Christine Gardner and Robert Maisto for their hospitality; to my typist, Rose Senior; and to my colleagues and friends at Bath Spa University, in particular, Alan Marshall.

Bookmarks would like to thank Hazel Sabey.

THE BLOOD NEVER DRIED

A People's History of the British Empire

John Newsinger

bookmarks publications

To the Leicester Old Comrades: Chris Lymn, Mal Deakin,
Andy Wynne, Jim Tolton, John Peach and the late Ken Orrill

The Blood Never Dried: A People's History of the British Empire
John Newsinger

First published July 2006
Reprinted April 2010
Bookmarks Publications Ltd,
c/o 1 Bloomsbury Street, London WC1B 3QE
Copyright © John Newsinger

ISBN 1905 192 126

Printed by Melita Press
Designed by Bookmarks Publications

Contents

Introduction:
the blood never dried

IN 2003 Niall Ferguson published his *Empire: How Britain Made The Modern World*, a volume intended to capture the spirit of the times. Empires and imperialism were being celebrated as a duty that powerful states owed to their weaker brethren. This duty was to be put into effect with catastrophic consequences with the invasion of Iraq. Ferguson followed this bestselling volume with another one, *Colossus: The Rise and Fall of the American Empire*, establishing himself as a latter day Rudyard Kipling, urging the American ruling class to take up "the white man's burden".[1]

One problem with contemporary apologists for empire, however, is their reluctance to acknowledge the extent to which imperial rule rests on coercion, on the policeman torturing a suspect and the soldier blowing up houses and shooting prisoners. It is the contention of this book that this is the inevitable reality of colonial rule and, more particularly, that a close look at British imperial rule reveals episodes as brutal and shameful as in the history of any empire. Indeed, a case in point is the methods the British used to suppress the Mau Mau rebellion in Kenya in the 1950s. This is especially pertinent, because in a personal reminiscence Ferguson tells his readers that "thanks to the British Empire, my earliest childhood memories are of colonial Africa". His father worked for two years in Kenya after independence, but as he observes, "scarcely anything had changed...We had our bungalow, our maid, our smattering of Swahili—and our sense of unshakeable security. It was a magical time." Indeed, he still has "the carved wooden hippopotamus, wart hog, elephant and lion which were once my most treasured possessions".[2] Now this is, of course, all very touching but his "magical time" was only made possible by one of the most ferocious episodes of colonial repression in British imperial history which does not merit so much as a mention in his book. The Mau Mau revolt of the 1950s was put down with terrible brutality, the routine use of torture, summary executions, internment on a massive scale, and the hanging of over 1,000 prisoners. How seriously should we take a history of the empire that somehow misses all this? Hopefully this volume will serve, at least in part, as an antidote to Ferguson's work.

First, however, let us make clear what we are primarily concerned with here. Imperialism has two dimensions: firstly, the competition between the great imperial powers, competition that in the 20th century produced two world wars and the Cold War. This competition is the driving force of modern imperialism, and it has wreaked terrible damage on the world, consuming millions of lives. What this book is primarily concerned with, however, is not the relationship between the British Empire and its imperial rivals, but with the second dimension—the relationship between the imperial power and its conquered peoples. The best description of this relationship was provided by George Orwell in his novel *Burmese Days*, where he wrote that imperialism consisted of the policeman and the soldier holding the "native" down, while the businessman went through his pockets.[3] Of course, countries were not invaded and occupied just for reasons of economic exploitation. Strategic considerations were also an important factor, although these strategic considerations invariably involved protecting colonies that were of economic importance.

It is the contention here that imperial occupation inevitably involved the use of violence and that, far from this being a glorious affair, it involved considerable brutality against people who were often virtually defenceless. For too long the image of imperial conquest that has prevailed in Britain is that propagated by the 1964 film *Zulu*. This tells the epic story of a small band of British soldiers battling against overwhelming odds at Rorke's Drift (in today's South Africa) in 1879. The British fight with both courage and honour and emerge victorious, more because of their national character than their superior weaponry. What the film conveniently leaves out is

THE BLOOD NEVER DRIED

the subsequent slaughter of hundreds of Zulus wounded, clubbed, shot and bayoneted to death, some hanged and others buried alive.[4] This was and remains the reality of colonial warfare.

It is worth remembering that the much trumpeted "Shock and Awe" that the United States promised to inflict on Iraq in 2003 had been inflicted by the British on city after city throughout the world in the course of the 19th and 20th centuries. Bombardments that left hundreds dead, districts reduced to rubble, and populations cowed are hardly worth the notice of most historians. If it had been British cities shelled by an invader, the story would have been very different. How many readers, one wonders, have even heard of the British bombardment of the Indonesian city of Surabaya in November 1945? A battle that is still celebrated as "Heroes Day", a vital episode in that country's struggle for independence, is altogether unknown in Britain, the country that carried out the attack.

Once a country was conquered, imperial rule was maintained by force. Whatever the particular architecture of imperial rule, it always rested in the end on the back of the policeman torturing a suspect. Those who affect surprise at the excesses of Abu Ghraib need to be reminded that these are the inevitable and unavoidable consequences of colonial rule. The aim in what follows is to provide evidence of this.

The book is also concerned to celebrate, dare one say "glorify", resistance to empire. From the slaves who overthrew slavery in the Caribbean, to the Indian rebels of the 1850s, from the Irish Republicans who took up arms during and after the First World War, to the Palestinian peasants fighting against the British and the Zionists in the 1930s, from the Mau Mau in the 1950s to the Iraqi resistance of today, brave men and women have resisted empire. The book also chronicles the extent to which radicals and socialists in Britain organised, demonstrated and protested in solidarity with these resistance movements. While the Stop the War Coalition can legitimately claim to be the largest and most powerful anti-imperialist and anti-war movement in British history, it stands in an honourable tradition. It was in the 1850s that the Chartist and socialist Ernest Jones responded to the claim that while the sun might never set on the British Empire, similarly "the blood never dried". Anti-imperialists today stand in the tradition of Ernest Jones and William Morris, another socialist and fierce critic of the empire—a tradition to be proud of.

And what of those who support and glorify the British Empire?

What they have to be asked is how they would respond if other states had done to Britain what the British state has done to other countries. How pro-imperialist would they feel for example if, instead of Britain forcing opium on the Chinese Empire, it had been the other way round? What would their response be if, when the British government had tried to ban the importation of opium, the Chinese had sent a powerful military expedition to ravage the British coastline, bombard British ports, and slaughter British soldiers and civilians? What if, instead of Britain seizing Hong Kong, the Chinese had seized Liverpool and Merseyside as a bridgehead from which to dominate Britain for nearly a hundred years? What if further British resistance provoked another attack that led to the Chinese occupying London, looting and burning down Buckingham Palace and dictating humiliating peace terms? What if today there was an Imperial Museum in Beijing that still put on display the fruits of the Chinese pillage of Britain? None of this is fanciful because it is exactly what the British state did to China in the 19th century.

The British Empire, it is argued here, is indefensible, except on the premise that the conquered peoples were somehow lesser beings than the British. What British people would regard as crimes if done to them, are somehow justified by supporters of the empire when done to others, indeed were actually done for their own good. This attitude is at the very best implicitly racist, and, of course, often explicitly so.

Which brings us to the invasion and occupation of Iraq. The argument in this book is that while Tony Blair, Gordon Brown and the New Labour government might well have dispensed with just about everything the Labour Party stood for, as far as domestic politics are concerned, with regard to imperialism they are very much in the Labour tradition. This may well surprise many readers, but the contention here is that the evidence is overwhelming. Labour politicians invented a tradition of anti-imperialism for the consumption of Labour Party members, but that is precisely what it is, an invention. While many individual Labour Party members, or more likely today, ex-members, and some Labour MPs certainly have been anti-imperialists and believe in this tradition, the fact is that every Labour government has been concerned with maintaining Britain's imperial position and has engaged in colonial repression. The bombardment of Surabaya, for example, was the work of a Labour government.

THE BLOOD NEVER DRIED

Moreover, Blair's participation in the American invasion of Iraq was, as we shall see, little different from Attlee's participation in the Korean War.

While this book is in the main concerned with the British Empire's relationship with its conquered peoples, it does also attempt to explore the process of British subordination to American imperialism that has taken place since the Second World War. There is a danger today that this policy of subordination will be personalised as Blair's policy. While his distinctive style (a combination of dishonesty and sincerity) and his personal domination over a supine cabinet and the most contemptible collection of Labour MPs in that party's history certainly contribute to this appearance, the reality is that this subordination is institutional and systemic. While the 1945-1951 Labour government hoped for some sort of equal alliance with the United States, in the aftermath of the Suez invasion of 1956, both Conservative and Labour governments have aspired to a subordinate role in the American Empire. This remains the situation today and it will continue when Blair is gone. In opposing our own government, we are participants in the global fight against American imperialism.

This book is not a comprehensive history of the British Empire. It is instead a study of particular episodes, from the struggle against slavery to the struggle against New Labour's Iraq adventure today. This struggle will go on as long as capitalism and imperialism are still with us.

The Jamaican rebellion and the overthrow of slavery

IN OCTOBER 1736 a slave conspiracy was discovered on the Caribbean island of Antigua. This was an extensive plot that had the support of a large number of slaves, both African and Creole (Antiguan-born). The instigators were an African named Court and a Creole named Tomboy. Their intention was to blow up the governor and the planter elite at the annual coronation ball on 11 October. Tomboy, a highly skilled carpenter, had ready access to the ballroom. Gunpowder would be hidden in the cellar and when it was exploded a general uprising would begin. The whites would be destroyed and an African kingdom established. Unfortunately the ball was postponed until the end of the month. Tomboy urged that they should rise on the 11th regardless, but Court argued that they should wait and carry out the original plan. Court won the argument. While they waited, the plot was betrayed and the ringleaders were rounded up. For the planters the discovery was a terrifying shock. There were less than 3,000 whites on Antigua, living among over 24,000 black slaves. Moreover, the ringleaders were from among the most trusted slaves, artisans and plantation drivers. Aware of their vulnerability the planters responded to the conspiracy with incredible ferocity. Altogether 88 slaves were to be executed for their part in what the judges described as "that unparalleled hellish plot": five were broken on the wheel, including both Court and Tomboy, 77 were slowly burned to death, and six were gibbeted (hung up in cages to die of thirst and starvation).[1] One of the planters, Dr Walter Tullideph, wrote to his brother in London complaining that "we are in a great deal of trouble on this island: the burning of negroes, hanging them up in gibbets alive, racking them upon the wheel, etc takes up all our time".[2] All that put a stop to the slaughter was that the treasury ran out of funds with which to compensate the owners of the butchered slaves.

The punishments meted out in Antigua were not out of the ordinary at the time, although the numbers killed were somewhat excessive. In 1707 Hans Sloane had conveniently listed the punishments for a variety of offences. For rebellion, slaves were usually punished "by nailing them down to the ground...and then by applying fire by degrees from the feet and hands, burning them gradually up to the head, whereby their pains are extravagant". For lesser crimes, castration or mutilation ("chopping off half the foot") was the norm. And as for negligence, "they are usually whipt...after they are whipt till they are raw, some put on their skins pepper and salt to make them smart; at other times their masters will drip melted wax on their skins, and use very exquisite torture".[3] Such cruelty was intended as a deterrent, as a way of terrorising the slaves into submission. It was the only way that the heavily outnumbered whites could feel safe. Torturing rebels and suspected rebels to death was a wartime measure used in what was for the planters a permanent state of emergency. An 1811 manual on the management of slaves made the point that "where slavery is established, and the population of slaves outnumbers their masters ten to one, terror must operate to keep them in subjection, and terror can only be produced by occasional examples of severity".[4]

From this point of view, the Antiguan conspiracy can be seen as one episode in what historian Hilary Beckles has described as a "200 Years War" between slave and slave-owner in the British Caribbean.[5] It is with the concluding stages of this war that we are concerned here, culminating in the great slave revolt of December 1831 in Jamaica, "the Baptist War" that sounded the death-knell for slavery throughout the British Empire.

The sugar empire

The British Empire in the Caribbean was founded on the production of sugar on plantations worked by black slaves. It was part of the so-called "Triangular Trade", whereby British manufactures were carried to Africa to buy slaves, who were then shipped to the Caribbean, where they produced sugar for export to Britain. The plantation system itself had first been established in Barbados. When sugar production was introduced in the 1640s, there were some 6,000 slaves at work. By 1680 the number of slaves had increased to 38,000 and by the end of the century to over 50,000. This economic model spread to Britain's other Caribbean possessions, but in the course of the 18th century Jamaica emerged as the cornerstone of the system. By the 1790s Jamaica was producing more sugar than all the other British islands put together. In 1700 Jamaica exported 4,874 tons of sugar to Britain; by 1748 the figure had risen to 17,399, and by 1815 to 73,849 tons. The enterprise sucked in slave labour.

British participation in the Atlantic slave trade is arguably the worst crime in British history. Estimates of the numbers shipped to the Americas by all the slave-trading countries range from a low of 10 million people to up as many as 15 million. Whatever the figure for those shipped, some 2 million is a conservative estimate for those who died while making the voyage whether from illness, violence, starvation, suicide or whatever. Although it extended over four centuries, the trade was revolutionised by sugar production. Whereas 10,000 slaves were being shipped annually in the 1650s, by the 1710s the figure had risen to 40,000 annually and by the 1740s to over 60,000 annually, a figure sustained into the 1800s. Moreover, by the middle of the 18th century, Britain had come to dominate the trade. From 1690 until the abolition of the slave trade in 1807, Britain shipped, according to the available figures, 2,943,356 slaves. The actual figure is certainly over 3 million, but there will never be a final accounting.[6]

James Walvin has warned against a recent tendency to "sanitise" the slave trade by treating it as just another business.[7] With the triumph of market ideology in the West, this tendency has increased. As eminent a historian as Herbert Klein, for example, can deprecate the portrayal of the slave trade in "popular literature" and insist as a corrective that while "violence and death were a significant factor…the overwhelming majority of slaves did reach America". Moreover "despite the *atmosphere* of violence, the experience may not have been as psychologically damaging as some have claimed" [author's emphasis]. Nevertheless, to be fair, Klein does acknowledge that it is "undesirable and a basic fact of the slave trade" that millions of Africans were shipped "to America against their will" and that this was not done "to better their lives".[8]

THE BLOOD NEVER DRIED

Given Klein's somewhat pathetic encounter with the slave trade, it is worth quoting Walvin's rather more forceful judgement:

We need to recall that every African shipped across the Atlantic (and more than 11,000,000 Africans survived the ordeal) had been violated physically. They had been held in chains, often branded, kept for weeks on end in the most wretched seaborne conditions, and all under the nose of threatening weapons and crew...They were held subservient by white men, who reduced them to unimaginable levels of suffering, who threatened them with weaponry of the most fearsome kind and who appeared to bring inexplicable ailments and death to the slaves huddled in their own filth on the slave decks... The experience of the crossing was dominated by violence. Indeed, the whole system was violent in its very essence.

And, of course, for women slaves there was in addition, sexual harassment and rape.[9]

Slave resistance began immediately. According to John Newton, the captain of a slave ship who became an opponent of slavery, an abolitionist, it was always "taken for granted that they will attempt to gain their liberty if possible". He wrote of how:

one unguarded hour or minute is sufficient to give the slaves an opportunity they are always waiting for. An attempt to rise upon the ship's company brings an instantaneous and horrid war: for, when they are once in motion, they are desperate, and when they do not conquer, they are seldom quelled without much mischief and bloodshed on both sides.

It has been estimated that there was a revolt on a British slave ship every two years.[10] To meet the challenge, weapons were always trained on the slaves and attempts to escape or rebel were punished with considerable ferocity.

For the modern reader, the *Zong* affair probably demonstrates the callous horror of the trade most graphically. The Liverpool-owned slave ship was carrying 470 slaves from West Africa to Jamaica in 1781. So that the owners could claim for the loss of sick slaves on their insurance, the captain, Luke Collingwood, decided to throw them overboard. On 29 November the first batch of 54 were drowned, the next day another 42, and on the third day another 26. Ten more slaves threw themselves overboard, effectively committing suicide in what must have been circumstances of complete despair. Collingwood ended up in court not to answer charges of mass murder, but as part of the insurance claim. At the trial, in May 1783, the Solicitor General, John Lee, went out of his way to insist that "the blacks were property" and that consequently no murder had taken place. This view was endorsed by Lord Mansfield, one of the presiding judges, who concluded "that the case of the slaves was the same as if horses had been thrown overboard".[11] While the number of Africans Collingwood and his crew murdered was high, the important point is that his attitude was unexceptional. The case attracted considerably less attention at the time than it does today.

What of the regime that the slaves found themselves living under once they had arrived in the West Indies? John Newton made an interesting comparison between slavery in West Africa and in the Caribbean:

> The state of slavery among these wild barbarous people, as we esteem them, is much milder than in our colonies. For as, on the one hand, they have no land in high cultivation like our West Indian plantations, and therefore no call for that excessive unintermitted labour which exhausts our slaves; so, on the other hand, no man is permitted to draw blood even from a slave.[12]

What the slaves found in the Caribbean was "excessive unintermitted labour" which was absolutely dependent on the "drawing" of blood. Elsa Goveia provides an account of the plantation slaves' working day towards the end of the 18th century. They would begin work at dawn and carry on until 9 when they would breakfast. After breakfast they would work until noon when they would have their midday meal. In the afternoon they continued working until about half an hour before sunset. Even once they had finished working in the fields, there were still other jobs to be done. She quotes John Luffman's observations in Antigua in the 1780s:

> The Negroes are turned out at sunrise and employed in gangs from 20 to 60, or upwards under the inspection of white overseers...subordinate to these overseers are drivers, commonly called

THE BLOOD NEVER DRIED

dog-drivers, who are mostly black or mulatto fellows of the worst dispositions; and these men are furnished with whips, which, while on duty, they are obliged, on pain of severe punishment, to have with them, and are authorised to flog wherever they see the least relaxation from labour; nor is it a consideration with them, whether it proceeds from idleness or inability, paying at the same time little or no regard to age or sex.[13]

The whip was the mainstay of the plantation work regime. As one historian puts it, the planters "could only squeeze a respectable profit out of their slaves by literally beating it out of them".[14] According to the Baptist missionary William Knibb, "flogging on the estates is as common as eating almost".[15] There were, of course, often refinements and personal idiosyncrasies involved in the administration of punishment. The Jamaican planter Thomas Thistlewood, for example, in 1756 had a slave caught eating sugar cane "well flogged and pickled, then made Hector shit in his mouth". This excremental punishment was used regularly enough on the estate to become known as "Derby's dose".[16] A visitor to another Jamaican plantation in 1790 witnessed the master nailing a house slave to a post by her ear for breaking a plate. She pulled herself free and ran away during the night. When she was caught, "she was severely flogged".[17] On another occasion on St Nevis two slave boys received 100 lashes each for stealing a pair of stockings and their sister 30 lashes "for shedding tears when she saw them beaten".[18] While this routine cruelty was primarily instrumental, to ensure submission and generate profit, there is no doubt that the master-slave relationship provided an opportunity for sadists and rapists to satisfy their desires. Sometimes they went too far. In 1811 a planter, Arthur Hodge, was hanged for having tortured and murdered perhaps as many as 60 of his slaves—men, women and children—on Tortola in the Virgin Islands.[19] The white community rallied to his support, outraged that one of their number could be executed for killing slaves. Troops had to be brought in and martial law declared to ensure that the sentence was carried out.[20]

Between 1700 and 1774 some 500,000 slaves were imported into Jamaica and yet the slave population only increased by 150,000. The reason was quite simple. The life expectancy of an African who survived the "Middle Passage" of the triangular trade was only some seven to ten years.[21] According to the planter and historian Edward Long, there was a 25 percent mortality rate for newly arrived slaves in the first 18 months of their Caribbean servitude.[22] It has been estimated that "for every African who became acclimatised to plantation slavery in America, at least one other African lost his life through such operations of the slave trade as warfare, the Middle Passage, and the seasoning".[23] Such an appalling casualty rate required a specific ideological justification. The pursuit of profit over so many corpses had to be clothed in racism. The key figure in the construction of planter racism was the same Edward Long who had lived through the great slave revolt of 1760 in Jamaica. In 1774 Long published his "negrophobic" History of Jamaica in which he argued that the blacks were a different species from the whites, closer to the apes. Indeed, he argued that an orang-utan husband "would not be a dishonour to a Hottentot female". Nevertheless, while the blacks were incapable of civilisation, if caught early enough, they could be taught to perform disciplined labour, although only "in a very bungling and slovenly manner, perhaps not better than an orang-utan might with a little pains be brought to do". Even the body lice of a black and a white were different (as the historian Richard Sheridan observes, presumably a white man's lice were superior). And, of course, unless kept constrained, the black was likely to resort to bestial savagery, to become monstrous.[24]

The other side of the oppression and exploitation of the slaves was, of course, slave resistance. This took many forms, ranging from a low level day-to-day resistance to labour discipline through to full-scale rebellion. As Emilia Viotta da Costa puts it, "Slaves and masters were engaged in permanent war—a cold war that took place every day in many forms, but from time to time burst into violent confrontation." As she insists, the idea of rebellion was always "latent…in slave societies…not as a clear and well-shaped notion, but as a mere possibility: an aspiration to be free that circumstances could crystallize into a concrete plot".[25] This was certainly the case with Jamaica. Indeed, Orlando Patterson has argued that:

Few slave societies present a more impressive record of slave revolts than Jamaica. During more than 180 years of its existence as a slave society, hardly a decade went by without a serious, large-scale revolt threatening the entire system. Between these larger efforts

THE BLOOD NEVER DRIED

were numerous minor skirmishes, endless plots, individual acts of violence against the master and other forms of resistance, all of which constantly pressed upon the white ruling class the fact that the system was a very precarious one, held together entirely by the exercise, or threat, of brute force.[26]

From the very beginning of their occupation of the island, the British faced a "Maroon" problem, the presence of armed runaway blacks establishing hidden communities outside white control, successfully resisting colonial military expeditions, and offering sanctuary to other runaways. The Maroons were a constant threat to the planters, both in themselves and in the example they offered. Having failed to destroy the Maroons after more than 70 years of warfare, in 1739 the British concluded treaties with both the Leeward and Windward communities. Subsequently the Jamaican Maroons became mercenaries, actively assisting the British in capturing runaway slaves and putting down slave revolts.[27]

The most serious 18th century slave revolt in Jamaica was Tacky's revolt, which broke out on 7 April 1760. At its height this involved some 30,000 slaves and for a while had the planters terrified. The revolt was not finally suppressed until October 1761. The rebels' purpose was, according to Edward Long, "the entire extinction of the white inhabitants…and the partition of the island into small principalities in the African mode". This was a more serious threat than the Maroons had constituted. Indeed, the Maroons played an important part in its suppression, with the rebel leader, Tacky, himself shot dead by a Maroon sharpshooter. By the time the revolt had been finally crushed some 60 whites had been killed, over 400 rebels had been killed, another hundred had been executed, many of them tortured to death, and some 500 deported to Honduras. According to Bryan Edwards, it was "thought necessary to make a few terrible examples of some of the most guilty of the captives". He describes how one prisoner was sat on the ground and "the fire was applied to his feet. He uttered not a groan, and saw his legs reduced to ashes with the utmost firmness and composure, after which, one of his arms by some means getting loose, he snatched a brand from the fire that was consuming him and flung it in the face of the executioner". Another prisoner, suffering the same fate, warned his executioners that "multitudes" had sworn to destroy them, "who now lay still, that if they failed of success in this rebellion to rise up again on the same day in two years". And indeed there were further outbreaks in 1765 and 1766 although not on the scale of Tacky's revolt.[28] The rebels deported to Honduras (today's Belize) themselves contributed to the slave unrest in that colony.[29]

The years of revolution

The great slave revolt on the French colony of St Domingue, the richest of the sugar islands, is one of the greatest revolutions of modern history. It was not only the first successful slave revolt, but it also survived massive assaults from both the British and the French, and struck a mortal blow at the heart of Caribbean slavery. One can only endorse Robin Blackburn's conclusion that "it is scarcely possible to exaggerate the impact of the Haitian Revolution on the fate of colonial slavery".[30]

The revolt broke out in August 1791. The failure of the French to crush it sent a wave of fear and hope across the Caribbean. In Jamaica the governor, the Earl of Effingham, responded to news of the outbreak by calling out the militia, establishing committees of security in each parish and requesting troop reinforcements from Britain. The planters even agreed to "some minor ameliorations in the slave laws".[31] Jamaica, according to one historian, "was on the brink of its own slave revolt, and the threat was real". In Kingston slaves were believed to be collecting weapons and were assembling to drink the health of "King Wilberforce" out of a cat's skull.[32] According to Adam Williamson, a future governor, Jamaican slaves were "very inquisitive and intelligent and are immediately informed of every kind of news that arrives". They had already "composed songs of the Negroes having made a rebellion in Hispaniola" and he had "not a doubt but there are numbers who are ripe for any mischief". One correspondent warned that "the ideas of liberty have sunk so deep in the minds of all Negroes, that whenever the greatest precautions are not taken they will rise".[33] In the event, there was no Jamaican slave revolt in 1791: the whites were too well prepared.

For the government in London, the St Domingue revolt was an opportunity as well as a danger. Embroiled in war with the French Republic, the seizure of France's Caribbean colonies proved an irresistible temptation. In September 1793 the first British troops landed in St Domingue, welcomed as saviours by the French planters. This was the beginning of what was to become a large-scale military commitment. Soon after, in December, the British occupied

THE BLOOD NEVER DRIED

Trinidad and St Lucia, and the following year, 1794, they occupied Martinique in February and Guadeloupe in March. This conflict was transformed when the revolutionary authorities in St Domingue declared slavery abolished in August 1793 and the Convention in Paris abolished slavery throughout all French possessions in February 1794. The British now found themselves confronting slave resistance sponsored by the French that for a while threatened to overwhelm them. The Jacobin revolutionary Victor Hugues played a leading role in raising a revolt against the British in Guadaloupe, and in encouraging resistance in St Lucia, St Vincent and Grenada. He had driven the British from Guadaloupe by early December 1794 and now made use of the island as a base for the spreading of the revolutionary message. By 1795, in the words of the military historian J W Fortescue, "the greater part of the Negroes in the West Indies were now in open revolt".[34] In March 1795 a revolt led by Julien Fedon broke out in Grenada and came near to expelling the British from the island. Thousands of slaves rallied to the rebel cause. While many British colonial governors have executed rebels, Fedon can claim the distinction of executing a British governor, George Home.[35] In June the British were forced to evacuate St Lucia. Even in Jamaica in July there was an outbreak of fighting with one of the island's Maroon communities, the Trelawny Maroons. The conflict was instigated by the government, which felt their independence to be a threat during a period of revolution. It proved a hard-fought campaign with some 300 Maroons waging an effective guerrilla war. According to Fortescue, after a month of fighting the British "had lost more than 70 killed, including two field officers…whereas there was no assurance that a single one of the Maroons had ever been touched".[36] By March 1796 the Maroons had agreed to surrender on generous terms, only for the government to renege on the agreement and deport them to Nova Scotia. The British military commander, General George Walpole, publicly condemned the government's treachery and refused any honours associated with the victory.[37]

The British responded to the setbacks of 1795 with the despatch of a massive expeditionary force of some 30,000 men. One of the most important British military campaigns of the Revolutionary and Napoleonic Wars was to be the attempt to finally conquer the French colonies and to restore slavery. To assist in this, the decision had been taken the previous year to raise regiments of black slaves to help fight against their revolted brothers and sisters. Between 1795 and 1808 the British state bought 13,400 slaves at a cost of £925,000 to serve as soldiers. Ironically, the only way these slave soldiers could be trusted to fight for their new masters was if they were themselves promised freedom at the end of their service.[38]

In April 1796 St Lucia was retaken, but the British quickly found themselves fighting a protracted guerrilla war waged by black revolutionaries. As the British commander, General John Moore, observed, "Men after having been told they were free, after carrying arms, did not easily return to slavery." Indeed, there were occasions when Moore feared that the island would once again be lost. This was not to be, but the last resistance was not finally extinguished until early 1798.[39] Grenada and St Vincent were also successfully reduced. Decisive, however, was the campaign in St Domingue, and here the British confronted the revolutionary army led by the former slave Toussaint L'Ouverture. The outcome was a humiliating defeat with the British being forced to withdraw in early October 1798.[40] The whole campaign in the Caribbean, from 1793 to 1798, cost the British over 55,000 casualties, dead, deserted or unfit for duty. It was one of the greatest disasters in British military history and consequently hardly figures in histories of the Revolutionary and Napoleonic Wars. The only consolation the British had was that Napoleon was to repeat their mistake, making a similar attempt to reconquer St Domingue and restore slavery. The result was the establishment of the black Haitian Republic in January 1804.

One last point worth briefly considering is why throughout all this revolutionary turmoil, with the British suffering serious setbacks at the hands of black revolutionaries, there was no revolt in Jamaica. In 1800, in response to Toussaint's takeover of power in St Domingue, slaves in Kingston were happily singing, "Black, White, Brown. All de same". Nevertheless, this sentiment never took up arms. The most convincing explanation is that there were, throughout this period, too many troops on the island for revolt to be seriously contemplated. Any rising would have been drowned in blood.[41] The Haitian Revolution still inspired hope, however. In January 1817 the seven-man slave crew of the schooner *Deep Nine* escaped to Haiti and claimed their freedom. The British demanded their return. The Haitian authorities returned the schooner, but the men remained free.[42]

The overthrow of slavery

The ending of the slave trade in 1807 and the resulting creolization of the slave population together with a supposed "amelioration" in slave conditions would, many planters hoped, eliminate slave unrest and weaken popular support for the abolitionists in Britain. This was not to be. Conspiracies and plots had continued throughout the Revolutionary and Napoleonic Wars, for example, the 1801 Tobago and 1805 Trinidad conspiracies.[43] What followed, however, was first to shake and then bring down the slave system. Three great revolts in Barbados in 1816, in Demerara in 1823 and in Jamaica in 1831 were to demonstrate that slavery was no longer viable in the British Caribbean. It could be ended peacefully or violently, but end it certainly would.

According to Hilary Beckles, slave resistance in Barbados in the 17th century had been characterised by "a small number of aborted rebellions, continuous attempts at marronage [running away], limited day-to-day socio-economic anti-planter acts, but no actual risings". There were "aborted rebellions" in 1649, 1675 and 1692. Reprisals were always savage. The 1692 conspiracy was punished by 92 executions carried out with all the usual cruelty. During the 18th century, while marronage and day-to-day anti-planter acts remained a problem, there were no significant conspiracies. Beckles puts this down to Barbados having "the most developed internal military system in the English West Indies". By the early years of the 19th century the planters were convinced that revolts were a thing of the past. There was a feeling that the slaves were becoming disrespectful and assertive but this was blamed on the pernicious influence of the abolitionist movement in Britain. On the eve of the revolt most planters "possessed an unshaken confidence in the strength and security of the regime".[44]

On Easter Sunday 14 April 1816 the slaves rose up and "more than half the island was engulfed by the insurrection". According to a senior British officer the slaves believed that "the island belonged to them and not to the white men whom they proposed to destroy". In the event, the rising was suppressed within four days although mopping up operations continued into June. Perhaps as many as 1,000 slaves were killed, some in the fighting, more shot out of hand in immediate reprisal, and 144 executed after trial. Admiral Harvey complained that the militia "put many men, women and children to death, I fear without much discrimination". One white man was killed, but 25 percent of the sugar cane was destroyed by fire. Even after the bloodletting a visitor to the island that June could still write that the slaves remained "sullen and sulky and seem to cherish feelings of deep revenge". He concluded that "we hold the West Indies by a very precarious tenure—that of military strength only".[45]

The outbreak in Barbados was followed soon after by another revolt in the recently acquired colony of Demerara. Demerara was one of three Dutch territories (the others were Berbice and Essequibo) seized in 1803 and which became British Guiana. According to Michael Craton, these territories had the dubious honour of possessing "the cruellest plantation regime in the hemisphere". The missionary John Smith wrote that the whip was "used with an unsparing hand" and that the planters believed the slaves must "be ruled by terror".[46] The revolt began on the Success plantation, one of seven owned by John Gladstone, on 18 August 1823. It quickly spread to some 60 plantations and involved some 12,000 slaves. The rebels showed considerable restraint, imprisoning or driving off the whites, rather than killing them. They demanded freedom. The governor, Major General John Murray, had encountered a party of 40 rebels himself and promised them reforms. They told him:

> These things were no comfort to them: God had made them of the same flesh and blood as the whites: they were tired of being slaves; their good King had sent orders that they should be free, and they would not work any more.[47]

While the slaves behaved with restraint, the whites (who were outnumbered in the colony by more than 30 to one) responded with predictable savagery. The revolt was put down by force, with over 200 rebels either killed in the fighting or shot out of hand, and a further 33 executed after a semblance of a trial. Ten slaves had their heads displayed on poles at the estates most heavily involved in the revolt.

As far as the planters were concerned, responsibility for the revolt rested with the abolitionist movement in general and with the London Missionary Society representative in the colony, the Reverend John Smith, in particular. His teaching of the story of Moses and the Exodus was regarded as particularly provocative. Smith was arrested and tried for his life with rebel prisoners being promised their own if

THE BLOOD NEVER DRIED

they implicated him. He was sentenced to death with a recommendation of mercy, but was to die in prison while awaiting the royal reprieve. Smith, a consumptive, was held in the most appalling conditions for six months and his death was really murder by deliberate neglect. John Gladstone welcomed his death, "as his release would have been followed by much cavil and discussion" in Britain. He urged the government to despatch troop reinforcements to Demerara and to have "ships of war stationed or cruising around". The slaves had to be kept "in due subjection and subordination" and it had to be made clear to them "that any renewed attempt will end in their own destruction".[48] The slaves, however, could not be reconciled to their servitude. Indeed, the following year (1824) the governor wrote to London that the "spirit of discontent is anything but extinct", that "it is alive as it were under its ashes" and that the slaves were "still agitated, jealous and suspicious".[49] Ten years later, when the brutal conditions on John Gladstone's Demerara plantations were criticised in the House of Commons, his son William, the future prime minister, sprang to his father's defence. He made it clear that "he deprecated slavery; it was abhorrent to the nature of Englishmen; but conceding all these things, were not Englishmen to retain a right to their own honestly and legally acquired property?" This was William Gladstone's maiden speech and it already displayed in full measure the hypocrisy that was to be one of the hallmarks of his long and distinguished career.[50]

The decisive episode in the overthrow of slavery in the British Caribbean was the great Jamaican revolt that began on 27 December 1831. It was the most serious slave revolt in British history, involving some 60,000 slaves, engulfing an area of up to 750 square miles, causing immense material damage, and costing many lives. Preparations for the rising had begun as early as April of that year, with the most privileged slaves on a number of estates, men with responsibility within the system, coming together to plan its overthrow. The conspiracy took shape in conditions of increasing hardship for the slave population, eventually embracing almost 100 estates. 1831 was a year of drought that seriously affected the slaves' own rations. The planters were intensifying the labour regime and they were refusing to implement some of the reforms being advocated by the British government. Even though flogging was legally restricted to 39 lashes at any one time, this was generally ignored, and the Jamaican Assembly had refused to even consider

London's proposal to prohibit the flogging of women. Moreover, the decision was taken to cut the number of days holiday at Christmas from three to two. At the same time, the slaves were aware of the growing abolitionist movement in Britain. They were even more aware of the planters' response to it. Planter threats of armed revolt and secession to join with the United States were common knowledge. There was even talk of a massacre of male slaves. One planter told a slave that "freedom was to come from England, but that he would shoot every d-d [damned] black rascal before they should get it".[51]

The underground network that bound the conspiracy together was provided by the Baptist church. The official Baptist church was controlled by white missionaries, and although they were abolitionist in sympathy, perhaps mindful of the fate of John Smith in Demerara, they preached a message of patient obedience and resignation. Alongside and within their church, however, there was the Native Baptist church, with its own black leadership, that preached a very different message. The leader of the conspiracy, Samuel Sharpe, was the chief deacon at the colony's most important Baptist chapel, Thomas Burchell's Montego Bay Baptist Chapel. He was also a native Baptist preacher. Sharpe, according to the white missionary Henry Bleby, was "the man whose active brain devised the project and he had sufficient authority with those around him to carry it into effect, having acquired an extraordinary degree of influence among his fellow slaves". He was "certainly the most intelligent and remarkable slave I ever met", Bleby later recalled, a man "possessed of intellectual and oratorical powers above the common order". Sharpe used his position as a privileged slave to spread the conspiracy, recruiting new adherents, preaching liberation and preparing for the coming day. At the end of prayer meetings on the plantations, selected individuals believed to be sympathetic would be invited to stay behind after the service, and either Sharpe himself or other leaders would attempt to win them over. One of those recruited in this way, Edward Hylton, later told Bleby that Sharpe had:

> Referred to the manifold evils and injustices of slavery; asserted the natural equality of man with regard to freedom; and referring to the Holy Scriptures as his authority, denied that the white man had any more right to hold the blacks in bondage than the black had to enslave the whites…

THE BLOOD NEVER DRIED

Once they were won over, the new recruits swore on the Bible not to return to work after Christmas except as free men and women.[52] Christianity had become a "revolutionary ideology", "a positive justification for action", that steeled them for the struggle ahead. Among the biblical texts that spoke to their aspirations was John viii: 36: "If the Son therefore shall make you free, ye shall be free indeed".[53]

Samuel Sharpe

What Sharpe and his fellow conspirators intended was a general strike that would continue until slavery was ended and the masters had agreed to a wage of 2s 6d (12.5p) a day. They had organised an "army" a few hundred strong to protect themselves, but there were no plans for revolutionary or guerrilla war. The signal for the strike to begin was the firing of the sugar trash on the Kensington estate on the evening of 27 December. Once this was lit, the trash was fired on estate after estate, as the slaves made their stand. The strike was almost immediately transformed into a rebellion, although the mechanism whereby this occurred is not altogether clear. Certainly, as far as the planters were concerned the strike was itself a rebellion to be put down by force, but there was also a widespread recognition on the part of the slaves that more militant action was necessary. With hardly any arms, there was no way that they could hope to defeat the military, so instead they struck at their oppressors by firing the plantations. According to one rebel, they would burn "the Blasted Estates and do away with all the sugarworks; it was them that kept them from getting freedom". A woman incendiary proclaimed, "I know I shall die for it, but my children shall be free." She was shot by the militia.[54] The burning of the estates dealt the planters a crippling blow with losses estimated at £1,154,590.

The revolt was effectively crushed by the end of the first week of January 1832, but the hunting down of fugitive rebels continued for weeks afterwards. Maroon mercenaries inevitably played their part in this mopping up exercise.[55] By the time the rebellion was officially over, the authorities claimed that 201 slaves had been killed. This number is much too low, as a number of districts never sent in returns. A figure of around 400 killed seems much more likely.[56] Many of them were shot out of hand. This was followed by a judicial massacre, which saw another 326 rebels executed after trials that were little more than a mockery. In addition to this, a number of the prisoners sentenced to be flogged also died, flogged to death, but were not listed as executed. Fourteen whites were killed in the revolt. Many slaves went to their deaths defiantly. Patrick Ellis told his firing squad to "fire for I will never again be a slave". Similarly, Samuel Sharpe, shortly before his execution, told Henry Bleby that he "would rather die on yonder gallows than live in slavery".[57] He was hanged on 23 May 1832, the last rebel to be executed. That same day a white Jamaican wrote that the slave "now knows his strength and will assert his claim to freedom. Even at this moment, unawed by the late failure, he discusses the question with a fixed determination".[58] Let us leave the last word on the revolt to the missionary Henry Bleby:

> The result failed of accomplishing the immediate purpose of its author, yet by it, a further wound was dealt to slavery which accelerated its destruction for it demonstrated to the imperial legislature that among the Negroes themselves the spirit of freedom had been so widely diffused as to render it most perilous to postpone the settlement of the most important question of emancipation to a later period...if the abolition of slavery were not speedily effected by the peaceable method of legislative enactment, the slaves would assuredly take the matter into their own hands, and bring their bondage to a violent and bloody termination.[59]

Abolition

Many planters blamed the white missionaries for the revolt that had left their estates smoking ruins. In the aftermath they responded by burning or pulling down nearly 20 chapels and arresting the missionaries who were manhandled and threatened. Henry Bleby was tarred and feathered and told he was to be burned alive, William Knibb was roughed up, insulted and prodded with a bayonet, and an attempt was made to frame Thomas Burchell by procuring perjured evidence of his involvement in the revolt. While these men had opposed the revolt, they now saw their chapels destroyed, had themselves been threatened, and had seen members of their congregation killed, as far as they were concerned, for their faith. The missionaries, in particular William Knibb, who was to become popularly known as "Knibb the Notorious", carried word of what had been done in Jamaica back to Britain. The abolitionist movement provided a mass audience.

What was the relationship between slave revolt, the abolitionist movement and the overthrow of slavery? While the contention here

THE BLOOD NEVER DRIED

is that slave revolt was the decisive factor, the importance of popular abolitionism should not be underestimated. Although usually personified in William Wilberforce, the abolitionist movement was, in fact, rooted among artisans particularly in the north and inspired by the ideas of the non-conformist church. It was a cross-class movement, but at the same time part of the popular working class radicalism of the day. Between 1830 and 1832 abolitionism became a mass movement. People "flocked" to the cause, and as James Walvin points out, "the extent and depth of anti-slavery feeling is difficult to overstress".[60] Public and private meetings were held (William Knibb toured the country on one occasion making the point that if Samuel Sharpe had been a Polish patriot fighting the Russian Tsar he would be celebrated as a hero), a huge amount of anti-slavery literature was sold, and mass petitions were organised. In 1833 Henry Whitely's *Three Months in Jamaica in 1832* sold 200,000 copies in two weeks. That same year 5,020 petitions, signed by 1,309,931 people, were submitted to parliament. This was a powerful movement at a time when the British political system was coming under tremendous popular assault culminating in the 1832 Reform Act. There were also radicals opposed to abolition, most notably William Cobbett, who combined democratic principles with a vicious racism—he had urged the French to hang Toussaint L'Ouverture and proclaimed slavery the African's fate. Even Cobbett, however, when standing for parliament in 1832 had to promise to support the abolition of slavery. This is a powerful testimony to the potency of the movement. Moreover, this explosion of support for abolition came at a time when the Caribbean plantocracy's position was weakening. The transformation of Britain into an industrial economy and society established the ideology of free labour with both the employing and the working class. The social, economic and political weight of this constituency was increasing, while that of the so-called West Indian interest, the plantocracy, was weakening. Indeed, the 1832 Reform Act dealt it a massive blow. Nevertheless, as Seymour Drescher has argued, just as it took the threat of revolution to secure the passage of Catholic Emancipation in 1829 and the threat of revolution to secure the passage of the 1832 Reform Act itself, so it took the threat of revolution in the Caribbean to secure the abolition of slavery.[61]

The threat was taken extremely seriously. It was assumed, certainly correctly, that failure to abolish slavery would inevitably result in further revolts. Indeed, they were thought imminent. On 7 July 1832 Lord Howick, under-secretary for the colonies and the son of the prime minister, Lord Grey, wrote to the new governor of Jamaica that his information was that:

> The slaves are not being in the least intimidated or cowed by the dreadfully severe punishments which have been inflicted, but on the contrary as being quite careless of their lives, and as regarding death as infinitely preferable to slavery, while they are exasperated to the highest degree and burning for revenge for the fate of their friends and relations...it is quite clear that the present state of things cannot go on much longer, and that every hour that it does so is full of the most appalling danger...my own conviction is that emancipation alone will effectively avert the danger, and that the reformed parliament will very speedily come to that measure, but in the meantime it is but too possible that the simultaneous murder of the whites upon every estate which Mr Knibb apprehends may take place.

In his journal, he wrote, "I would not be surprised any time to hear that Jamaica is in the possession of the negroes".[62]

The Jamaican revolt had finally made it clear that slavery was no longer a viable system of exploitation in the British Caribbean. Fear of further outbreaks made the passage of the Emancipation Act a matter of urgency and the legislation was carried through both Commons and Lords by large majorities in the summer of 1833. Slavery was formally abolished on 1 August 1834 with some 750,000 men, women and children set free. Their freedom came very much on the planters' terms, however. They received £20 million in compensation for their lost property, an astonishing sum at the time, and over £2.2 billion in today's money. John Gladstone, for example, received £85,600 for his 2,183 slaves. The slaves, of course, received no compensation. On top of that, slavery was replaced by what one historian has described as "unfreedom", an apprenticeship system whereby ex-slaves continued to be compulsorily bound by law to work for their former owners for over 40 hours a week without pay. The apprenticeship was to last for four years for domestic slaves and artisans and six years for agricultural slaves. Apprenticeships met with immediate opposition. In St Kitts there was a general strike that had to be put down by troops.[63]

THE BLOOD NEVER DRIED

Elsewhere, in Dominica, Trinidad and Jamaica, there were more limited strikes. The apprenticeship scheme became the source of continual conflict.[64] How tense the situation had become was shown when a rumour circulated that Knibb had been murdered by the planters. Hundreds of armed blacks assembled to take revenge, only dispersing when assured that it was untrue.[65] Apprenticeship was eventually abolished for *all* ex-slaves after only four years on 1 August 1838. Freedom at last!

Morant Bay, 1865

Freedom did not end exploitation and oppression. Even with the abolition of slavery, political and economic power remained in the hands of the white plantocracy. Moreover, there were continual rumours that the colony was going to secede to the United States and later the Confederacy of the Southern States as a first step in the restoration of slavery. Economic, social and political grievances came to a head on 11 October 1865 in Morant Bay with clashes between the militia and protesters led by Paul Bogle. The governor of Jamaica, Edward Eyre, responded with overwhelming force and incredible brutality. As far as he was concerned, one moment's hesitation "might have lit the torch which would have blazed in rebellion from one end of the island to the other". If unchecked, he feared the revolt might spread throughout the Caribbean.[66] Troops were sent into the disturbed areas where they imposed a reign of terror. There were hundreds of executions, over 600 prisoners were flogged, including pregnant women, and a thousand houses were burned down. Twenty nine whites were killed in the outbreak and between 500 and 1,500 blacks. Officially, 353 people were executed after court martial and some of these were used as target practice by the troops. In case the reader should think this an exaggeration, we have the testimony of Captain Spencer Field, that after being sentenced to death Arthur Wellington was tied to a tree while soldiers using the Enfield rifle fired at him from a distance of 400 yards. The provost sergeant acted as a marker and signalled that the seventh shot had "passed through the rebel's throat, the ninth or tenth shot entered his heart or thereabouts".[67] Bogle himself was hanged on 25 October. The Assembly member for Morant Bay, George William Gordon, was in Kingston throughout the outbreak and had no involvement in it whatsoever. He was, however, a champion of the poor and a vocal critic of Governor Eyre. He was arrested and taken to Morant Bay where he could be tried by court martial and hanged without the inconvenience of a jury hearing the evidence or rather lack of it. This was a barely disguised political murder.

The scale of Eyre's repression provoked outrage in Britain. A Royal Commission investigated his conduct, and while it praised his speedy response to the outbreak, nevertheless condemned the use of capital punishment as excessive, the floggings as "reckless" and the house burning as cruel.[68] Eyre was dismissed and returned to England. He arrived at Southampton on 12 August 1866 to find a group of respectable, wealthy supporters, many of them titled, proposing to hold a dinner in his honour. While the mayor welcomed Eyre and his supporters on 21 August, working class protesters gathered outside. They condemned the "Banquet of Death", assaulted the guests and stopped and searched their coaches, looking for Eyre so they could lynch him. Elsewhere a protest meeting, "the largest working-class meeting that the city of Southampton had ever known", passed resolutions condemning him and the disgrace his welcome had brought on the city.[69] A Jamaica Committee was established in London to demand that Eyre be prosecuted, and a rival Eyre Defence Committee to celebrate his heroism. There was a fierce controversy with Eyre's supporters arguing a viciously racist defence. They did not deny the murderous brutality of his martial law regime but championed such methods as the only way to keep the blacks down. Middle class and working class radicals fought back to good effect, but no prosecution took place. This campaign was part of the radical upsurge that was to culminate in the 1867 Reform Act.

The Irish famine

I N 1798 a full-scale rebellion against British rule in Ireland was only put down with considerable violence and the deliberate encouragement of sectarian conflict. The United Irishmen, an underground movement of both Catholics and Protestants, had mounted a powerful revolutionary challenge, looking to the French for assistance, but had been brutally crushed. A later attempt in 1803 was to misfire and the British were able to restore order with little difficulty.[1] In the interim Ireland's separate Protestant legislature had been abolished and the country had been formally incorporated into the United Kingdom by the 1801 Act of Union. Ireland was now represented at Westminster, but in practice it continued to be governed as an occupied country. In the 1820s Daniel O'Connell had successfully built up a mass movement demanding Catholic emancipation. The movement triumphed in 1829. O'Connell subsequently took up the demand for the repeal of the Union and once again put himself at the head of a powerful mass movement. While ostensibly a constitutional movement, the intention was to intimidate the British government into repeal by the threat of violence. On this occasion the British called O'Connell's bluff and in 1843 saw off the challenge by making it clear that they would put the repeal movement down by force if necessary. But while the movement had suffered a serious defeat, the likelihood was that this was only a temporary setback. All the conditions were ripe for renewed resistance. In 1844 a young Tory MP, Benjamin Disraeli, told the House of Commons that anyone looking at the condition of Ireland, with its "starving population", "absentee aristocracy", "alien church" and "the weakest executive in the world", would inevitably conclude that "the remedy was revolution". All that prevented revolution was "the connexion with England".² Certainly, if the British government had found itself confronted by a revived mass Repeal movement in the revolutionary year of 1848 then the history of both Ireland and Britain in the 19th century would have been very different. Instead the Irish landscape was to be changed altogether by famine.

The Great Hunger
Potato blight (the fungus phytophthora infestans) first appeared in Ireland in 1845 when it destroyed between 30 and 40 per cent of Ireland's potato crop. The potato was the staple food of the poor and the blight caused great hardship. The following year the blight ruined almost the whole crop and great hardship became terrible famine. In 1847 the blight was less severe, but the farmers now had few seed potatoes to sow, with the result that the yield was only 10 percent of a pre-famine harvest. In 1848 the blight returned once again with devastating consequences that continued into the following year. The effects of the famine lasted into the early 1850s. This was Western Europe's worst modern peacetime catastrophe, with a million people dying of starvation, disease and exposure, and another million fleeing their homeland as refugees, seeking safety in England and Scotland, Canada and the United States. The hardest hit were inevitably the rural poor, the landless labourers, cottiers and small farmers, most of whom already lived in the most appalling poverty. According to the economic historian Cormac O Grada, for the Irish poor, "life on the eve of the famine was at least as grim as for the poor in much of the Third World". For some half of the Irish people, life was "harsh and comfortless".³ West Munster, South Ulster and Connaught were the areas worst affected, but in every district where subsistence farming predominated there was terrible suffering. Even the Wicklow Mountains, in sight of Dublin, were devastated by hunger and disease.

How did the British state respond to this crisis? How did the richest country in Europe, "the workshop of the world" and the ruler of a great empire respond? Robert Peel's Tory government took limited relief measures to cope with the partial failure of the potato crop in 1845, measures that were sufficient to ensure that despite considerable hardship there were few actual deaths. The complete failure of

THE BLOOD NEVER DRIED

the crop in 1846 coincided with Peel's replacement by a Whig government headed by Lord John Russell. This development was enthusiastically welcomed by the repealers who regarded Russell as a friend, as someone committed to a policy of reform and amelioration in Ireland. The new government was also doctrinally committed to laissez-faire, free trade and market forces, even to the extent of refusing to introduce such an elementary measure as a prohibition of food exports from Ireland. Russell ended the Tories' food relief measures and subsidies to Irish public works and left the provision of food to the free market. The results were disastrous, and the government was reluctantly and grudgingly forced to adopt emergency measures. The scale of the catastrophe overwhelmed its public works scheme, with the numbers employed increasing from 250,000 in the autumn of 1846 to 750,000 in the spring of 1847. When this policy collapsed, it was replaced by soup kitchens, which by August 1847 were feeding 3 million people a day. This initiative, which saved the lives of tens of thousands of people, was only intended as a stopgap measure while a system of workhouse relief, which it was intended would be paid for out of Irish resources, was made effective throughout the country. All of these measures were, moreover, implemented in a harsh and mean-spirited manner with the lead being given by the chancellor of the exchequer, Charles Wood, and the under-secretary at the Treasury, Charles Trevelyan, certainly two of the most monstrous figures in modern British history.[4] In effect, a million people died because government relief measures were too little and too late. And, they were too little and too late because of a fatal and deadly interaction between the government's economic ideology and Ireland's colonial situation.

The harsh truth is that the Irish poor were sacrificed on the altar of free trade and economic liberalism. At a protest meeting in Cork in the terrible winter of 1846-47 Horace Townsend suggested that the coroner's verdict on the famine dead should be that they had "died from an overdose of political economy administered by quacks".[5] Of course, it has been argued that those responsible, the Whig ministers and their officials, did, in fact, do all that was believed to be possible at the time. The ideological universe these men inhabited, so the argument goes, simply did not provide solutions to the catastrophe that confronted them. This led to the remarkable situation where a delegation from Ireland visited Russell to plead for more relief for the starving poor, only to have the prime minister read to them from Adam Smith's *The Wealth of Nations*. The relief they were asking for would, according to Russell's political economy, only make the situation worse and actually result in more deaths.[6]

The problem, one historian, Gearoid O Tuathaigh, has agreed, was that by the 1840s the British governing classes were united in the belief that private enterprise, the sanctity of property rights, free trade and the laws of supply and demand "constituted the optimum conditions for economic activity… The disciples of laissez-faire ruled the roost." This account is compromised by its idealist approach, that is it wrenches the "conventional wisdom" of the time free of the social and political forces within which it was formed. Within the context of British politics the Irish Famine was not of sufficient moment to call into question the conventional wisdom. This was the essence of Ireland's colonial situation. The fate of the Irish poor never became a central concern for the British government or the governing classes generally. As O Tuathaigh himself notes, the pressure of events did actually force the Whigs to abandon certain of their cherished principles, but not enough to save the famine dead.[7] The viceroy of Ireland, Lord Clarendon, made the point that even in Ireland the British government could not allow the numbers starving to rise above a certain number.[8] Moreover, there were many contemporary critics of British government policy, but they never had sufficient political weight to make a difference. One does not have to turn to Republicans such as John Mitchel for an indictment of Russell's government. In March 1849 Edward Twistleton, the eminently respectable Chief Poor Law Commissioner for Ireland, resigned. Clarendon wrote to London explaining that Twistleton considered "the destitution here is so horrible, and the indifference of the House of Commons so manifest that he is an unfit agent of a policy that must be one of extermination".[9]

If the famine had occurred in part of England there can be no doubt that the British government would have taken whatever measures necessary to prevent mass starvation regardless of cherished economic principles. The threat to the social and political order would have been too great for any other course to be have even been contemplated. Mass starvation in Ireland, however, was just not important enough to shift the conventional wisdom. Moreover, Ireland was already perceived as a hotbed of disaffection and, if anything, the famine was to actually help preserve British rule rather than pose a threat to it.

THE BLOOD NEVER DRIED

There was, of course, popular protest against the conduct of the authorities, but historians have barely started to examine this dimension of the famine years. One notable exception is Ciaran O Murchadha's *Sable Wings Over the Land*, a study of Ennis in County Clare. Here the agrarian secret societies, the Whiteboys or Terry Alts, took steps to prevent the export of grain from the district in the winter of 1846-47. Farmers were threatened and if they ignored the warning the horses that had carried their grain to market were shot. In October 1846 some 50 horses were shot and over the next two years hundreds more shared the same fate. An organised attempt was made to prevent grain being shipped from the port but troops were brought in to disperse the blockading crowds. There were protests about the administration of relief and access to the public works. Early in December 1846 an unsuccessful attempt was made to assassinate the overseer at the Clare Abbey works. In reprisal, the Poor Law inspector, Captain Edmond Wynne, closed the works and let starvation teach the people a lesson. Two weeks after he closed the works, Wynne visited the district:

> Although a man not easily moved, I confess myself unmanned by the extent and intensity of the suffering that I witnessed, more especially among the women and children, crowds of whom were to be seen scattered over the turnip fields, like a flock of famishing crows, devouring the raw turnips, mothers half-naked, shivering in the snow and sleet, uttering exclamations of despair, whilst their children were screaming with hunger. I am a match for anything else that I may meet with here, but this I cannot stand.

But stand it he did. The collective punishment was considered a great success and the works were reopened for a cowed population. Similar action was subsequently taken elsewhere, with works closed at Ruan and Kilmaley. Trevelyan was full of praise for Wynne's "undaunted spirit" and considered that he was all that stood "between the people of Clare and complete anarchy".[10]

What of the expense of keeping the Irish alive? Altogether the British government spent some £8 million on famine relief. This contrasts sharply, as was pointed out at the time, with the £20 million spent on compensating the slave owners when slavery was abolished in 1834. This money was disbursed to uphold the right of property and went to the deserving rich rather than to the undeserving poor, and the Irish poor at that. As Twistleton observed in 1849, the House of Commons was more concerned with "the conquest of Scinde or of the Punjab" than with keeping the Irish alive.[11] As if to prove the point, soon after the famine the British government was to find, without too much difficulty, £70 million to wage the Crimean War. Most telling of all perhaps was the comment by the Irish nationalist MP William Smith O'Brien in the House of Commons, that "if there were a rebellion in Ireland tomorrow, they would cheerfully vote 10 or 20 millions to put it down, but what they would do to destroy life, they would not do to save it".[12]

Evictions

Compounding the hunger and disease was the way the famine became the occasion for dramatic land clearances that amounted to a concerted landlord offensive against the poor. The large Catholic farmers joined in this assault and in fact emerged as important beneficiaries in the post-famine period. Exactly how many people were evicted during these grim years is unknown and is inevitably the cause of controversy. The figure certainly exceeds half a million people, an astonishing number by any standard.[13] This is one of the most terrible acts of class war in modern European history even without the accompanying starvation. How does one of the standard histories, Roy Foster's much-praised *Modern Ireland 1600-1972*, deal with it? The whole famine receives pretty minimal treatment, but the clearances get one sentence in 596 pages of text.[14] It is inconceivable that a general history of Scotland would treat the Highland Clearances in such a fashion, but perhaps Scottish history is not so politically sensitive.[15]

In December 1849 the correspondent for the *London Illustrated News* reported from Moveen, a village in the Kilrush Poor Law district:

> There is nothing but devastation…the ruthless destroyer, as if he delighted in seeing the monuments of his skill, has left the walls of the houses standing, while he has unroofed them and taken away all shelter from the people. They look like the tombs of a departed race, rather than the recent abodes of a yet living people, and I felt actually relieved at seeing one or two half-clad spectres gliding about as evidence that I was not in the land of the dead.

The people, he went on, were "resigned to their dooms...One beholds only shrunken frames scarcely covered with flesh—crawling skeletons." He emphasised "the vast extent of the evictions".[16]

An account by a parish priest in September 1847 described one eviction scene. The tenant was:

Confined to bed, being for a considerable time in a declining state—the result of destitution. The Sheriff, on seeing the extreme debility of the man, hesitated to execute his orders—he came out and remonstrated: but Mr Walsh was inexorable. Duffy was brought out and laid under a shed, covered with turf, which was once used as a pig cabin, and his house thrown down. The landlord, not deeming the possession complete while the pig cabin remained entire, ordered the roof to be removed and poor Duffy, having no friend to shelter him, remained under the open air for two days and two nights, until death put an end to him.[17]

This sort of spectacle even appalled members of the government. Russell himself, on one occasion, complained that "the murders of poor cottier tenants are too horrible to bear" and that the government "ought to put down this lynch-law of a landlord".[18] Bear it he did, however. The Poor Law inspector in the Kilrush district, Arthur Kennedy, was even more appalled, later recalling "that there were days...when I came back from some scene of eviction so maddened by the sights of hunger and misery I had seen in the day's work that I felt disposed to take the gun from behind my door and shoot the first landlord I met".[19]

Russell's government actually included two Irish landlords, Lords Palmerston and Clanricarde, both of whom were determined to uphold the rights of property and favoured a policy of systematic clearance. Palmerston urged that "ejectments ought to be made without cruelty" but the harsh fact was that any improvement in Ireland "must be founded upon...a long continued and systematic ejectment of smallholders and of squatting cottiers". Clanricarde was not so bothered about the cruelty side of things and told the cabinet on one occasion that sometimes if a tenant would not "go away by daylight, nothing is left but to force him out by night, and so he is forced out on a winter night and dies of cold and starvation by the roadside".[20] Even more extreme were the sentiments the viceroy,

Lord Clarendon, gave voice to in August 1848: "I would sweep Connacht clean and turn upon it new men and English money just as one would to Australia or any freshly discovered colony." This, the forcible removal of some 2 million people, was the only solution he could see to "the Irish Problem".[21]

There was, of course, resistance to eviction. Some landlords were shot. The most notorious case was the shooting of Major Denis Mahon of Strokestown in County Roscommon on 2 November 1847. He was an evicting landlord and had paid passage for some 500 of his tenants on a "coffin ship", the *Virginius*, to Canada. Over 150 of the emigrants were dead by the time the vessel arrived and most of the survivors were in such a poor condition that they had to be carried ashore, where over a hundred more of them subsequently died. In the British press, however, Mahon was celebrated as a humane landlord cut down by a murderous assassin urged on by the parish priest. The death by shooting of this one man eclipsed the death by starvation of tens of thousands. A government-orchestrated press campaign was launched with the *Times* leading the way, a campaign that was intended in part to intimidate and silence those clergy publicly critical of government policy. One priest, Father James Maher, replying to the press assault, asked whether the 16 ounces of food a day provided by the Carlow workhouse was not in itself an incitement to revolt and, more particularly, how many murders such a diet would provoke if it were imposed on the poor in England.[22] Palmerston considered the Mahon shooting to be part of "a deliberate and extensive conspiracy among the priests and peasantry to kill or drive away all the proprietors of land, to prevent and deter any of their agents from collecting rent, and thus practically to transfer the land of the country from the landowner to the tenant." Unfortunately there was no such conspiracy. Nevertheless, Palmerston went on to argue quite hysterically that there had never been in modern times, outside of Africa, "such a state of crime as now exists in Ireland". His proposed solution to this law and order crisis was that "whenever a man is murdered in Ireland, the priest of the parish should be transported. A more generally popular proposal would be that he should be hung, and many who clamour for martial law fancy, I have no doubt, that by martial law this latter process could be adopted".[23] He somewhat predictably showed considerably more concern for protecting his rents than he did for relieving the hunger of his tenants.

Palmerston was himself an evicting landlord and offered many of his tenants passage to Canada. One biographer of the great man describes how in:

> The summer and autumn of 1847 nine ships arrived at Quebec and St John carrying a total of two thousand of Palmerston's tenants from Sligo. The Canadians were shocked at the conditions of the immigrants who arrived in a state of complete destitution...though Palmerston had announced that every family would be paid between £2 and £5 on arrival at Quebec, no representative was there to meet them or provided them with any assistance, and they were left to be in the snow, barefoot and in rags, during their first Canadian winter.[24]

Adam Ferrie, chairman of the Emigration Committee in Canada, complained that Palmerston had "forgot that duty which he owed to God, his sovereign and his country". His transported tenants were "victims to that cruel system of maritime imprisonment and the only destination they could have was an early grave". Ferrie regretted "that men pretending to be Christians, and especially British, could be guilty of such barbarity".[25] None of this was to hinder Palmerston's subsequent political career and as far as most historians of the period are concerned it leaves no stain on his reputation.[26]

While the people starved and the land was being cleared, the Irish upper class continued to enjoy a life of great luxury and extravagance. The Republican John Mitchel later observed that:

> You may imagine that Dublin city would show some effect or symptom of such a calamity. Singular to relate, that city had never before been so gay and luxurious; splendid equipages had never before so crowded the streets; and the theatres and concert rooms had never been filled with such brilliant throngs... Any stranger arriving in those days, guided by judicious friends only through fashionable streets and squares, introduced only to the proper circles, would have said that Dublin must be the prosperous capital of some wealthy and happy country.[27]

The same Lord Clarendon who presided over mass starvation, who could write to Russell that "these people...deserve to be left to their fate", also presided over Dublin's social life.[28] In February 1848, there were three large balls at Dublin Castle, attended by 1,300, 400 and 45 guests and five large dinner parties. March saw two balls for 900 and 550 guests and four large dinner parties. The spectacle was to drive some to revolution.

John Mitchel and the famine

Looking back on the famine in 1854, John Mitchel wrote that while now "I can set down these things calmly...to see them might have driven a wise man mad". He described:

> How families, when all was eaten and no hope left, took their last look at the sun, built up their cottage doors, that none might see them die nor hear their groans, and were found weeks afterwards skeletons on their hearths; how the law was vindicated all this while...and many examples made; how starving wretches were transported for stealing vegetables by night...and how every one of those years, '46, '47 and '48, Ireland was exporting to England food to the value of 15 million pounds sterling.

He accused the British government of deliberately starving the Irish people, of making use of the potato blight to "thin out these multitudinous Celts". While the potato crop might have failed, there was, Mitchel insisted, still more than enough grain, cereals and livestock in the country to have fed the population, but it was exported to England. He wrote of how "insane mothers began to eat their young who died of famine before them; and still fleets of ships were sailing with every tide, carrying Irish cattle and corn to England." This was what "free trade did for Ireland in those days".[29] If such a disaster had befallen the south of France, he argued elsewhere, then the whole reserve of the country would have been used to provide "labour upon works of public utility" and to provide "such quantities of foreign corn as might be needed". Similarly, if the north of England had been afflicted "there is no doubt such measures as these would have been taken promptly and liberally".[30] Ireland's colonial position was the key.

Mitchel was radicalised by the famine. He was one of a number of intellectuals associated with the *Nation* newspaper, who had become known collectively as "Young Ireland". They were cultural

THE BLOOD NEVER DRIED

and literary nationalists, Protestant and Catholic, who had begun by supporting O'Connell and repeal, but had become disillusioned by his retreat from confrontation in 1843 and his friendly relations with the Whigs in London. They finally broke away from the Repeal Association in July 1846 and soon after, in January 1847, established the Irish Confederation. This was not a revolutionary organisation. While it refused to rule out the use of force (which was one of the causes of the break with O'Connell), it certainly was not planning to use it, but rather saw it as a threat not to be given up. The Irish Confederation's strategy was to win over the Protestant landlords to the Nationalist cause and hopefully force the British into making concessions, without violence or disorder. They certainly had no ambitions to replicate the United Irishmen of the 1790s. Their vision was of an independent Ireland where landlords fulfilled their social obligations to a grateful tenantry who recognised their natural claim to leadership. It was a deeply conservative vision. For Mitchel, the horrors of the famine swept it away.

Mitchel came to recognise that the struggle for land had to be central to any successful strategy for national liberation. His embrace of social revolution is a testimony to the impact that mass starvation and mass eviction had on his thinking. Much later, looking back on this period, he argued that revolution could "only be justified by desperate necessity", but that this had been the situation during the famine years. He went on: "When the system was found to work so fatally— when hundreds of thousands of people were lying down and perishing...society itself stood dissolved." Circumstances propelled him and his comrades into confrontation. They were all, he remembered, possessed by a "sacred wrath... They could endure the horrible scene no longer, and resolved to cross the path of the British car of conquest, though it should crush them to atoms".[31] Mitchel's radicalism led him to embrace democracy, social revolution and an alliance with the Chartists in England.[32]

The Irish Confederation's leadership did not share Mitchel's radicalism. While William Smith O'Brien, Charles Gavan Duffy and the others were bitterly critical of the British government, they were not revolutionaries. Indeed, Mitchel's call for social revolution was seen as as much of a threat to their wealth and position as it was to the British. Inevitably there came a parting of the ways. Mitchel established his own newspaper, the *United Irishman*, proclaiming that "the deep and irreconcilable disaffection of his people to all British laws, lawgivers and law administrators shall find a voice".[33] In a letter to the moderate Duffy, he explained that his intention was "once and for all, to turn men's minds away from the English parliament, and from parliamentary and constitutional agitation of all kinds". He made the point that "most of the people have no franchise and are not very likely to get any", indeed the electorate was "growing smaller and poorer continually". And as for any "combination of the gentry with the people", this "is now and henceforth impossible". Instead he proposed to promulgate "sound instruction in military affairs…a deliberate study of the theory and practice of guerrilla warfare" as "the true and only method of regenerating Ireland".[34]

1848 in Ireland

The political situation was transformed by the revolutionary overthrow of the regime of Louis Philippe in Paris in February 1848. This signalled the beginning of a revolutionary wave that was to shake governments throughout Europe. Mitchel enthusiastically welcomed the outbreak, celebrated it in the pages of the *United Irishman* and fervently hoped that the revolutionary contagion would spread to Ireland. On 4 March Mitchel told his readers that the earth "was awakening from sleep: a flash of electric fire is passing through the dumb millions. Democracy is girding himself once more like a strong man to run a race; and slumbering nations are arising in their might." He went on: "The blessed words 'Liberty! Fraternity! Equality!'…are soon to ring out from pole to pole." His readers were urged to make ready for the coming fight for freedom: "Let the man amongst you who has no gun, sell his garment and buy one".[35] Even the moderate leadership of the Irish Confederation felt that a revolutionary outbreak was now inevitable, that the old order was about to be swept away. The fear that increasingly gripped them was that the coming revolution would be led by the radicals. As Duffy put it to William Smith O'Brien, his great fear was that "you and I will meet on a Jacobin scaffold, ordered for execution as enemies of some new Marat or Robespierre".[36] If revolution was to come, they were determined it should be neither democratic nor socially levelling, but a moderate respectable affair.

How realistic were the hopes of revolution? In Dublin the Irish Confederate clubs were dominated by the artisan trades, with many

THE BLOOD NEVER DRIED

members sympathetic to Chartism. Serious preparations for rebellion were under way with demonstrations and meetings throwing down a challenge to the authorities. It was here that Mitchel's influence was strongest, with the *United Irishman* reminding its readers that the "trades unions now govern France".[37] Certainly, Clarendon was seriously alarmed, writing to Russell in London that "a spirit of disaffection...among the lower orders is universal". The people, he complained, actually thought that a revolution would lead "to a government that feeds the whole nation".[38]

Mitchel was arrested on 13 May 1848, tried before a carefully picked jury of government supporters and sentenced to 14 years transportation on the 27th. Within hours of the sentence being passed he was taken in chains on board a government steamer, beginning his journey to Van Diemens Land, now Tasmania. He had hoped that his arrest would provoke an insurrection, that it would occasion Dublin's "day of the barricades". O'Brien, Duffy and the moderates prevailed, however, opposing a proposed armed rescue and urging caution and patience. In this way, as Alexander Sullivan put it, "the Irish insurrectionary movement of 1848 was put down".[39] Certainly, the best moment for a revolutionary attempt was missed. As Justin McCarthy later observed, had "there been another Mitchel out of doors as fearless and reckless as the Mitchel in prison a sanguinary outbreak would probably have taken place".[40] Even after this success Clarendon was worried. The men who served on Mitchel's jury were subsequently boycotted and, he told Russell, "have suffered severely and some of them are quite ruined". One of them had "a respectable looking, well-dressed lady" visit him: she spat "in his face and said, Take that for what you did to Mitchel".[41] As far as he was concerned, "in any real danger we have only the Protestants to rely on". He told one correspondent that he would only have "to hold up my finger to have re-embodied all the Orange yeomanry and to have set them in march upon the south". The trouble was that their "exuberance of loyalty" was as much trouble as "the excess of sedition" in the south.[42]

After Mitchel had been transported, any hope of insurrection in Dublin was abandoned. The city was filled with troops. Instead the Irish Confederation leadership looked to the countryside. Their hand was forced when internment was introduced on 25 July 1848. William Smith O'Brien, a most unlikely revolutionary, set out to raise the standard of revolt in Kilkenny. O'Brien, according to one biographer, had "an almost pathological fear of anarchy and revolution from below".[43] While the circumstances in which he tried to rally the peasantry were certainly difficult, to say the least, his own limitations made failure certain. The rebellion collapsed after a skirmish with the police at Ballingarry on 26 July. The rebels dispersed and their leaders fled. Another attempt was to be made the following year in August 1849, but this too ended in failure.

Was this outcome inevitable? Certainly a successful insurrection in Ireland in 1848 was most unlikely. The famine had ravaged the rural population and starvation was not the best preparation for rebellion. What was possible, however, was a serious attempt that could have at least shaken, even if not overthrown, British rule. The best opportunity was missed in Dublin at the time of Mitchel's arrest. O'Brien's attempt amounted to little more than a half-hearted gesture. What has to be acknowledged is the extent to which the famine actually helped preserve British rule. If the famine had not decimated and demoralised the Irish people then there can really be no doubt that Ireland would have been one of the countries overwhelmed by the revolutionary wave of 1848, with the British either conceding repeal or being swept away.

Irish Republicanism

The famine and the revolutionary attempt of 1848 were the context within which modern Irish Republicanism was formed, and Mitchel was its first spokesman. His ferocious hatred of the British Empire, "the Carthaginian sea-monster"[44] as he called it, that he held responsible for the mass starvation and mass evictions, was to inform the revived Republican movement of the 1860s, the Fenians, and afterwards. Yet Mitchel protested that he was not motivated by "mere hatred of England". He made a crucial distinction between "the British nation" and "what Cobbett called the Thing [the British establishment]", and insisted that the best friend of the British people "is simply he who approves himself the bitterest enemy of their government and all their institutions". He never mistook the British people for Britain's pirate empire. His alliance with the Chartists is proof of this. He escaped from Van Diemens Land in July 1853 and arrived in the United States that October. Here he still looked forward to a revived European revolutionary movement. In January

1854 he proclaimed that "Europe is again ripening fast for another bursting forth of the precious and deathless spirit of freedom". In Britain the Chartists "are finding voice and spirit again". The Crimean War, he believed, provided an opportunity for revolutionaries, and he urged preparation of an Irish military expedition from America to once again raise the standard of revolt in Ireland.[45]

There was no fresh revolutionary outbreak, however, and Mitchel was condemned to remain an exile in the United States. His stay had a corrosive effect on his radicalism, and John Mitchel, one of the most powerful voices of 1848, was to become a fierce supporter of black slavery and advocate of the Confederacy in the American Civil War. All that remained of his radicalism was his support for an Irish Republic.[46]

The efforts of Irish revolutionaries in both Ireland and the United States continued culminated in 1858 in the establishment of the Irish Republican Brotherhood (IRB—better known as the Fenians) in Dublin. This was an underground movement that by 1864 had over 50,000 sworn members. The IRB successfully infiltrated the British army, established links with the radical movement in Britain and prepared for armed rebellion. Once again the attempt, in February 1867, was to misfire.[47] The IRB survived, however, and was to play a major part in the Land Wars of the 1880-1900s and go on to organise the Easter Rising in 1916. The IRB, under the leadership of Michael Collins and others, was to provide much of the sinew, muscle and brain of the Republican movement during the War of Independence.[48]

The Opium Wars

THE BRITISH Empire was the largest drug pusher the world has ever seen. By the 1830s the smuggling of opium into China was a source of huge profits and these profits played a crucial role in the financing of British rule in India and were the underpinning of British trade and commerce throughout the East. This is one of those little details that are often overlooked in general histories of the empire, where the opium trade is generally played down and sometimes ignored altogether. Denis Judd's acclaimed volume, *Empire*, a 500-page history of the British Empire, has no discussion of either the trade or the wars it occasioned.[1] More recently, the prestigious *Oxford History of the British Empire: the 19th Century*, edited by Andrew Porter, barely acknowledges the trade in over 700 erudite pages.[2] This is despite its tremendous economic importance: opium is estimated to have been "the world's most valuable single commodity trade of the 19th century",[3] and despite the fact that the Second Opium War actually brought about the overthrow of the government of the day in a vote of confidence and forced the holding of a general election, something not even the massive opposition to the recent Iraq war managed. Moreover, the opium trade was, in the words of the historian John K Fairbanks, without any doubt, "the most long-continued and systematic crime of modern times".[4]

"The safest and most gentlemanlike speculation I am aware of"
The production of opium in India had come under British control towards the end of the 18th century. In 1775 the British gave the East

India Company a monopoly over its production and sale, and towards the end of the century the company established an opium agency to manage the business. Sale and consumption of the product in India itself were successfully discouraged, something which seems to show a clear awareness of its disastrous consequences.[5] The export of opium to China, however, was to develop into a massive concern. In the 1760s some 1,000 chests of opium (each weighing 140 lbs) were smuggled into China, and this figure gradually increased to around 4,000 chests in 1800. In the years from 1800 to 1820 the trade stagnated with an average of 4,500 chests being shipped each year. Expansion only really began after 1820 so that by 1824 over 12,000 chests were being smuggled into China, rising to 19,000 in 1830, to 30,000 in 1835 and to 40,000 chests (an incredible 2,500 tons of opium) in 1838.[6] By this time the opium trade had become a vital national interest, "the hub of British commerce in the East".[7]

The opium trade was one corner of an Eastern "triangular trade" that mirrored the 18th century Atlantic slave trade. The smuggling of opium turned a large British trading deficit with China into a substantial surplus, paying for British imports of tea and silk, for the export of manufactured goods to India and for a substantial proportion of the costs of British rule in India. According to one authority, the opium trade was absolutely crucial "to the expansion of the British Empire in the late 18th and 19th centuries". This was both because of the revenues it produced and because of the powerful network of "narco-capitalists", merchants and financiers it created, "who profited from the trade, and whose influence buttressed the imperial lobby throughout the 19th century". For the British administration in India, opium was its second most important source of revenue and, for most of the 19th century, its most important export.[8] The trade kept the East India Company "afloat financially".[9] Moreover, as John Wong has shown, it not only turned a British trade deficit with China into a substantial surplus and generated massive profits, but also provided substantial revenues for the British government in London. The duty that was levied on the tea imports, which was paid for by smuggled opium, was sufficient to finance a considerable proportion of the costs of the Royal Navy during the 19th century.

The opium trade was clearly not a small-scale affair carried out by small-time crooks and gangsters. Instead it was a massive international commerce carried out by major British trading companies under the armed protection of the British state. According to William Jardine of Jardine Matheson, the most important of the companies involved in the trade, it was "the safest and most gentlemanlike speculation I am aware of". In a good year profits could be as high as $1,000 a chest. His wealth was sufficient to buy him a seat in the House of Commons and, as we shall see, to get him the ear of the government.[10]

Jardine Matheson and Co was founded in 1832 and was the most successful of the opium smuggling companies. It is still a major financial and trading company today. Jardine's partner in the enterprise, James Matheson, shows the uses to which the profits from the trade could be put. In the 1840s he too became an MP, sitting in the Commons for some 25 years. He bought the Hebridean Island of Lewis for £500,000, had Stornoway Castle built and cleared more than 500 families off the land, shipping them to Canada. He went on to become chairman of the great P&O shipping line, the major opium carrier for most of the 19th century, a governor of the Bank of England and the second largest landowner in Britain. His successor in the company, Alexander Matheson, a nephew, was likewise to settle on extensive estates in Scotland, bought for £773,000, and was to be an MP for nearly 40 years. Another nephew, Hugh Matheson, was to found Rio Tinto Zinc in the early 1870s. Clearly drug pushing was no obstacle to advancement and respectability in Victorian Britain.

The First Opium War
The importation of opium into China was, of course, illegal, prohibited by the Manchu Emperors, but the British companies engaged in the trade systematically corrupted or intimidated the Chinese authorities so that it was able to continue with little interruption. Depot ships were anchored off the coast, selling the drug to Chinese smugglers, who carried it ashore for distribution. By the 1830s the scale of the problems caused by the trade forced the Chinese government to respond. The country was being drained of silver to pay for the opium, its administration was being corrupted and the extent of addiction (estimates of the number of addicts go as high as 12 million) was seen as a threat to both state and society. In March 1839 the emperor sent a special commissioner, Lin Zexu, to Canton to enforce the ban on the opium trade and stamp it out once and for all.

THE BLOOD NEVER DRIED

Lin cracked down ferociously both on Chinese pushers and addicts, effectively suppressing the use of the drug, before proceeding to action against the British merchants who were bringing it in. He confined them to the area of the European territories in Canton, holding them hostage until they surrendered the opium they held. After six weeks the British superintendent of trade, Captain Charles Elliot, who himself regarded the trade as one "which every friend of humanity must deplore", capitulated and ordered the surrender of over 20,000 chests, which the Chinese destroyed. For the merchants, who for months had been unable to sell their product because of Lin's crackdown, this was a tremendous opportunity to practise massive fraud, an opportunity that they found irresistible. The British government would compensate them for their losses so they exaggerated their losses in every way possible, making huge profits from the confiscations. One trading house was rumoured to have made £400,000 from the episode.[11] And, of course, Lin's attempt at enforcing China's laws was to precipitate war with Britain.

Lin expelled the British from Canton, only for them to establish themselves on the island of Hong Kong, which they were determined to hold even in the face of Chinese hostility. At the same time the British government responded to Chinese actions by demanding compensation for the confiscated opium, the opening of more Chinese ports to trade, the legalisation of the opium trade, and the handing over of Hong Kong. They also demanded that China paid the full cost of the British military effort necessary to enforce these demands. A powerful expeditionary force was despatched to bring the Chinese to their senses, first blockading the coast and then proceeding up the Yangtze River to Nanjing. Advising the government in London was one of the opium barons himself, William Jardine. The foreign secretary, Lord Palmerston, was later to thank him for "the assistance and information...so handsomely afforded us" and to which "it was mainly owing that we were able to give to our affairs, naval, military and diplomatic, in China, those detailed instructions which have led to these satisfactory outcomes". Palmerston celebrated the war and its outcome as an episode that "will form an epoch in the progress of the civilization of the human races" and which incidentally would "be attributed with the most important advantages to the commercial interests of England".[12]

The British had an overwhelming technological superiority in this

First Opium War that turned every engagement into a one-sided massacre. As one British officer observed, "The poor Chinese" had two choices, either they "must submit to be poisoned, or must be massacred by the thousands, for supporting their own laws in their own land".[13] The British capture of the port of Jinhai in early October 1841 provides a useful example of the character of the conflict. The port was bombarded by the *Wellesley* (74 guns), the *Conway* and the *Alligator* (28 guns each), the *Cruiser* and the *Algerine* (18 guns each) and another dozen smaller vessels each carrying ten guns. In nine minutes they fired 15 broadsides into the effectively defenceless town before landing troops to storm the ruins. According to one British participant, "the crashing of timber, falling houses and groans of men resounded from the shore" and when the smoke cleared "a mass of ruins presented itself to the eye". When the troops landed on the beach, they found it deserted, save for "a few dead bodies, bows and arrows, broken spears and guns..."[14] With the bombardment of the town still under way, the troops moved in to rape and pillage. According to the *India Gazette*, "A more complete pillage could not be conceived...the plunder only ceased when there was nothing to take or destroy".[15] It was during this war that the Hindi word "lut" entered the English language as the word "loot". The taking of Jinhai cost the British three men killed, while the number of Chinese dead was over 2,000. Close behind the warships came the opium ships, restarting their trade.

There was a similar outcome when the Chinese made a surprise attack on the British-occupied port of Ningbo on 10 March 1842. John Ouchterlony, a young British officer, described the attackers as "men whose gallantry and determination could not have been excelled". Nevertheless, the result was a massacre with the British driving the Chinese off and then pressing them into the suburbs. Here they met a large force of Chinese soldiers and brought up an artillery piece which immediately opened fire:

> Upon the living wall before them with case shot at a distance not exceeding 20 to 30 yards. The effect was terrible, for the street was perfectly straight, and the enemy's rear, not aware of the miserable fate which was being dealt out to their comrades in front, continued to press the mass forward, so as to force fresh victims upon the mound of dead and dying which already barricaded the street...the

THE BLOOD NEVER DRIED

howitzer only discontinued its fire from the impossibility of directing its shot upon a living foe, clear of the writhing and shrieking hecatomb which it had already piled up.

The British did not suffer a single fatality, while some 400 Chinese had been killed. According to Ouchterlony, this "merciless carnage in the street of the western suburb proved too fearful a tension to be soon forgotten by the Chinese troops".[16]

More successful were the Chinese guerrilla tactics whereby individual soldiers and sailors were attacked. According to an officer stationed in Ningbo, the Chinese became "most expert" in the art of kidnapping and beheading British troops. On 18 April 1842 he wrote of how the body of a soldier kidnapped five weeks earlier "had been found in a canal without its head". This low-level guerrilla campaign cost the British more casualties than all the full-scale battles and engagements, and they responded with ferocious reprisals, burning villages and summary executions. Following the assassination of a soldier on 28 April ("He had been murdered in broad daylight, strangled, bound and bagged"), "the whole of the north suburb was burnt down", although the officer thought they might be "playing the game of the Mandarins, whose aim is to make us odious to the people".[17] And indeed this was beginning to happen towards the end of the war when large numbers of peasants began to mobilise against British depredations.

One interesting question is the extent to which the British were aware of the consequences of the trade they were intent on imposing on China. Lord Jocelyn, the military secretary to the expedition, in his account of the war, described visiting an opium den in Singapore whilst en route to China:

> One of the objects, at this place that I had the curiosity to visit, was the opium-smoker in his heaven; and certainly it is a most fearful sight... On a beginner, one or two pipes will have an effect, but an old stager will continue smoking for hours... A few days of his fearful luxury, when taken to excess, will have a pallid and haggard look to the face; and a few months, or even weeks, will change the strong and healthy man into little better than an idiot skeleton. The pain they suffer when deprived of the drug, after long habit, no language can explain... The last scene in this tragic

play is generally a room in the rear of the building, a species of dead-house, where lie stretched those who have passed into the state of bliss the opium-smoker madly seeks—an emblem of the long sleep to which he is blindly hurrying.

Nevertheless, he went on to insist that, "however hateful it may appear", the trade is "a source of great benefit to the Indian government, returning I have heard a revenue of upwards of two million and a half yearly".[18]

At home the war was strongly opposed in the Chartist press with the *Northern Star* newspaper condemning this "opium war".[19] In the House of Commons the Tory opposition put down a motion of censure on the Whig government's conduct. The secretary of state for war, Thomas Babington Macauley, proceeded to wrap himself in the Union Jack. He reminded MPs that the opium traders "belonged to a country unaccustomed to defeat, to submission, or to shame", that they had flying over them a "notorious flag" and he urged "that this most rightful quarrel may be prosecuted to a triumphal close".[20] One of the government's critics, William Gladstone (a young Tory MP at that time), condemned the war in the most uncompromising language: "A war more unjust in its origins, a war more calculated in its progress to cover this country with disgrace, I do not know and I have not read of." The flag, he went on, is being "hoisted to protect an infamous contraband traffic" while justice was with the Chinese and "whilst they, the pagans and semi-civilised barbarians have it, we, the enlightened and civilised Christians, are pursuing objects at variance with both justice and religion". Macauley's shabby prostitution of his oratorical talents in the cause of massacre and drug pushing carried the day and the government won the vote by 271 to 262. Gladstone recorded in his diary that he was "in dread of the judgement of God upon England for our national iniquity towards China".[21]

When the Whig government finally fell in June 1841, the Tories led by Robert Peel took office and in the best traditions of British politics continued the very same policy that they had condemned earlier. The war continued until the Chinese were forced to accept British terms, conceding everything except the legalisation of the opium trade. Public opinion in Britain resented the pressing of this demand, but it was made clear to the Chinese that interference with the trade would not be tolerated. James Matheson summed up the situation:

THE BLOOD NEVER DRIED

"The opium trade is now so very important in England that we cannot be too cautious in keeping as quiet and out of the public eye as possible".[22] The most important gain made by the British was the gaining of Hong Kong.

The Taiping rebellion

Defeat at the hands of the British seriously weakened the Chinese Qing dynasty and was certainly one of the factors prompting the Taiping rebellion, the greatest revolutionary movement of the 19th century. While it is virtually unknown in the West today, in June 1853 Karl Marx had welcomed this "Chinese Revolution", which he had hoped would "throw the spark into the overloaded mire of the present industrial system and cause the explosion of the long-prepared general crisis". "It would", he went on, "be a curious spectacle, that of China sending disorder into the Western world".[23] Of course, his hope that the Taiping rebellion would precipitate a fresh revolutionary wave in Europe, reviving the movement of 1848, was to remain unfulfilled. Nevertheless, he recognised the importance of the revolt.

The Taiping rebellion swept up millions of people into a 14-year struggle to overthrow the Manchu emperors and establish a messianic Christian theocracy. Inspired by their reading of the Bible, the rebels called for the abolition of landlordism and the establishment of a form of primitive communism with all the wealth held in common in the "sacred treasury". They prohibited prostitution, infanticide, slavery, the binding of women's feet and the smoking of opium. While certainly not feminist in any modern sense, the position of women in the Taiping movement went a considerable way towards establishing women's equality. The rebels were to come close to victory but in the end were defeated and totally destroyed by the Manchu armies, which were armed and assisted in this by the British. The war to destroy the Taipings was the most terrible in human history before the First World War, costing 20 million people their lives.

The movement had its origins in the preaching of Hong Xiuquan, the son of a peasant farmer, who came to believe that he was the son of God and the brother of Jesus. Hong's messianic Chinese reworking of Christianity found an eager audience in the China of the 1840s. Increasing hardship, poverty and oppression were the lot of the poor, unrest was widespread and revolt endemic, and the Qing dynasty was discredited by its defeat at the hands of the

British. Hong's condemnation of the ruling class "demons" and his promise of social justice, all dressed up in the trappings of divine revelation and promising salvation and the kingdom of heaven now, fired the imagination of thousands of desperate people in his home province of Guangxi.[24] A British consular official, Thomas Meadows, writing in 1856, noted the Taiping intention "to adopt institutions of equality and communism" and recognised that for the poor "the institution of equality of property, or at least of a sufficiency for every man...is of course peculiarly attractive". He compared the movement to the English revolutionaries of the 1640s and observed that inevitably "the property-holding classes" took the side of the Manchus.[25] Another contemporary account argued that the Taipings had "the spirit of the Fifth Monarchy", the English revolutionaries of the 1650s.[26] The first armed clashes between the Taipings and Qing troops took place in December 1850 with the rebels emerging triumphant. Recognising that this was a serious threat, the authorities sent a larger force to crush the movement. In early January 1851 a 10,000-strong rebel army, with men and women fighting side by side, routed the imperial troops at the town of Jintian. Soon afterwards Hong proclaimed the Heavenly Kingdom of Peace (Taiping Tianguo) with himself the Heavenly King (Tian Wang).

With imperial troops beginning to concentrate against them, the rebels abandoned their homes and began an incredible march that was only to end with their storming of the great imperial city of Nanjing in March 1853. They broke through the imperial lines in August 1851 and made their way overland and by river, beating off attacks and capturing towns and cities. All the while they grew stronger as thousands and thousands of the poor and downtrodden rallied to their cause. At Chansha in September 1852 the authorities estimated their numbers at 120,000; by the time they captured Wuchang in January 1853 they were 500,000 strong; and when Nanjing fell, the authorities estimated they numbered 2 million. Hong proclaimed Nanjing his capital.

At this point the Qing regime was close to collapse, but Hong decided to call a halt rather than press on to attack Beijing. This was a fateful decision. Augustus Lindley, a British volunteer who fought in the Taiping ranks, later concluded that the occupation of Nanjing had "proved fateful to the success of the Taipings" because they surrendered the initiative to their enemies. "Insurrection", he argued, "of whatever kind, to be successful, must never relinquish the aggressive movement; directly it acts upon the defensive, unless possessing some wonderful organisation, its power is broken." He thought that Hong's decision to establish his capital at Nanjing "lost him the empire".[27]

What was the British attitude to the Taiping rebellion? For a while the movement was regarded sympathetically because it helped weaken the Manchus and, moreover, the Taipings were Christians—although not of a sort that was to prove acceptable to Europeans. The idea that Jesus had a Chinese brother smacked too much of racial equality. The overriding British concern, however, was the safeguarding of the opium trade which the Taiping prohibited wherever they took control. This was to lead to British military action against them, even while the British continued to proclaim their neutrality. As we shall see, this was to result in a remarkable situation in the summer of 1860 whereby the British were fighting the Manchus on one front and fighting on their behalf against the Taiping on another.

The Second Opium War

Even after their defeat in the First Opium War, the Manchus continued to resist British efforts to incorporate them into their informal empire. The Chinese refusal to allow access to Canton, in violation of their treaty with Britain, came to be seen as the key to relations between the two countries. If the Chinese could be forced to back down over this it would consolidate British influence and be a step towards opening up the rest of the country. What was required was a pretext to force the issue, and the *Arrow* incident was to provide it.

On 8 October 1856 Chinese police seized a suspected pirate vessel, the *Arrow*, and arrested its crew. The British consul protested, claiming that the *Arrow* was a British ship registered in Hong Kong and that the police had forcibly lowered the Union Jack. An apology was demanded which the Chinese refused. The governor of Hong Kong, John Bowring, responded with military action, sending warships to destroy Chinese forts and to bombard Canton. This action was taken despite the fact that the crew had been released, that the vessel's Hong Kong registration had lapsed and that it had indeed been engaged in piracy. Moreover, as John Wong has shown, in a masterly piece of historical detective work, Chinese denials that the Union Jack had even been flying on the *Arrow* were almost certainly true.[28] Nevertheless a war was required and this was the pretext. One point worth making here is that Bowring was not some sort of arch-reactionary, but one of the most notable liberal intellectuals of the day. He had been a close friend of the philosopher Jeremy Bentham, who had died in his arms, and had been a Radical MP. Bowring had supported the People's Charter, had opposed the First Opium War and was a stalwart of the Peace Society. He was a noted linguist and a committed non-conformist, author of the hymn "In The Cross of Christ I Glory". He was also a passionate believer in the case for free trade. Indeed, he combined this passion with his religious enthusiasm, on one occasion actually insisting that "Jesus Christ is Free Trade and Free Trade is Jesus Christ". By the time he came to precipitate the Second Opium War, he was personally indebted to Jardine Matheson and his son, John, was a partner in the firm. Many of his former associates and friends regarded him as having sold himself to the opium merchants.[29]

The British attitude to China was perhaps best expressed by Palmerston a few years earlier, commenting on how one should deal with "half-civilized governments such as those of China, Portugal, Spanish America". They all required "a drubbing every eight or ten years to keep them in order…they must not only see the stick but actually feel it on their shoulders".[30] What he found on this occasion, however, was that the pretext Bowring had provided was widely derided and that his government faced growing opposition in both the Lords and the Commons. Palmerston survived a vote of censure over the issue in the Lords, but in the Commons Richard Cobden's motion was carried by 263 votes to 247. This was a remarkable result. Palmerston responded by dissolving parliament and fighting a fiercely jingoistic general election campaign. His widely circulated election address began: "An insolent barbarian wielding authority in Canton has violated the British flag".[31] The result in April 1857 was a landslide victory that swept away many of his opponents, including Richard Cobden. Cobden complained bitterly to his fellow radical John Bright that "I consider that we as a nation are little better than brigands, murderers and poisoners in our dealings at this moment with half the population of the globe".[32] The war had barely started.

The man sent to bring the Chinese to heel was James Bruce, the eighth Earl of Elgin. He considered the *Arrow* incident to be a "scandal" and a "contemptible" occasion for war, but nevertheless was determined to do his duty and force the Manchus to accept British

THE BLOOD NEVER DRIED

terms.[33] Preparations were held up by his troops being diverted to India to help suppress the Great Rebellion (see Chapter Four), but by the end of December 1857 an Anglo-French army had finally assembled. The bombardment of Canton began on the 28th. Shells and rockets from 32 warships battered the walls for 27 hours. The next day the city was stormed in the face of nominal resistance. Once Canton was taken, the expedition proceeded to take the Dagu forts guarding the mouth of the river Baihe and advanced up river to Tianjin which was occupied at the end of May 1858.

British methods of maintaining order in the territory they had occupied were best demonstrated in Canton where they encountered a guerrilla insurgency. Most of the population had fled, but according to Colonel Frederick Stephenson, there were bands of insurgent "braves" concealed about the city, "intimidating the people that remain, and trying, as they publicly proclaim, to cut us off by assassination". Individual soldiers were being caught on their own and beheaded. The response to these attacks was to "burn a large number of houses around the spot where they took place". Following a particularly daring attack on a patrol, they "burnt the whole neighbourhood to a distance of three quarters of a mile". The persistence of the attacks inevitably led to reprisals being stepped up. On 20 July, which was after peace had been officially concluded, Stephenson wrote home that the troops were carrying out two reprisals at that moment, destroying a district of Canton "covering a space equal to a moderately-sized town, and the other not very much smaller". He went on to say that the Chinese were an "odious and contemptible" race.[34]

The Chinese finally came to terms after Elgin threatened to advance on Beijing. On 26 June 1858 the Treaty of Tietsin was concluded, awarding Britain a £1 million indemnity, opening up the Yangxi River and five new treaty ports. The emperor also agreed to the appointment of a British ambassador to Beijing—the post was given to Elgin's brother, Frederick Bruce—and at last opium was legalised. Elgin fully acknowledged in the privacy of his journal that British conduct towards the Chinese was scandalous, but excused himself because he had, at least, tried to minimise the loss of life whereas there were many, including some missionaries, who wanted China subdued by fire, sword and massacre. He capitalised on his success at Tianjin by crossing to Japan where its rulers, the Shogunate, were

suitably impressed by the fate of the Manchus and signed the Treaty
of Yedo on 26 August 1858. This opened up a number of Japanese
ports to trade. He returned to Britain a hero with a position in the
cabinet, the rectorship of Glasgow University and the Freedom of
the City of London.

The Third Opium War

Back in China, however, Elgin's achievement was already beginning
to unravel. His brother, Frederick Bruce, insisted that his progress to
Beijing, where he was to be installed as ambassador, should be a military demonstration. The Chinese refused to accept this new
humiliation and so Bruce decided to teach them a further lesson in
compliance. He ordered the Baihe route cleared. On 25 June 1859 the
overconfident British once again attacked the Dagu forts, but on this
occasion suffered a serious defeat, with five ships sunk or disabled and
over 500 British soldiers and seamen killed. It was one of the worst
British military disasters of the 19th century. Encouraged by this victory, the emperor promptly repudiated the treaty and Elgin was once
again sent out to bring the Chinese to terms.

Once again an Anglo-French army was assembled (13,000 British
and 7,000 French) and preparations were made to renew the attack on
the Dagu forts. On 21 August 1860 the British attacked the northern-
most fort. After a ferocious bombardment the fort was stormed with
a least 2,000 Chinese killed. The Reverend R J L M'Ghee, chaplain to
the expedition, wrote of the horrors to be seen inside the fort where
the new Armstrong artillery had performed to deadly effect: "It was
indeed an awful sight, limbs blown away, bodies literally burst asun-
der, one black and livid mess of blood and wounds." He could only be
thankful that, "since there were such weapons in existence, they were
in our hands—ours, who would use them more to preserve the peace
of the world than ever to make an aggressive or unjust war".[35] British
honour had been besmirched by the so-called "Dagu Repulse" and
now it was publicly restored. No less than six Victoria Crosses were
awarded for this and the storming of the fort.

The Anglo-French army advanced on Beijing, an advance punctu-
ated by massacre and looting. At last on 5 October 1860 it arrived
before the walls of the city. What followed was, in the words of one
British officer, "a memorable day in the history of plunder and
destruction".[36] With the French leading the way the army fell on the

THE BLOOD NEVER DRIED

emperor's Summer Palace—a huge ornamental park with numerous palaces and pavilions, outside the city. According to Colonel Garnet Wolseley, both officers and men "seem to have been seized with a temporary insanity; in body and soul they were absorbed in one pursuit which was plunder, plunder".[37] The British established a prize fund for the benefit of the whole army and auctioned off their loot. This raised £26,000, a fraction of the value, and private soldiers received £5 each. Individuals still managed to enrich themselves, however. Lieutenant James Harris, for example, had to surrender his seven large baskets of plunder to the prize fund, but was allowed to keep a quantity of gold for himself that was subsequently valued at £22,000. According to Harris, the China campaign was "truly...the most enjoyable picnic in which I have taken part".[38]

In reprisal for the torture and death of a number of prisoners who had fallen into Manchu hands, Elgin ordered that the Summer Palace should be destroyed altogether. This unearthed yet more plunder. Among those sent to carry out the work was Major Charles Gordon: "We accordingly went out, and after pillaging it, burned the whole place, destroying in a Vandal-like manner most valuable property which could not be replaced for four millions... You can scarce imagine the beauty and magnificence of the places we burnt. It made one's heart sore to burn them; in fact, these palaces were so large, and we were so pressed for time, that we could not plunder them carefully. Quantities of gold ornaments were burnt, considered as brass. It was wretchedly demoralising work... Everybody was wild for plunder." Gordon himself took possession of a throne which he donated to his regiment.[39]

On 24 October Elgin entered Beijing in triumph, carried in a sedan chair and accompanied by a cavalry and infantry escort. The Manchus were now forced to ratify the Treaty of Tientsin, opening up Tianjin as a further treaty port and ceding the Kowloon peninsula to Britain, together with an additional Convention of Peking that increased the size of the indemnity. And while Elgin could not claim a trophy as valuable as the Parthenon Marbles, stolen by his father, "the Summer Palace's robes and thrones were brought back to England where they grace that monument to British imperialism, the Victoria and Albert Museum".[40] But it was not just a matter of material reward. As one officer put it, the news "of the fall of Peking will resound through Asia and produce in India an excellent effect".[41]

Crushing the Taiping rebels

Even while British troops were fighting against the Manchus, they were also fighting on their behalf against the Taipings. What the British wanted was a compliant Qing government in Beijing, which would, however reluctantly, accept British hegemony. What they did not want was a revolutionary Taiping government that would among other things prohibit the opium trade. When, in the course of 1860, the Taipings moved against Shanghai, the British resolved to stop them. The Taiping intention was to capture what was the country's most important port, giving them control of substantial customs revenues, access to supplies of modern weapons and, hopefully, Western allies. Somewhat naively they expected the British in Shanghai to welcome them both because they were fellow Christians and because they were also enemies of the Manchus.

A Taiping army led by their ablest general, Li Xiucheng, arrived before Shanghai in mid-August 1860. They had dispersed all the Manchu forces in the area and expected an unopposed takeover of the Chinese districts of the city. Li had no idea that the British had decided to defend Shanghai against him. The first he knew of their decision was when they opened fire on his troops. Augustus Lindley, the British volunteer fighting with the Taipings, described how "they were met with a storm of shot, shell and musketry" without any warning. Some 300 rebels were killed outright in this unprovoked onslaught, "mowed down by the savages on the walls" and never retaliating "with a single shot". Li was convinced the attack was a terrible mistake, but as his casualties mounted he was forced to retreat. According to Lindley, over three days the British killed some 3,000 rebels without suffering a single casualty. The Taipings never returned fire and even after they were driven off still hoped for friendly relations. Lindley recounts how a missionary, Mr Milne, fell into Taiping hands as this one-sided slaughter was taking place. Li gave him an escort to see him safely to the city gate, whereupon British troops massacred the escort.[42]

The British proceeded to proclaim a 30-mile exclusion zone around Shanghai. This led to continual fighting with the Taiping rebels. Li Xiucheng made two more attempts to occupy Shanghai, and although he inflicted some defeats on British and French forces, in the end he was always driven off by their overwhelming firepower. As for the British, they intervened more and more openly on the side of the

THE BLOOD NEVER DRIED

Manchus. In May 1862 the Taiping-held port of Ningbo, a hundred miles from Shanghai, was attacked by an Anglo-French force who handed it over to Manchu troops. The British stood by while the population, including women and children, were massacred. An important part in the British war on the Taiping rebels was played by a mercenary force, the Ever Victorious Army. This consisted of Chinese troops but equipped with modern weapons, including artillery, and under British and American officers. Charles Gordon eventually succeeded to command of the force and became a popular hero in Britain where he was celebrated as "Chinese" Gordon. This celebration was seriously misplaced, according to Lindley, who actually captured one of his gunboats, the *Firefly*. In his account of the Taipings, Lindley described how Gordon captured the town of Taitsan in May 1863 and promptly handed it over to the Manchus, who proceeded to massacre the population. The imperial troops were guilty of "the most revolting barbarities" and Lindley held that Gordon himself was "criminally responsible".[43] A number of rebel leaders were tortured to death in full view of Gordon and his officers. One should not make too much of this, however, because as one of Gordon's contemporary admirers assured his readers, it was astonishing how little the Chinese "suffer in comparison with more sensitive races".[44]

Gordon's reputation did suffer some damage when he negotiated the surrender of Suzhou in December 1863. Despite his having guaranteed the safety of the garrison, the Manchu troops carried out their usual massacre. Perhaps as many as 30,000 people were slaughtered, including the men Gordon had negotiated with. As Lindley observed, all of Gordon's victories were accompanied "by the wholesale massacre of the vanquished".[45] This was an acceptable price to pay for the suppression of the Taipings.

At the time, and for many years afterwards, Gordon was given credit in the West for having destroyed the Taipings almost single-handedly. The reality was that the rebels were finally overwhelmed by the massive Qing armies under Zeng Guofan, who finally captured Nanjing in July 1864. Nevertheless, the British did play an important role. The denial of Shanghai was a fatal setback for the revolutionary cause. The British administered the customs service, which guaranteed the government's revenues. They supplied modern weapons. And, of course, British military intervention cost the lives of thousands of rebels. While the British did not defeat the Taipings, it is most unlikely that the Manchus would have been able to defeat them without British help.

What of the opium trade? By the 1860s the British were exporting 60,000 chests of opium to China annually, rising to 100,000 chests (over 6,000 tons of opium) annually in the 1880s. After this the trade began to decline in the face of competition from Chinese produced opium. It still remained a profitable business for the rest of the century and beyond. The British opium trade with China did not finally come to an end until 1917. As for Britain's pre-eminent position in China, this began to come under pressure from rival imperialist powers towards the end of the 19th century and from Chinese revolutionary nationalism in the early decades of the 20th century. But Britain's influence was only finally eclipsed in the 1930s.

The Great Indian Rebellion, 1857-58

MICHAEL EDWARDES has argued that during the Indian Rebellion "the English threw aside the mask of civilisation and engaged in a war of such ferocity that a reasonable parallel can be seen in our times with the Nazi occupation of Europe".[1] This was the considered opinion of a historian who had spent his life studying and writing about India. How valid is his assertion? Certainly there can be no comparison between British methods of pacification and the Holocaust, and this was surely not what Edwardes intended. However, between British methods and the Nazi repression of the European resistance, there are very striking parallels. Let us consider the memoir of a certain Thomas Lowe. In his *Central India During The Rebellion of 1857 and 1858* he laments that on one occasion the column in which he was serving had become encumbered with prisoners. While the policy was to take no prisoners, he told his readers that:

> We must remember that flesh and blood—even the hardy Anglo-Saxons—cannot go on slaying from sunrise to sunset. However willing the spirit may be, physical force cannot endure it. Soldiery tire in the limb after great exertion as well as other good people, and thus it happens after a battle when the animal spirit is exhausted by heat and long-continued excitement, that many prisoners must be made.

Not to worry though. On this occasion all 76 of the men taken prisoner "were tried, sentenced and executed". They were "ranged in one long line and blindfolded" with their executioners positioned "a couple of yards" in front of them. When the bugle sounded "a long rattle of musketry swept this fleshy wall of miscreants from their earthly existence". Lowe himself acknowledges how "terrible" the scene was.

This was not an exceptional occurrence. It was routine, repeated on numerous occasions, sometimes with fewer victims, sometimes more, often with greater brutality. Much of the killing was carried out in the heat of battle, but there was also the execution on a large scale of rebels, suspected rebels and those executed solely to make an example, regardless of participation in the rebellion. Lowe himself was to participate in yet another mass disposal of prisoners, on this occasion the execution of 149 men. They were once again "ranged in one long line" and then simultaneously shot down from a few yards distance. One prisoner made a break for it and happily escaped.[2]

The violence with which the British put down the Indian Rebellion has only been approached in the history of the empire by the suppression of the United Irish rebellion in the 1790s and of the Mau Mau rebellion in the 1950s.[3] What this chapter is primarily concerned to do is to establish the dimensions of that violence and to consider the reasons for it, to examine the nature of the Indian Rebellion, without any doubt the most serious challenge to British colonial rule in the 19th century and to look at the response in Britain to this most terrible of colonial wars.

By the sword

The British conquest of India, begun in the 18th century, was completed in the 19th century by a succession of bloody wars of aggression. One historian has described the campaigns conducted in a 30-year period from 1824 until 1852-53 somewhat over enthusiastically as "little short of awe-inspiring". In 1824-26 there was the first invasion of Burma, in 1839-42 the disastrous invasion of Afghanistan, in 1843 the conquest of Sind, in 1844 the occupation of Gwalior, in 1845-46 the first war with the Sikhs for control of Punjab, followed soon after in 1848-49 by the second Sikh War that completed that conquest, and in 1852-53 another invasion of Burma.[4] These wars involved countryside laid waste, cities sacked, civilians robbed, raped and murdered, and tens of thousands of soldiers killed and mutilated. The wars with the Sikhs were particularly bloody affairs. One contemporary wrote of the siege of Multan in 1848 that "seldom or never in any part of the world has a city been exposed to such a terrific shelling as the doomed city of Multan".⁵ What this succession of aggressions demonstrates, of course, is the predatory nature of the British state. Whereas Britain after 1918 was a "satisfied" empire, concerned to hold what it had rather than seize more, in the 19th century the British Empire, despite the liberalism of its metropolitan rulers, was a predatory empire engaged in continuous warfare. This was apparent to at least some commentators at the time. Richard Cobden, the radical MP whose opposition to the Opium Wars we have already encountered, argued that just as "in the slave trade we had surpassed in guilt the world, so in foreign wars we have been the most aggressive, quarrelsome, warlike and bloody nation under the sun". In October 1850 he wrote to fellow radical Joseph Sturge that if you looked back over the previous 25 years "you will find that we have been incomparably the most sanguinary [bloodthirsty] nation on earth". Whether it was "in China, in Burma, in India, New Zealand, the Cape, Syria, Spain, Portugal, Greece, etc, there is hardly a country, however remote, in which we have not been waging war or dictating our terms at the point of a bayonet". Indeed, he believed that the British, "the greatest bloodshedders of all", had in this period been involved in more wars than the rest of Europe put together. Cobden blamed this militarism on the aristocracy that had "converted the combativeness of the English race to its own sinister ends". This last claim revealed the limits of the radical critique of the empire.⁶

The invasion of Burma in 1852 was, Cobden believed, a particular outrage. The pretext was the treatment of two British sea captains and the demand for £1,000 compensation from the Burmese. Their failure to immediately capitulate led to escalating threats that culminated in January 1852 with the Royal Navy seizing the royal yacht, shelling Burmese forts and incidentally killing hundreds of Burmese soldiers, and imposing a blockade. Lord Dalhousie, the governor general of India, now demanded compensation of £100,000 and, when this was refused, war was declared in April.⁷ When he came to examine the causes of the war Cobden was, he admitted, "amazed at the case":

I blush for my country, and the very blood in my veins tingled with indignation at the wanton disregard of all justice and decency which our proceedings towards that country exhibited. The violence and wrongs perpetrated by Pizarro or Cortez were scarcely veiled in a more transparent pretence of right than our own.

It was not a war, but a massacre. The Burmese had "no more chance against our 64 pound red-hot shot and other infernal improvements in the art of war than they would in running a race on their roads against our railways". And, moreover, "the day on which we commenced the war with a bombardment of shot, shell and rockets…that the natives must have thought it an onslaught of devils, was Easter Sunday!"[8]

Cobden published a savage indictment of the war, *How Wars are got up in India: The Origins of the Burmese War*, in 1853. Here he made the point that similar disputes with the United States had never ended in war for the simple reason "that America is powerful and Burma weak". Britain, he insisted, quite correctly, "would not have acted in this manner towards a power capable of defending itself".[9] The war ended in 1853 with the annexation of another large slice of Burmese territory, which fortuitously included the Pegu gold mines.[10]

Within India itself, after the defeat of the Sikhs, Dalhousie had no more enemies to conquer, but instead followed a policy of annexing the territory of Britain's princely allies. This was his policy of "lapse" whereby if a ruler died without a direct heir Britain took over his territory and, more importantly, his revenues. In five years he annexed five princely states—Satara, Nagpur, Jhansi, Tanjore and, lastly, in 1856, Awadh. This last annexation was not as a result of lapse, however, but on the pretext of the mismanagement of the king, Wajid Ali Shah. As Dalhousie proudly observed, "Our gracious Queen has 5,000,000 more subjects and £1,300,000 more revenue than she had yesterday".[11] In fact, this last annexation was a huge mistake. It was regarded as an act of naked aggression against an ally, as an act that revealed the British as absolutely untrustworthy. Moreover, two thirds of the largest of Britain's "native" (or sepoy) armies, the Bengal Army, some 60,000 men, were recruited from Awadh. Dalhousie's last aggression was one of the most important grievances that provoked the Great Rebellion.

Company rule

British rule in India was exercised through the agency of the East India Company, an early private-public partnership, that had conquered and now ruled the subcontinent. Although it was originally a trading company, by the 19th century company revenues derived less from trade and more from the exploitation of the rural population through the levying of oppressive land taxes. By 1818 Indian revenues were worth some £22 million, dwarfing the profits made from trade. In 1820 the company remitted £6 million to Britain, tribute paid to the conqueror, a form of exploitation the Romans would have recognised. One important aspect of the company's operations was, of course, the production and sale of opium. The revenues accruing from this trade were, as we have seen, great enough to be worth going to war for.[12]

By the 1850s India was still relatively undeveloped as a market for British exports. According to Karl Marx, writing in the summer of 1853, this was explained by the fact that the British had "a double mission in India: one destructive, the other regenerating". They had accomplished the destructive in a way that "unveiled before our eyes" all the "profound hypocrisy and inherent barbarism of bourgeois civilisation...turning from its home, where it assumes respectable forms, to the colonies, where it goes naked". Indeed, he wrote, "the historic pages of their role in India report hardly anything beyond that destruction". Nevertheless, he believed that the work of regeneration had begun. Crucial to this was the interest that the British capitalist class had in fostering economic development in India. Once the "millocracy" had destroyed the Indian textile industry, it "discovered that the transformation of India into a reproductive country has become of vital importance". Railways were necessary to effectively exploit India's natural resources. Moreover, it had become apparent to British capitalists that "you cannot continue to inundate a country with your manufactures, unless you enable it to give you some produce in return". British manufactured exports to India actually fell in the course of the 1840s. Consequently, India had become "the battlefield" in the contest between "the industrial interest on the one side" and the financial and aristocratic interests represented by the East India Company.[13]

For Marx, the nature of company rule was best demonstrated by its seldom acknowledged reliance on torture. Writing after the outbreak of the Great Rebellion, he discussed "the official Blue Books on the subject of East India torture, which were laid before the House of Commons during the sessions of 1856 and 1857". These reports established "the universal existence of torture as a financial institution of British India". It was admitted that revenue officers and the police routinely used torture in the collection of taxes. As he observes, while this was freely admitted, "the admission is made in such a manner as to shield the British government itself". The practice of torture "is entirely the fault of the lower Hindu officials", while British officials were not only not involved, but had "done their best to prevent it". This claim, as Marx points out, was contradicted by much of the evidence assembled in the reports. He concluded that here we have a chapter:

> From the real history of British rule in India. In view of such facts, dispassionate and thoughtful men may perhaps be led to ask whether a people are not justified in attempting to expel the foreign conquerors who have so abused their subjects.[14]

What did this torture involve? It ranged from rough manhandling through to flogging and placing in the stocks and then on to more extreme measures:

> Searing with hot irons…dipping in wells and rivers till the victim is half suffocated…squeezing the testicles…putting pepper and red chillies in the eyes or introducing them into the private parts of men and women…prevention of sleep…nipping the flesh with pincers…suspension from the branches of a tree…imprisonment in a room used for storing lime…[15]

What is remarkable is how little this regime of torture has figured in accounts of British rule in India. It is a hidden history that has been unremarked on and almost completely unexplored. Book after book remains silent on the subject. This most surely calls into question the whole historiography of the Raj.[16]

One last point is worth noting here: the extent to which everyday relations between the British and their Indian subjects were characterised by abuse and violence. Servants were routinely abused as "niggers" and assaulted and beaten by their masters, something that

THE BLOOD NEVER DRIED

worsened during and after the Great Rebellion. Lord Elgin, writing in August 1857, described British feelings towards the Indians as consisting of "detestation, contempt, ferocity". Their feelings were ones of "perfect indifference", treating their servants, "not as dogs because in that case one would whistle to them and pat them, but as machines with which one can have no communion or sympathy". This indifference when combined with hatred produced "an absolute callousness...which must be witnessed to be understood and believed".[17] The war correspondent William Howard Russell witnessed a fellow Briton attacking with "a huge club" a group of coolies for idling, leaving them maimed and bleeding. He thought murder might have been done had he not intervened to restrain the assault.[18] Sometimes there was regret. One British officer confided to his diary how he had kicked and injured his servant: "I must never kick him or strike him anywhere again, except with a whip, which can hardly injure him".[19] This everyday abuse and violence continued until the end of the British Raj.

The Great Rebellion

Speaking in the House of Commons on 27 July 1857, Benjamin Disraeli, one of the leaders of the Conservative Party, asked, "Does the disturbance in India indicate a military mutiny, or is it a national revolt?" It was, he concluded, answering his own question, a national revolt.[20] This interpretation of the outbreak was subsequently endorsed by the governor general, Lord Canning, who made it clear that as far as he was concerned the struggle "had been more like a national war than a local insurrection...its magnitude, duration, scale of expenditure, and in some of its moral features it partakes largely of the former character".[21] From a different point of view, Karl Marx argued that in their creation of a sepoy arm, the British themselves had inadvertently created "the first general centre of resistance which the Indian people were ever possessed of". There had been mutinies before, but "the present revolt" was different in that "Mussulmans and Hindus, renouncing their mutual antipathies, have combined against their common masters". Indeed, he saw the revolt as part of "a general disaffection against English supremacy on the part of the great Asiatic nations".[22]

The contemporary recognition that the Great Rebellion had many of the features of a national uprising later became an embarrassment to the British once arguments for their continued rule became predicated on the claim that there was no such thing as an Indian nation. Increasingly, it was Indian nationalists who claimed the rebellion as a national movement, as the first blow in India's national struggle. In 1909 V D Savarkar published his *The Indian War of Independence, 1857*, the first substantial statement of this position. The book was, of course, banned in India, but still appeared "on the Indian bookstalls, wrapped in a cover labelled *Random Papers of the Pickwick Club*".[23] Academic disputes concerning the character of the rebellion continue to this day, with many historians arguing that while there was certainly a rebellion or rebellions, it was not a national movement. Certainly, the rebellion had many components, military mutiny, peasant revolt, legitimist insurrection, artisan rebellion, religious uprising, but these were all given shape by a ferocious popular hostility to British rule. The problem is that those historians who emphasise these various components have a static view, whereas the rebellion has to be regarded as a dynamic phenomenon. It can best be seen as a national revolt in a particular phase of development, full of contradictions certainly, but put down by the British before these could be resolved. If the rebels had been more successful in spreading the revolt, marching on Calcutta, for example, instead of consolidating at Delhi, the story might have been very different. Instead they were destroyed.

The rebellion was precipitated by a mutiny in the Bengal Army over the infamous issue of the greased cartridges for the new Enfield rifle. This proved to be the great fear into which all the sepoys' other grievances (pay and allowances, abuse at the hands of British officers, the annexation of Awadh) were poured. Increasing resentment against British domination was given a religious expression with all their very real transgressions being summed up as their perceived determination to forcibly convert Hindus and Muslims to Christianity. What is astonishing in retrospect is that the mutiny took the British by surprise. There had been plenty of warning. In September 1855 a senior officer, Colonel Colin Mackenzie, had interfered with a religious procession and was nearly beaten to death by outraged sepoys. The men's worries regarding the cartridges had been made known to their officers, but were disregarded. Moreover, the fear that the cartridges were greased with cattle and pig fat was justified, showing a disregard for caste sensitivities that is astonishing. In February 1857 troops at Berhampur and at Barrackpur had refused to use the cartridges. The

THE BLOOD NEVER DRIED

first sign of what was to come, however, took place on 29 March when a young soldier, Mangal Pandy, tried to raise the standard of revolt at Barrackpur. He fought with and wounded two British officers before being overpowered, but while the other sepoys did not join the revolt, neither did they take action against him. Pandy was hanged and for the British his name was to become a generic term for rebels.

The explosion finally came on 10 May at Meerut. Men here refused to handle the cartridges and 85 of them were placed in irons. Their comrades mutinied, according to one account, urged on by a British woman, the widow of a British sergeant, known as "Mees Dolly". She was summarily hanged.[24] The mutineers freed their comrades, killed or drove off their officers and then marched on Delhi. The decision to march on the old Mughal capital turned the mutiny into a rebellion. They seized the city and its arsenal on the 11th with the sepoy garrison joining the revolt. The Mughal emperor, Bahadur Shah, a man in his eighties, who had spent his adult life as a helpless pensioner of the British, found himself reluctantly installed as the figurehead for a full-scale rebellion.

The revolt spread across northern and central India with the beleaguered British managing to hold out only at Kanpur, Agra and in the residency compound at Lucknow (the city itself was in rebel hands). Wherever sepoys mutinied, the local population rose up, artisans and labourers in the cities and the peasantry in the countryside. A number of historians have pointed out the unevenness of this popular mobilisation, but this is true for every revolutionary outbreak. The popular movement compelled a number of princes and rulers, with varying degrees of reluctance, to embrace the rebellion, Bahadur Shah as we have already seen, but also Nana Sahib at Kanpur and the Rani Lakshmi at Jhansi. Most of the rulers remained loyal to their British patrons, however.[25] More to the point, British rule collapsed across a huge area, swept away as the company's means of repression slipped from its grasp. The rebellion engulfed 150,000 square miles with a population of 45 million.[26] It was, without doubt, one of the largest revolutionary outbreaks of the 19th century, arguably only exceeded in scale by the contemporaneous Taiping revolt in China. Of course, one reason for the rebellion's defeat was that it did not spread further, a point to which we will return.

To the extent that the rebellion is remembered at all in Britain, it is remembered for the Kanpur (or Cawnpore) massacre. The attack on

General Wheeler's small force as it evacuated under negotiated terms on 27 June is portrayed as the height of treachery. More important though is the fate of the survivors of this attack, the 180 people, overwhelmingly women and children, who were massacred, hacked to death, on 15 July, as the British approached the city. Rudrangshu Mukherjee, in his *Spectre of Violence*, has made a convincing attempt at contextualising these events. He shows that the attack on Wheeler's force at Satichaura Ghat was a popular collective affair, celebrated as a great victory over the oppressor. The massacre of the women and children at the Bibighar, however, was something very different. The sepoys refused to take part and the killing was instead carried out by men procured by Nana Sahib's retainers.[27] They were killed on the orders of people who had nothing to lose, because their lives were already forfeit if they should fall into British hands.[28] This is, of course, not to minimise the horror of what took place. Indeed, wherever rebellion broke out, the popular fury often involved killing all the British, men, women and children that the rebels could lay their hands on. According to Marx, this was:

> Only the reflex, in a concentrated form, of England's own conduct in India, not only during the epoch of the foundation of her Eastern Empire, but even during the last years of a long-settled rule…it is a rule of historical retribution that its instrument is forged not by the offended, but by the offender himself.

He went on to complain of the reporting of the rebellion in the British press that "while the cruelties of the English are related as acts of martial vigour, told simply, rapidly, without dwelling in disgusting details, the outrages of the natives, shocking as they are, are still deliberately exaggerated".[29]

Events at Kanpur and elsewhere were indeed wildly exaggerated into stories of rape and torture. It was widely reported that British women had been cooked alive, forced to eat their children, horribly mutilated with noses and ears cut off and eyes put out, and stripped naked and publicly raped. These stories were untrue. Exhaustive investigations carried out by the British authorities themselves produced no evidence whatever of rape and torture and it was subsequently accepted that none had occurred. At the time, however, the stories were used to justify the most fearsome reprisals,

THE BLOOD NEVER DRIED

although it is important to remember that these reprisals were already well under way before the massacre at the Bibighar. One last point worth making is that, terrible though it was, the Bibighar massacre was a small-scale affair put alongside the British sack of Allahabad, Delhi, Lucknow and Jhansi. Its prominence derives, as Russell put it, from the fact "that the deed was done by a subject race".[30]

War

Why did the Great Rebellion fail? The most important reason is that it failed to spread. Of course, this begs the question of why this was the case. In Punjab the British response to unrest, orchestrated by John Lawrence, was both determined and absolutely ruthless. They effectively stamped out the movement before it could master sufficient strength to make a fight of it.[31] This was a serious blow to the rebel cause because, once successfully pacified, Punjab was to supply large numbers of troop reinforcements, including many Sikhs, for the attack on Delhi. Equally serious was the rebels' own concentration of their forces at Delhi, rather than despatching mobile columns to spread the revolt and, in particular, to strike at Calcutta. As Eric Stokes has put it, this tendency "to congregate at Delhi...was to deprive the rebellion of its expansive proclivities". Their strategy saw them "surrender the initiative" at the very time that they had the British on the run, effectively forfeiting "the option of a war of movement at the most opportune hour".[32] The establishment by the British of a fortified camp at Delhi, described quite correctly by one historian as "a knight's pawn move against the enemy king", only reinforced the tendency to rally on Delhi.[33] Delhi was not really under siege until August, but in the meantime the rebels wasted their strength making brave but futile assaults on the British position, suffering heavy losses when they should have been spreading the revolt. This strategic failure was decisive.

To a considerable extent the strategic failure derived from the failure to establish an effective revolutionary government in Delhi. An attempt was made to establish a democratic regime, the Court, under the auspices of Bahadur Shah, but it never succeeded in establishing its authority, in becoming a revolutionary regime on the model of the French Revolution.[34] Similarly, the military leader in the capital, Bakht Khan, was never able to take effective command of the rebel forces. When it came to the conduct of military affairs, although the rebels had an overwhelming numerical superiority, this was often not realised on the actual battlefield because of problems of command and control. Lack of experienced officers and a weak chain of command meant that rebel forces were often defeated piecemeal without individual units supporting each other. On the field of battle numbers were often more equal than appeared on paper. And, of course, the British had an overwhelming technological advantage. The Enfield rifle had a far greater range than the Brown Bess musket, and although not all British troops were equipped with it, enough were to enable the British to inflict heavy losses on the rebels before they were even close enough to return fire. Moreover, thousands of rebels did not have firearms at all, but were equipped with swords, shields, spears and even bows and arrows. Most important, however, was the British superiority in artillery, the decisive weapon in the war, which enabled the British both to batter down rebel defences and to slaughter them in the open. One historian has remarked that in the circumstances the wonder was that the rebels "won any battles at all".[35]

Repression

British military operations were accompanied by the most savage repression. In Punjab, John Lawrence proceeded to disarm those sepoy regiments considered unreliable, accompanied by the execution of individuals believed to be sympathetic to the rebellion. One disarmed regiment, the 26th, mutinied, broke out of camp and fled with their families. They were hunted down with 150 of them killed in the process and another 282 handed over to Frederick Cooper, the deputy commissioner of Amritsar. He proceeded to execute them in batches. When over 200 had been shot, the remainder barricaded themselves in their prison and were left overnight. The next morning, they were found "dead from fright, exhaustion, fatigue, heat and partial suffocation". Undeterred, Cooper had the last 20 survivors shot. Another 40 were eventually rounded up and sent to Lahore where they were blown from the guns. Within 48 hours nearly 500 men had been executed and the entire regiment had been destroyed. The natives who were witness to the executions, according to Cooper, "marvelled at the clemency and justice of the British". He was much congratulated, with Lawrence himself commending his "energy and spirit". Cooper also recounts the fate of another regiment that broke out and was hunted down. Within 30 hours 659 soldiers of the 51st

Native Infantry had been slaughtered. As he observes, "no misplaced leniency was extended to any captures. The offence was mutiny, the design treason, the punishment—death".[36] This was how Punjab was kept quiet.

Elsewhere things were not so civilised. At Benares, Colonel James Neill, a particularly brutal Christian psychopath, crushed the 37th Native Infantry on 4 June and instituted a reign of terror. Hundreds of people were hanged. Parties of armed British civilians set themselves up as "volunteer hanging parties", helping to pacify the city and surrounding districts with summary executions. Among those hanged were some young boys who had paraded in rebel colours. From Benares, Neill proceeded to Allahabad, where news of his approach actually provoked a rising. He shelled the city and put it to the sack. Once again hundreds were hanged, some, as F A V Thurburn, the deputy judge advocate general, observed, with "slight proofs of criminality".[37] His troops carried the terror into the surrounding countryside, burning villages and hanging "niggers". By the time his terror had exhausted itself some 6,000 men, women and children had been killed. As Neill piously observed, "God grant I may have acted with justice. I know I have with severity, but under the circumstances I trust for forgiveness".[38]

Neill sent off a column under Major Sydenham Renaud to relieve Kanpur, terrorising the countryside on the way. Renaud was explicitly ordered to attack and destroy all the villages of the Mubgoan district: "Slaughter all the men; take no prisoners." He was ordered to make "a signal example" of the town of Futtehpore, "all in it to be killed".[39] Renaud proceeded to burn and hang (12 men were hanged because their faces were "turned the wrong way") until ordered by General Havelock to burn "no more villages unless occupied by insurgents". As Russell was to observe, Renaud's "severities could not have been justified by the Cawnpore massacre, because they took place before that diabolical act".[40] John Sherer, the resident magistrate of Futtehpore, described the scene:

> Many villages had been burned by the wayside and of human beings there were none to be seen. A more desolate scene than the country we passed through can scarcely be imagined...the blackened ruins of huts...the utter absence of all sound that could indicate the presence of human life...the occasional taint in the air

from suspended bodies upon which, before our eyes, the loathsome pigs of the country were engaged in feasting; all these things, appealing to our different senses contributed to call up such images of desolation and blackness and woe as few, I should think, who were present will ever forget.[41]

Havelock's forces entered Kanpur unopposed on 17 July, the rebels having fled. He left Neill in command and marched on to attempt the relief of the besieged residency at Lucknow. Neill proceeded to exact a terrible vengeance for the Bibigher massacre. On 25 July he ordered that prisoners were to be taken to the house and forced to lick clean a portion of the bloody floor, beaten until they complied, and then hanged. He saw himself guided by "the finger of God in this". This procedure continued in operation until early November when General Colin Campbell finally put a stop to it. By then Neill himself was dead, shot in the second attempt to relieve Lucknow. He received a posthumous knighthood from Queen Victoria. For some, Neill's retribution did not go far enough. Colonel John Nicholson, another Christian soldier, soon to become a popular hero, urged the passing of "a bill for the flaying alive, impalement, or burning of the murderers of women and children". If he had his way, "I would inflict the most excruciating tortures I could think of on them with a perfectly easy conscience".[42]

Delhi was finally stormed on 13 September, although fighting continued for another week, as the city was put to the sack. According to one officer, Lieutenant Charles Griffiths:

There is no more terrible spectacle than a city taken by storm. All the pent-up passions of men are here let loose without restraint. Roused to a pitch of fury from long-continued resistance and eager to take vengeance on the murderers of women and children, the men in their pitiless rage showed no mercy.

Looting began even while the fighting continued and many British troops were soon drunk. If the rebels had been able to organise a counter-attack, the British would have been driven from the city. Instead it was given over to looting, rape and murder. British and Sikh troops actually began fighting among themselves. Griffiths described the scene:

THE BLOOD NEVER DRIED

Not content with ransacking the interior of each house, the soldiers had broken up every article of furniture, and with wanton destruction had thrown everything portable out of the windows. Each street was filled with a mass of debris consisting of household effects of every kind... Not a single house or building remained intact.

This continued for three weeks, leaving Delhi to all appearances "a city of the dead on which some awful catastrophe had fallen". There were dead bodies "in almost every street, rotting in the burning sun, and the effluvium was sickening". As for the population, those who survived were driven from the city:

Old men, women and children...half-starved...the most wretched-looking objects I ever saw...by order of the general, they were turned out of the gates of Delhi and escorted into the country... I fear that many perished from want and exposure.

Meanwhile, "executions by hanging were a common occurrence in the city",[43] and similar scenes were to be repeated at Lucknow and Jhansi.

The worst massacre carried out by the British is not even acknowledged as such, but was instead celebrated as a heroic epic with no less than eight Victoria Crosses being awarded to the participants. This was the storming of the Sikander Bagh, a walled garden, during the second relief of Lucknow. There were over 2,000 rebels in the enclosure and they were attacked by troops from the 93rd Highlanders and the 4th Punjab Infantry. According to the future Field Marshal Lord Roberts, then a young officer, the scene required "the pen of a Zola to depict". The rebels found themselves trapped and, according to Roberts, "fought with the desperation of men without hope of mercy". He wrote:

Inch by inch they were forced back to the pavilion, and into the space between it and the north wall where they were all shot or bayoneted. There they lay in a heap as high as my head, a heaving surging mass of dead and dying inextricably entangled. It was a sickening sight... The wretched wounded men could not get clear of their dead comrades, however great their struggles, and those near the top of the ghastly pile of writhing humanity vented their rage and disappointment on every British officer who approached by showering upon him abuse of the grossest description.[44]

Another officer wrote of "hundreds of sepoys dead or dying, many on fire…a suffocating, burning, smouldering mass". He saw 64 prisoners lined up "and bayoneted…God forgive us".[45] The next day another future field marshal, Garnet Wolseley, saw a handful of survivors surrender to the Sikhs who "made them kneel down and …killed them with their tulwars [sabres]".[46] According to Malleson, "more than 2,000 corpses lay heaped around… It is said that of all who garrisoned it, only four men escaped, but even the escape of four is doubtful".[47] Some 60 Scottish and Sikh troops were killed. This was clearly not a battle, but a massacre. Hundreds of men, who had ceased to offer any resistance, were killed without mercy. There were women and children, shot and bayoneted, among the dead.[48]

This was a war of innumerable horrors: prisoners blown from the guns, mass hangings (Sergeant William Forbes-Mitchell saw 130 men hanged from one giant banyan tree)[49] and the merciless sack and pillage of ancient cities. William Howard Russell recounted another incident in Lucknow where a young boy approached a British officer and asked for his protection. The man put his pistol to the boy's head and shot him. What made the crime worse was that the weapon misfired three times before the boy could be killed. Muslims were smeared "with pork-fat before execution" and "Hindus were forced to defile themselves". There were things being "done in India which we would not permit to be done in Europe".[50] Lord Canning, the governor general, complained to Queen Victoria of "a rabid and indiscriminate vindictiveness" having gripped the British in India. People seemed to think "that the hanging and shooting of 40 or 50,000 mutineers besides other rebels can be otherwise than practicable and right". He confessed to "a feeling of shame for one's fellow countrymen". Canning's attempts to urge, not so much restraint, as some discrimination, in the slaughter, earned him the derisive nickname of "Clemency Canning".[51]

Let us close this section by looking at the letters home of Major Harcourt Anson. They provide a horrific chronicle of the pacification of rebel India. On one occasion, he told his wife, they surrounded a village with orders to kill every man found there:

THE BLOOD NEVER DRIED

Fathers are shot with all their womenkind clinging to them, and begging for their lives, but content the next moment to lie in their blood howling... Unarmed cowherds were mercilessly pistolled together with about 20 armed men. What the poor women and children in this place are to do without their men who are being killed in every house, I cannot say.

On 4 January 1858 he wrote home telling her how the rebel leader Nazir Khan was hanged. He was surrounded by "soldiers who were stuffing him with pork...well flogged and his person exposed, which he fought against manfully... He died game." On the 10th he told of how there were "14 men hung or rather tortured to death" and the following day he described "one of the most remarkable sights I ever in my life beheld; no less than 20 men all hanging naked on one tree". On 25 February he wrote of how another village was punished with "a number of women...killed while clinging to and trying to hide their delinquent husbands". Other women died when they refused to leave a house that was set on fire, although, as he observes, "their fate was preferable to two unfortunates who were ravished to death". He confided that he was worried he would return home "without a heart or feelings of any soft humanising tendency". On another occasion, he wrote home, "The only real wonder to me in this land is that all do not at once rise upon us and exterminate the hated Feringhees [the British] who so grievously oppress them".[52]

The war at home
Public opinion in Britain was inevitably mobilised behind the war to suppress the Great Rebellion by the atrocity stories that appeared in the press. On 30 October 1857 Lord Shaftesbury, in a widely reported speech, told of how "day by day ladies were coming to Calcutta with their ears and noses cut off and their eyes put out" and that children were being "put to death under circumstances of the most exquisite torture". The speech was immediately published as *Lord Shaftebury's Great Speech on Indian Cruelties*. Prompted by this, Lord Ellenborough, himself a former governor general of India, called in the House of Lords for every man in Delhi to be castrated and for the city to be renamed "Eunochabad".[53] Even Charles Dickens could long for the opportunity "to exterminate the race upon whom the stain of the late cruelties rested...to blot it out of mankind and raze it

off the face of the earth".⁵⁴ Inevitably, the Radicals retreated in the face of this surge of opinion. Although privately Richard Cobden could still confess that if he were an Indian "I would be one of the rebels" and that "Hindustan must be ruled by those who live on that side of the globe", discretion proved the better part of valour. He reluctantly came to accept that the rebellion had to be put down, although he still thought it "terrible to see our middle class journals and speakers calling for the destruction of Delhi, and the indiscriminate massacre of prisoners".⁵⁵

There were still voices raised in support of the Indian cause, however. The Chartist and socialist Ernest Jones, on the public platform and in his newspaper, the *People's Paper*, campaigned in support of the rebels in what has been described as "a magnificent climax to his revolutionary career". Earlier, in 1851, he had written a long poem, "The New World", which was now republished as "The Revolt of Hindostan". It was in the preface to this poem that Jones made his celebrated observation that "the blood never dries" on the British Empire. Now as early as 4 July in the *People's Paper*, he argued that the Indian rebels "are now fighting for all most sacred to men. The cause of the Poles, the Hungarians, the Italians, the Irish, was not more just and holy." The rebellion was "one of the noblest movements the world has ever known". And the working class in Britain was being asked to pay for its suppression, sustaining "one of the most iniquitous usurpations that ever disgraced the annals of humanity". On 1 August he wrote to insist that the rebellion was "not a military mutiny but a national insurrection" and urged recognition of "the independence of the Indian race".⁵⁶

Jones returned to these themes regularly, as Karl Marx's daughter Jenny put it, "making Kossuths [after the Hungarian revolutionary hero] of all the Hindus". The East India Company, he pointed out, collected taxes by the use of torture. If you could not pay, "they hung you up with your heads downwards in the burning sun, lashed you, tortured you, tied scorpions to the breasts of your women, committed every atrocity and crime". What, he asked, would the British people do if subjected to such a tyranny? He replied:

You would rise—rise in the holy right of insurrection, and cry to Europe and the world, to heaven and earth, to bear witness to the justice of your cause.

THE BLOOD NEVER DRIED

As for the atrocities committed by the rebels, he elsewhere insisted that their conduct, "throughout the mutiny, has been in strict and consistent accordance with the example of their civilised governors".[57] Jones continued his powerful support for the rebellion through its defeat.

One last point worth making is that there were Britons who fought in the rebel ranks against British rule. In Delhi a former British sergeant major named Gordon served with the rebels and was captured in September 1857. His fate is unknown. In Lucknow, Felix Rotton and his three sons fought against the British. And there was a widely held belief at the time that Brigadier Adrian Hope had been killed by a British soldier in the rebel ranks owing to his cockney accent and slang when taunting his opponents. There were undoubtedly other "unofficial Europeans", Britons who lived among and had married into Indian communities, fighting against the British Empire.[58]

The aftermath

Only when the rebellion had already been effectively defeated did rebel leaders, most notably Tanti Topi, adopt the methods of mobile warfare. As one historian has observed, however, "this display of tactical brilliance was too late to influence the outcome of a war which had already been decided by British victories in Delhi and Awadh". If mobile columns had been sent out to spread revolt when the rebellion was at its height, the story might well have been different.[59] Even so, guerrilla warfare continued well into 1859. Indeed, the hunt for rebels hiding out in the villages continued into the 1860s, a demonstration that much of the countryside still remained outside effective British control.[60]

What did the rebellion accomplish? The answer is best left to one of the rebel leaders, Mahomed Ali Khan, awaiting execution in February 1858. Sergeant Forbes-Mitchell was in charge of the guard detachment. He prevented Ali Khan's defilement and the two men became friendly. On one occasion when Ali Khan faltered in the face of death, he steeled himself with the words, "I must remember Danton [a leader of the Great French Revolution] and show no weakness." As far as Mahomed Ali Khan was concerned, the rebellion might have been defeated but it had destroyed company rule and this was a first step. He was duly hanged. And, as he had foreseen, in August 1858 the British ended company rule in India.[61]

The invasion of Egypt, 1882

IN THE late autumn of 1879 William Gladstone began his celebrated "Midlothian campaign". Over a two-week period the 69 year old veteran spoke at 27 meetings to an audience estimated at over 80,000 people. His speeches were fully reported in both the national and local press. According to one historian, the old man's "charismatic power" reached its zenith during the campaign and he brought about what could almost be described as "an uprising of the populace".[1] On 25 November Gladstone spoke at the Music Hall in Edinburgh. He condemned "the established dietary of the present government" which consists of "a series of theatrical expedients, calculated to excite, calculated to alarm, calculated to stir pride and passion". What, he wondered, would be their "next quasi-military operation"? The Conservatives were setting up "false phantoms of glory" which were leading people to believe that they were better than the rest of the world. More specifically, he condemned the annexation of the Transvaal, the attack on the Zulus, the assumption together with France of "the virtual government of Egypt" and "the most wanton invasion of Afghanistan". The Afghanistan adventure had "broken that country to pieces, made it a miserable ruin".[2] These were to be recurrent themes in the wide-ranging indictments of Conservative misrule that were taken up by Liberals and Radicals throughout the country. Gladstone presented a crushing indictment on both moral and practical grounds. When the general election was finally held in April 1880 the Conservative government was routed, with 351 Liberal MPs returned and only 239 Conservatives.

Gladstone's repeated condemnation of the government's actions in Egypt in his Midlothian speeches is especially noteworthy because he was to order a full-scale invasion of that country some two years into office. This turnaround should not come as a complete surprise. Even in his Midlothian speeches Gladstone made it clear that he was condemning ill-considered imperial adventures rather than the empire as such. In a speech in Glasgow on 5 December 1879 he had actually promised "to consecrate" the empire "to the Almighty by the strict application of the principles of justice and goodwill, of benevolence and mercy".[3] More to the point, every government he had been a member of in his long career had invaded somewhere and he had always managed to square it with his conscience. Moreover, his own first government had sent a military expedition to the Gold Coast in west Africa in 1873-74 ("the Ashanti War") and had been preparing to annex Fiji when it lost office. Even so the turnaround from condemning the assumption of the "virtual government" of Egypt to full-scale invasion still requires some explanation.

Ismail and the bankers

Egypt had been delivered up into the hands of the French and the British by the efforts of its ruler, the Khedive, to modernise the country. At the time of his succession in 1863 Egypt was benefiting from a boom in the demand for its cotton brought about by the disruption of supplies from the Southern States during the American Civil War. This created what has been described as the "Klondike of the Nile" with European banks rushing to "spoil the Egyptians" with loans. Ismail, the Khedive, invested heavily in improvements to the country's infrastructure. During his reign 112 irrigation canals were dug totalling 8,400 miles in length, the railway system was extended from 275 to 1185 miles, 430 bridges were built and the harbour at Alexandria was modernised. He increased the amount of agricultural land from some 4 million acres in 1862 to nearly 5.5 million in 1879. Ismail also invested heavily in education with the number of elementary schools increasing from 185 to 4,685. And he presided over the construction of the Suez Canal.[4]

The Suez Canal can be seen as the first step along the road to eventual bankruptcy and the takeover of Egypt by the British. Construction, which took from 1859 until 1869, cost some £16 million of which shareholders subscribed £4,500,000 and the Egyptian government the rest. The bulk of the profits from the operation of the canal nevertheless went to the shareholders, not the government. Even worse, the Egyptian government had to borrow the money for its own investment on ruinous terms so that by 1873 it had paid £6 million in interest on these loans alone.[5] According to one economic historian, "Egypt's financial difficulties originated with the building of the Suez Canal" and moreover, while its construction was of considerable benefit to European, particularly British commerce, it "could not possibly be of any benefit" to Egypt.[6]

By 1876 the Egyptian government had foreign loans amounting to £68 million, internal loans of over £14 million and a floating debt of £16 million. Of the amounts borrowed something like a third had never made it into the Egyptian treasury but had been siphoned off by the banks as "discounts and commissions which were exaggerated and inflated to the verge and beyond the verge of fraudulence".[7] The Marxist Theodore Rothstein provided a useful account of the "methods of modern finance" with regard to a loan for £32 million that Ismail negotiated with Rothschild's investment bank in 1873. The Rothschilds kept nearly £12 million as security and, of the £20 million actually handed over, some £9 million was in substantially overvalued bonds of Egyptian floating debt. The Egyptians received less than half of what they had borrowed and, of course, had to pay interest on the whole of it. This was fraud on a massive scale that goes unmarked by most historians. The 1873 loan, instead of alleviating the Egyptian position, seriously weakened it.[8] Bankruptcy was only avoided in 1875 by the sale of the Egyptian government's share in the Suez Canal to the British government for a derisory £4 million.

This merely postponed the inevitable, and the following year Ismail announced his intention of postponing of the bondholders' coupon. The Egyptian government was effectively bankrupt. Egypt was delivered into the hands of European financial interests, who, with the support of the British and the French governments, progressively took over the running of the country. Egypt was to be governed for the benefit of the bondholders, the investors who had bought into the Egyptian debt, and its population despoiled to ensure the payment of their interest. British investors owned a third of the debt. This constituted a significant section of the British upper class, including William Gladstone, who was one of the bondholders. Their exactions were to provoke revolution.

The scale of the problem is demonstrated by the budget for 1877. Egyptian revenue was £9,526,000 extracted from the peasantry, the fellahin, often with considerable brutality. Of this, most, £7,474,000, went to the bondholders; £470,000 went as tribute to the Ottoman Sultan in Istanbul (this tribute was also owned by European bondholders) and £200,000 went as interest on the Suez Canal shares sold to the British. This left £1,400,000 to pay for the government, administration and defence of the country.[9] Under pressure from the European powers Ismail was forced to agree to the appointment of two controllers-general, one British and one French, to supervise the government, although Ismail did his best to obstruct this system of "Dual Control". As early as February 1878 George Goschen, MP for the City of London, a senior Liberal politician and Gladstone's personal financial adviser (and one of the architects of this dual control) wrote in his diary that Ismail would have to be "deposed if he won't give way".[10]

Ismail was bullied into accepting the appointment of an Englishman, Rivers Wilson, as minister of finance and a Frenchman, de Blignieres, as minister of public works. Increasing popular hostility to European influence encouraged him to try and retrieve the situation and in April 1879 he dismissed them both. Only shortage of troops prevented the then Conservative government intervening militarily, with Lord Salisbury complaining that "all our force is locked up" in Zululand and Afghanistan.[11] Instead a diplomatic offensive in Istanbul secured Ismail's removal and he was replaced by his son, Tewfik, on 25 June 1879. From the very beginning Tewfik was aware that his fate was dependent on the British.

"Egypt for the Egyptians!"

The late 1870s were a period of the most appalling hardship for the Egyptian fellahin. A series of crop failures produced famine in Upper Egypt in 1878 during which thousands starved to death. At the very same time the exactions of the tax collectors, whip in hand, were stepped up in order to ensure the payment of the bondholders' interest. Rivers Wilson records in his memoirs being told by one Egyptian official of the plight of the people. When he insisted that the taxes had to be collected he was told that it would be done but "I must beg that you make no inquiry into the means which I will employ".[12] These means were flogging, torture and imprisonment. None of this caused serious problems of conscience for most Europeans. There were, of course, individual exceptions. Wilfred Scawen Blunt wrote that the fellahin "were in terrible straits of poverty…the European bondholders were clamouring for their 'coupons' and famine was at the door". "We did not", he went on, "as yet understand, any more than did the peasants themselves, the financial pressure from Europe which was the true cause of these extreme exactions." Even less, he later confessed, did he suspect "our English share of the blame".[13]

Opposition to European exactions grew and was given voice in the Chamber of Notables that Ismail had established in 1866. This body was a sort of pseudo-parliament that was never intended to have any influence. Now as unrest grew, many Egyptians came to see it as a means of curbing both Ismail's despotism and European influence. An important feature of this emerging nationalist opposition was what has been described as "Muslim Modernism". The key figure espousing this doctrine was the Persian, Sayyid Jamal al-Din al-Afghani, who called upon Muslims to resist Western domination, to establish popular representative governments and to embrace the scientific advances of the modern world. The man who tried to interpret this "Muslim Modernism" to the British was Wilfred Scawen Blunt.[14]

One of Tewfik's first acts on becoming Khedive was to order the deportation of al-Afghani. The cause was taken up by others, however, most notably by Shaikh Mohammed 'Abdu. All Tewfik achieved was to bring together the various opposition factions and interests around the demand of "Egypt for the Egyptians".

The opposition embraced all levels of Egyptian society, fuelled by a variety of grievances. For many, the privileges accorded to the over 90,000 Europeans resident in the country by 1880 were intolerable. They were exempt from taxation and, to all intents and purposes, from Egyptian law. Once Tewfik was installed their influence increased until "by mid-1880 there was scarcely an aspect of Egyptian domestic affairs over which the French and the British, and to some extent other Europeans, did not exercise substantial, if not complete sway".[15]

While Egyptian officials were dismissed or had their pay held in arrears as an economy measure, European officials were taken on, paid considerably more and regularly. The salaries of 1,300 Europeans, overwhelmingly British and French, swallowed a twentieth of

THE BLOOD NEVER DRIED

government revenue.[16] And while the economy measures that left Egyptians impoverished were ruthlessly enforced, the little luxuries that made life bearable for Europeans were left untouched. As Blunt pointed out, the £1,000 a year paid by the government to the Reuters news agency was sacrosanct because how else would it be possible "to know at Cairo the odds on the Oxford and Cambridge boat race or even on the Derby and Grand Prix". Similarly, the £9,000 subsidy to the European Opera House was essential.[17] Even the more wealthy Egyptians turned against the Europeans complaining of excessive taxation and the government's decision to leave debts to Egyptians unpaid so that the European bondholders could receive their interest. This growing unrest inevitably adopted an Islamic rhetoric, provoked not just by the takeover of the country by Christians, but by the racist attitudes that accompanied it. The French occupation of Tunisia in April 1881 gave added impetus to the opposition because it seemed clear that Egypt was destined for a similar fate.

The classic mistake the British and French made in their takeover of Egypt's "virtual government" was to alienate the army. The economy measures taken to ensure the payment of the coupon involved a reduction in the size of the army and the dismissal of large numbers of officers and men whose pay was generally months in arrears. To many this seemed to be preparing the way for a European military occupation of the country. The result was to throw the army into the hands of the opposition. Instead of the army being available to crush the opposition and, if necessary, close down the Chamber of Notables, the army put itself at the service of the opposition and became a champion of the chamber. The greed of the bondholders and their representatives had seriously exceeded their political judgement. The man who emerged as the key figure in the military opposition was Colonel Ahmed Urabi, who was to give his name to what was to become a revolutionary movement. In May 1880 Urabi put himself at the head of protest against the government, giving notice that the army had become an independent political actor. In February 1881 an attempt to arrest him and other officers sympathetic to the opposition provoked open mutiny, forcing Tewfik into a humiliating climbdown. And in September the army intervened to force Tewfik to dismiss his European ministers and appoint a nationalist government responsible to the Chamber of Notables. The historian of the Urabist movement, Juan Cole, insists that while the army "became a pivotal ally of the civilian revolutionaries, intervening at crucial points...the evidence does not support the charge that it was a martial law dictatorship at any time in 1881-82".[18] This is an important point because one of the main British justifications for invading Egypt was that they were saving the country from military tyranny.

Blunt met with Urabi in Cairo in December 1881 and agreed to represent the nationalist case to the Liberal government in London. After their conversations, together with Mohammed Abdu and others, he drew up a "Programme of the National Party of Egypt". Copies were sent to Gladstone and to *The Times*. The programme was deliberately moderate, intended to win over liberal opinion and persuade the British government to support constitutional reform in Egypt. The nationalists were not proposing to repudiate Egypt's debt; what they were proposing was an end to European control of the administration, the ending of Khedival autocracy and the introduction of constitutional government, and the assembly's control over that part of the budget not committed to servicing the foreign debt. While there was some expression of sympathy on the part of the British Liberals, including Gladstone himself, in the end the British government realised that only a despotism under European control could safely protect the bondholders' interests.

On 8 January 1882 the British and French governments issued a "Joint Note" that made clear their support for Khedival autocracy and opposition to the constitutional claims of the Chamber of Notables. This completely alienated the nationalists and strengthened the position of the army as the one body that could force Tewfik to submit to the chamber and defend the country against European invasion. With the nationalist movement defiant, European invasion became inevitable. The British consul general in Cairo, Edward Malet, wrote to the foreign secretary on 23 January 1882 informing him of discussions he had had with the president of the Chamber of Notables, Mohammed Sultan. When the president made it clear that the chamber was determined to secure control over the budget, Malet warned him that he was entering on the path of the French Revolution, "the consequence of which was that the country was inundated with the blood of its citizens" and its government overthrown "by an European coalition against it". The warning was ignored. Malet went on to confess that he personally disliked the idea of "a war engaged in on behalf of bondholding and which would have for effect to repress the first

THE BLOOD NEVER DRIED

attempt of a Mussulman country at a parliamentary government. It seemed unnatural for England to do this".[19] At this stage, it is clear that the British objection was not to any supposed military dictatorship, but to the establishment of parliamentary government in Egypt.

The Liberal response

Gladstone's government responded to Egyptian defiance in a very traditional way. Warships were despatched (an Anglo-French force) to Alexandria in May 1882 in an attempt to intimidate the nationalists and bolster the authority of the Khedive. In the circumstances, this only made the situation worse. Intervention was inevitable. Gladstone is often portrayed as an opponent of military action, only reluctantly brought to accept it by more determined colleagues. A better way of regarding the situation is that Gladstone hoped to intimidate the nationalists into compliance and only when this approach had clearly failed did he finally embrace intervention, with, as we shall see, considerable enthusiasm. Within the Liberal government there was no serious disagreement over the need to maintain Khedival autocracy as the instrument of European control.

Towards the end of May the British and French demanded that Tewfik dismiss the nationalist government and exile Urabi. Popular protest forced him to retreat once again, fearful that the country was on the edge of revolution. Even so, popular anger finally burst onto the streets of Alexandria on 11 June. Following a clash between an Egyptian youth and a Greek, Egyptian crowds set about the Europeans. The assault was provoked by resentment at the privileged position of the Europeans and their racist arrogance, and by fury at the continued intimidatory presence of the Anglo-French warships. For Juan Cole, the image "of a furious Egyptian crowd attempting to overturn the carriages of the European consuls, who had superciliously lorded it over them for two decades, eloquently expresses the entire revolution".[20] By the time Urabi's troops had restored order, 50 Europeans had been killed, including three British seamen on shore leave. At the same time some 250 Egyptians had also been killed, shot down by the city's well-armed European population.

There was outrage in Britain at a native population daring to attack Europeans. Reprisals were necessary or else the British living among native populations throughout the empire and beyond would be at risk. Moreover, it was widely perceived as a Muslim attack on

Christians. Something had to be done. Charles Dilke, one of the radical members of Gladstone's government, wrote in his diary, "Our side in the Commons are very Jingo about Egypt. They badly want to kill somebody. They don't know who".[21] The people of Alexandria had to be taught a lesson.

Egyptian improvements to their coastal forts at Alexandria were seized on as a suitable pretext for military action. They were to be presented as a threat to British warships that could not be tolerated. In fact, the forts posed no credible threat. Indeed, only days before the riots Lord Northbrook, the First Lord of the Admiralty, had written that the navy did not "entertain the slightest apprehension with regard to them".[22] Now, however, they were seized on as a convenient excuse for military action. Ministers were quite explicit in this regard. As Lord Northbrook candidly informed the foreign secretary, "If we want to bring on a fight we can instruct B Seymour [the admiral] to require the guns to be dismantled. My advisers do not think they will do much harm where they are".[23] This is an important point. Charles Royle, a contemporary observer, later admitted in his history of the invasion of Egypt that "the actual danger to Admiral Seymour's ships…was at the time simply nil". Nevertheless, he insisted that the bombardment of Alexandria was "a necessity if only to restore European prestige".[24] And it was not just Liberal ministers and MPs who wanted bloody retribution. The Khedive himself was privately urging the British to shell his subjects into submission.

Seymour actually demanded that the Egyptians surrender the forts. When they refused, he prepared for an attack. At this point the French withdrew their ships. At 7am on 11 July Seymour's eight ironclad warships began their bombardment. After a relentless ten-hour bombardment the Egyptian guns fell silent. Although the Egyptians mounted a brave defence, the battle was completely one-sided, providing further testimony that the forts posed no threat. The British had five men killed and 28 wounded, while Egyptian casualties were in the region of 2,000 men killed and wounded.

By the time the bombardment ended, much of Alexandria itself was in ruins. The British blamed this on Egyptian mobs, but there is overwhelming evidence that most of the damage was the result of the British shelling. One young naval officer was detailed to recover unexploded shells from the town. "Our gunnery, during the bombardment", he acknowledged, "had not been very good, and the town

THE BLOOD NEVER DRIED

appeared to me to have suffered more from the misses than the hits".[25] An army officer on the scene later recalled that though he could see that "considerable damage had been done to the town of Alexandria by the bombardment, and the fire which followed it, the forts that lined the coast had suffered but little".[26] Another officer reported that "the huge shells flew wide and high, some of them reaching Lake Mariout, two miles inland".[27]

Clearly this was a shameful episode costing hundreds of lives, many of them defenceless civilians. What is of interest is how little it has affected the reputations of those involved. The horror of a city under bombardment is airbrushed out, an incidental detail in the careers of great men. The reality was somewhat different. Those responsible delighted in what they had done. Dilke wrote in his diary at the time, "My room at the House [of Commons] presented a most animated appearance while the bombardment of Alexandria was going on... Hartington, Brett, Childers and other members of our Jingo gang kept coming in to hear the news by telephone from the FO".[28] The bombardment, he was to observe, "like all butchery is popular".[29]

One member of the cabinet, the veteran Radical, John Bright, felt obliged to resign in protest. A few days before the bombardment he had written in his diary of how painful it was "to observe how much of the Jingo or war spirit can be shown by certain members of a Liberal cabinet".[30] Gladstone tried to persuade him to stay, arguing that the bombardment had "taught many lessons...shown the fanaticism of the East that the massacre of Europeans is not likely to be perpetrated with impunity, and greatly advanced the Egyptian question towards a permanent and peaceable solution". Gladstone insisted that he felt "that in being party to this work I have been a labourer in the cause of peace".[31]

The problem was not that Gladstone was a liar, but rather that he had the very useful facility of being able to convince himself that anything was right. Wilfred Scawen Blunt wrote of there being two Gladstones—"a man of infinite private sympathy" and an "opportunist statesman". He went on to write that Gladstone's:

Public life was to a large extent a fraud...the insincerities of debate were ingrained in him...if he had a new distasteful policy to pursue his first objective was to persuade himself into a belief that it was really congenial to him, and at this he worked until he had made himself his own convert... Thus he was always saved the too close consciousness of his insincerities, for like the tragedian in Dickens, when he had to act Othello he began by painting himself black all over.[32]

"Vast numbers of Egyptian dead"

The bombardment of Alexandria did not end the crisis. Although Tewfik promptly defected to the British, the nationalist government remained defiant in revolt against both the Khedive and his masters. Urabi prepared to defend the country against invasion. Accordingly, Gladstone despatched an expeditionary force under General Garnet Wolseley to put down the Egyptian revolution. The vote authorising the invasion was carried by 275 votes to 21 in the House of Commons on 27 July. The spirit of Midlothian that had swept Gladstone into office was well and truly dead.

The Egyptian army was decisively defeated at the battle of Tel-el-Kebir on 13 September 1882. The British overwhelmed their defences in a surprise attack just before dawn and carried out a textbook massacre, a model of well-executed colonial warfare. British casualties were 57 killed and 382 wounded. Estimates of the Egyptian dead, as is the way with colonial wars, range from 2,000 to 10,000 dead. No one counted. According to one British officer, Colonel William Butler, an Irish Catholic and admirer of the Irish nationalist leader Charles Stewart Parnell, the Egyptians had put up a brave but hopeless resistance against a British attack that had fallen on them like "a thunderbolt". There was, he felt, no glory in this sort of one-sided encounter. It was a "gift war-horse which the Stock Exchange is now able to bestow" and which one could not afford to examine "too severely in the mouth". What, he asked, was "the bad revolting star of this Egyptian business...which guided us to overwhelm the sleeping fellaheen host at Tel-el-Kebir? The Egyptian peasant in revolt against his plunderers or an English Liberal government in revolt against Liberalism?" He remembered "vast numbers of Egyptian dead".[33]

Butler was not alone in being appalled at the slaughter. The Presbyterian chaplain with the expedition, the Reverend Arthur Male, wrote of "a strange and horrible sight" on the battlefield: "as far as the eye could reach, a line of bodies lying or kneeling or reclining against the parapet, from end to end. There they had stood till the rush of

THE BLOOD NEVER DRIED

our men was upon them, and there they had fallen." Although Male's commitment to the British soldier was absolute, he could not accept that this was a just war. The Urabist movement was "really a national protest against the tyranny of a government with a weak viceroy at its head and men alien to its country as its ministers". Urabi had the Egyptian people behind him and as for his being an adventurer as was alleged in Britain, Male observed that he "was a poor man when he began his movement; he was no richer when he ended—a strange fact, indeed, had he been nothing but an adventurer". But for the British, Urabi would, in Male's view, have been an Egyptian Oliver Cromwell.[34] Another officer, Colonel William Hicks, confessed himself "ashamed of the fuss" made over such a one-sided victory and was convinced that it had been "magnified...to make political capital for Mr Gladstone...honours and decorations in bushels". It was "enough to make one sick".[35]

Making political capital out of the victory was, indeed, Gladstone's intention. He wanted guns fired in Hyde Park and church bells rung in celebration. One of his private secretaries, Edward Hamilton, described him as being "in the highest possible spirits" after this "brilliant little campaign". He remarked on Conservative rage because Gladstone had "adopted their policies and taken leaves out of their books which he cut up to pieces so when he was in opposition". Now it had all come good and "has given a great 'fillip' to the government". Queen Victoria was, of course, absolutely delighted and both she and Gladstone hoped that Urabi "could be hung without any inclemency".[36]

One last point here: Gladstone benefited financially from the invasion of Egypt. As we have already noted, he had a substantial investment in the Egyptian debt and this appreciated in value once the country had been occupied. Was this corrupt? The point has been made in his defence that at this time "almost anyone with a substantial portfolio would have held one or other issue of the Egyptians".[37] It was inconceivable to this class, of which Gladstone was a member, that their interests would not be protected. This was, after all, what the British state was for. As far as Gladstone was concerned he was not protecting his personal investment—this was incidental—he was protecting the investments of his class. To do otherwise would not have occurred to him. Moreover, the battle of Tel-el-Kebir, with its piles of Egyptian dead, precipitated a "rush to get into Egyptian securities" and for several days this was "the one feature of Stock Exchange business".[38]

The Mahdi and Sudan

Success soon turned to dust. On 29 October 1882 Edward Hamilton recorded in his diary the first intimations that all was not well. "There seems to be reason to fear that we are not out of our difficulties in Egypt", he wrote. "News has arrived which is calculated to raise grave apprehensions, that the so-called 'false prophet' in the Sudan is, with large forces at his back about to march on Egypt... This may mean a most serious business".[39]

In Sudan, Muhammad Ahmad had taken advantage of the crisis in Egypt to proclaim himself the Mahdi in June 1881 and raise the standard of revolt against Anglo-Egyptian rule. Having put down a modernising Islam in Egypt, the British now confronted a fundamentalist Islam in Sudan. Wilfred Scawen Blunt made the connection admirably:

> The revolt in the Sudan stood in close analogy with that in Lower Egypt. Both had a double character, beginning as the natural rebellion of a people against long misgovernment, and taking a religious complexion when Christian Europe had intervened in support of the tyrannical ruler against the people. The only difference between the two cases lay in the fact that whereas in Egypt the reformers were enlightened men, representing the humane and more progressive side of Islam, the Sudanese reformers were reactionary and fanatical. It cannot be too strongly insisted on that the great, the capital wrong committed by our English government in 1882, was less the destruction of the hopes of free government in Egypt as a nation, than the treacherous blow its armed intervention struck everywhere at the aspirations of liberal Islam... What wonder then that the defeat at Tel-el-Kebir should have been taken through all Mohammadan lands as a setback to reform, an impulse to reaction.[40]

Blunt's criticism of the "reactionary and fanatical character" of the Mahdist movement did not compromise his support for their revolt against oppression in the slightest.

The British meanwhile continued to consolidate their control over

THE BLOOD NEVER DRIED

Egypt by means of "all the now-familiar techniques of overcoming peasant resistance...military raids, secret police, informants, massive imprisonment (the country's jails were filled to four times their capacity) and the systematic use of torture".[41] While this was accomplished, a hastily assembled Egyptian army under the command of Colonel William Hicks was despatched to crush the Mahdi. In early November 1883 Hicks's force was destroyed by the Mahdi's armed followers, the Sunni Ansar, at Shaykan. The British government responded to the crisis by sending the popular hero General Charles Gordon to Khartoum to supervise the evacuation of most of Sudan. A law unto himself, Gordon was cut off and very reluctantly Gladstone recognised that an expedition would have to be sent to rescue him. Wolseley, by now Baron of Cairo, was put in command. This was to prove a much more hard-fought campaign than his conquest of Egypt and on a number of occasions the expedition was close to disaster. In the end, it arrived too late. Khartoum fell to the Mahdi on 26 January 1885. The British had been humiliated and Gladstone became the villain of the hour for his failure to save Gordon. As Edward Hamilton observed "The gloom and rage of London knows no bounds".[42]

There were, however, voices raised against British intervention in Sudan. When Khartoum fell, *Commonweal*, the newspaper of the Socialist League, carried an article "Gordon and the Sudan" by the Marxist Ernest Belfort Bax. This roundly attacked Gordon, criticised the British relief expedition for its slaughter of "ill-armed and ill-disciplined barbarians" and condemned "the great god Capital" for being responsible for "this wretched business war".[43] This stand flew in the face of public opinion which regarded Gordon as a martyr, "our boys" as above criticism and the empire as a glorious enterprise. William Morris, one of the leaders of the league, wrote to his daughter at the time that "Khartoum has fallen—into the hands of the people it belongs to". On 26 March 1885 he wrote a letter defending the Socialist League's position, in particular its stance regarding the death of Gordon. "It was", he wrote, "quite necessary to attack the Gordon worship, which has been used as a stalking horse for such widespread murder" in Sudan. He went on to provide a fine statement of the Marxist position:

We assume, as we must, that the Mahdi is the representative of his countrymen in their heroic defence of their liberties; on that assumption we may well approve of him if we are not to condemn Garibaldi... As to his fanaticism (which it seems must be condemned in him though praised in Gordon) you should remember that any popular movement in the East is bound to take a religious form; the condition of development of the Eastern peoples forces this on them. Surely it must be considered an article of faith with us to sympathise with all popular revolutionary movements though we may not agree with the all the tenets of the revolutionists.[44]

Reconquest

Sudan was not to be reconquered by the British until Kitchener's campaign of 1898 that culminated in the battle of Omdurman on 2 September. On this occasion the Sudanese conveniently launched a frontal assault on the invading army and were massacred in a display of overwhelming firepower. Modern rifles, machine guns and artillery destroyed the Sudanese army before it even got close enough to the British to begin inflicting casualties. The British themselves were very much aware of how one-sided the battle was. One NCO described the slaughter (his words) as "dreadful", "I thought it was like murder", and another considered the battle "more like a butcher's killing house than anything else". After the battle the bodies of some 10,800 Sudanese were counted but many more who had fled the scene would have subsequently died of their wounds. The British themselves estimated the final Sudanese death toll from the battle at 16,000. British losses were 48 killed and over 400 wounded.

The aftermath of the battle saw prisoners and wounded being shot and bayoneted out of hand. The troops were ordered "to bayonet and shoot everyone we saw" in revenge for Gordon and some of them entered into the killing with considerable enthusiasm. One soldier later boasted of killing "about 25, I think," and after each one "I said 'Another one for Gordon'".[45] The young Winston Churchill, a participant in the battle, wrote home that the victory was "disgraced by the inhuman slaughter of the wounded" for which he blamed Kitchener. He singled out in particular for censure the troops under the command of Colonel John Maxwell. Maxwell was subsequently put in charge of the occupation of the town of Omdurman where, he privately admitted, he "quietly made away with a bunch of Emirs".[46] Some 18 years later the by then General Sir John Maxwell was to command the British forces suppressing the

Easter Rising in Dublin. Meanwhile, as part of the revenge for Gordon, the Mahdi's tomb was broken into and subsequently blown up, his skeleton thrown into the Nile and his skull presented to Kitchener as a trophy. Even Queen Victoria thought that this "savours...too much of the Middle Ages" and complained that as the Sudanese had respected British graves so theirs should also have been respected. The Mahdi's skull was buried in secret.[47]

The post-war crisis, 1916-26

THE BRITISH Empire emerged victorious from the First World War in 1918. The most terrible conflict in human history, until the Second World War that is, had been fought not for democracy, liberty or freedom, but to protect the British Empire from its powerful German rival. To this end, millions of lives had been sacrificed, including those of 900,000 British and imperial soldiers. Nevertheless, the war had ended in triumph, with Germany and its allies forced to surrender. Britain proceeded to divide up the Middle East with the French, took its pick of Germany's colonies and even cast acquisitive eyes over parts of the Russian Empire, a former ally, that had collapsed in revolution in 1917. There were those in the Lloyd George government, including the foreign secretary, Lord Curzon, who advocated the establishment of British protectorates over the Caucusus and Transcaspia. British supremacy seemed assured.[1]

Celebration was short-lived, however. Almost immediately the empire was plunged into crisis. The British found themselves confronting revolutionary outbreaks in Ireland, Egypt, India, Mesopotamia (modern day Iraq) and China. And this took place at a time when the government was seriously worried that some sort of revolutionary working class outbreak was inevitable in Britain itself. Moreover, the international context had been transformed by the Bolshevik Revolution. By 2 June 1920 the chief of the Imperial General Staff (CIGS), General Henry Wilson, could write that he feared "the loss of Ireland to begin with; the loss of empire in the second place; and the loss of England itself to finish with". He had not, he admitted, "been so nervous about the state of affairs in regard to the British Empire since July 1914, and in many ways I am more anxious today than I was even that fateful month".[2] Soon after he wrote this, the threat of a general strike was to force the Lloyd George government to retreat from its policy of military support for the Poles in their war with the Soviet Union.[3]

In this chapter we shall examine the challenge the British Empire faced in each of these storm centres between 1916 and 1926. Having extended the empire to its greatest expanse of territory and influence, the British found that they did not have the resources to sustain this achievement. Nevertheless, the British Empire was to emerge from the crisis intact and to survive until shaken apart by another World War 30 years later.

The Irish struggle

To a considerable extent Irish Republicanism had been successfully marginalised by an alliance between the Home Rulers and the British Liberals. Ever since William Gladstone's 1886 promise of "Home Rule", the Liberal Party had been committed to carrying out the measure, in reality a scheme for devolved power as an alternative to calls for independence. Even such a limited measure was opposed with hysterical ferocity by the Ulster Unionists. In the years immediately before the First World War they threatened and prepared for civil war with the enthusiastic support of the Conservative Party. The Liberal government refused to coerce the Ulster Unionists in the way that Irish nationalists had been routinely coerced for over 100 years. The partition of Ireland seemed the most likely outcome. The Liberal retreat dealt the first of a number of damaging blows to the Home Rulers' domination of Irish politics, creating space for the re-emergence of Irish Republicanism.

The underground Irish Republican Brotherhood was instrumental in establishing the Irish Volunteers during the Home Rule crisis of the 1910s. Although it had lost control of most of that organisation on the outbreak of war in 1914, it kept control of an armed rump. The Republicans determined to commit this force, by 1916 some 15,000 strong, to an armed insurrection in alliance with the German Empire. The small working class militia, the Irish Citizen

Army, led by the revolutionary socialist James Connolly, allied itself with the attempt.[4] In the event, the Easter Rising that was staged in Dublin in April 1916 seriously miscarried. It took place without any popular support, and serious divisions within the volunteers resulted in less than 1,000 men and women taking up arms. The rebels held out for a week while the British assembled an overwhelming force and effectively shelled them into submission. Once they had surrendered, they were marched through the streets to the jeers and catcalls of a hostile population. Even in defeat, however, the rebels had begun a transformation in Irish public opinion, a transformation that was dramatically assisted by the British decision to execute the rebel leadership: Padraic Pearse, James Connolly, Tom Clarke, Sean MacDermott, Joseph Plunkett and ten others. The British general in charge in Dublin was John Maxwell, whose troops, as we have already seen, had massacred the wounded and summarily executed prisoners in the aftermath of the battle of Omdurman.[5]

The Russian Bolshevik leader, Vladimir Lenin, provided the starting point for any analysis of the Easter Rising when he lamented the fact "that they rose prematurely, when the European revolt of the proletariat had not yet matured".[6] If the rebels had only waited, 1917 would have provided them with a rapidly changing situation as war weariness gripped Europe's peoples and popular opposition to the war increased, reaching breaking point in Russia. This was the context in which a regrouped republican movement, led by Eamon de Valera, Arthur Griffiths and Michael Collins, prepared for a fresh challenge to British rule. The Home Rulers were to be challenged electorally by Sinn Fein, while Collins organised an underground resistance, the Irish Republican Army (IRA), for guerrilla war. As far as Collins was concerned, the Easter Rising had been "a Greek tragedy...bungled terribly". The rebels had been "a corporal's guard planning to attack the armed forces of an empire".[7] This would not happen again. Collins was to prove himself one of the great guerrilla leaders of the twentieth century.[8]

The Home Rule party was destroyed in the general election of November 1918. This proved a triumph for Sinn Fein, an alliance including both hard-line republicans and those who prepared to settle for dominion status, that is self-government within the British Empire. They were united only in opposition to the Home Rulers. Sinn Fein MPs, including the first woman MP, Constance Markiewicz, refused to sit at Westminster and instead established the revolutionary Dail in Dublin towards the end of January 1919. The prime minister, Lloyd George, was confronted by a revolutionary movement with an overwhelming democratic mandate, many of whose leaders were eager to open negotiations. Even though Home Rule had been decisively rejected by the Irish people, the British government decided to impose it regardless. Instead of exploiting the differences within Sinn Fein between the hardline Republicans and those prepared to compromise (Collins was complaining at the time of Sinn Fein becoming "ever less militant and ever more theoretical political"), the British insistence on devolution made war inevitable. The IRA launched their guerrilla war.[9]

The IRA campaign was always a comparatively small-scale affair of assassinations and ambushes, confined, moreover, largely to Dublin and Munster. The Republican leadership, both military and political, was opposed to actively involving the mass of the population in the struggle, not least for fear that this would radicalise the movement.[10] Instead a small elite of a few thousand guerrilla fighters would defeat the British, first by making the country ungovernable, and, second by turning public opinion both in Britain itself and internationally (particularly in the United States) against British government policy. There was never any prospect of the IRA militarily defeating the British Empire. Instead they would inflict enough damage to make the British position politically untenable. Popular support was crucial and this was evident even in those areas where there was little IRA activity. There was widespread rejection of the institutions of British rule, which effectively collapsed in many parts of the country. Boycotts, strikes and demonstrations were the other side of the military campaign. This popular support was given its most dramatic expression during IRA hunger strikes, most notably that of Terence MacSwiney, who died in Brixton Prison on 25 October 1920. These occasions prompted massive outpourings of sympathy for the martyred dead that helped consolidate support for what was portrayed as a sacred cause.[11]

The problem for the British was that combating the IRA's campaign required intelligence, and this was not forthcoming. Indeed, the extent of the Republicans' popular support meant that it was they who had the more effective intelligence apparatus, serviced among others by both policemen and civil servants. In these circumstances, unable to identify their antagonists, troops and police increasingly retaliated against the civilian population, carrying out both official and unofficial reprisals. In an attempt to strengthen the police, the British created new paramilitary formations, the "Black and Tans" and the Auxiliaries. These became a byword for brutality, arson and murder. And there was a well-documented and incontrovertible resort to the use of "murder squads", troops or police in civilian clothes, assassinating known Republicans. This was authorised by Lloyd George himself. Interestingly, the military authorities objected to these activities. In his diary Henry Wilson recorded an argument with Winston Churchill, the secretary of state for war, at the end of August 1920. Wilson condemned the "wild reprisals" carried out by the Black and Tans as a scandal, while Churchill defended the unit as "honourable and gallant officers". Later, on 23 September, he recorded a conversation with Churchill and Major General Henry Tudor, the officer running the murder gangs:

> Tudor made it very clear that the Police and the Black and Tans and the 100 Intell officers are all carrying out reprisal murders. At Balbrigan, Thurles and Galway yesterday the local police marked down S[inn] F[ein], as in their opinion actual murderers or instigators and then coolly went and shot them without question or trial. Winston saw very little harm in this but it horrifies me. During the day Winston took Tudor over to see L[loyd] G[eorge] and Winston told me tonight that LG told Tudor that he would back him in this course through thick and thin.

Wilson, of course, was no humanitarian. He advocated the proclamation of martial law and the shooting of Sinn Fein members by properly constituted firing squads![12]

Churchill certainly thought his methods were working. On 16 November 1920 he told Wilson that "we have nearly won in Ireland".[13] Only five days later, on the 21st, Collins's men carried out coordinated raids in Dublin that left 14 British servicemen dead, of whom four were army intelligence officers and four MI5 or MI6 agents. This was a tremendous success. Reprisals soon followed. That afternoon a Gaelic football match at Croke Park was cordoned off by police and troops, who proceeded to fire randomly into the crowd. Eleven spectators and one player were killed. Later that evening two IRA officers,

Dick McKee and Peadar Clancy, together with an unfortunate civilian, Conor Clune, arrested with them, were tortured and summarily executed in Dublin Castle. This was "Bloody Sunday", 1921.[14]

The British responded to the events of Bloody Sunday with increased repression and a renewed attempt to win the intelligence war.[15] This certainly had some successes, with the number of IRA men interned without trial rising dramatically to 4,500. Claims that the Republicans were all but beaten in 1921 were premature, however. Despite setbacks there can be little doubt that the IRA was capable of reorganising and regrouping to sustain a protracted struggle. Its popular base was strong enough for it to replace its losses. Moreover, it continued inflicting casualties on the British. Whereas in 1920 the IRA had killed 182 police and 57 soldiers over the whole year, from January until April 1921 they killed 94 police and 45 soldiers. And the Republicans were winning the propaganda war. On 11 December 1921, for example, the Auxiliaries burned down the centre of Cork in reprisal for an IRA attack. While the chief secretary, Hamar Greenwood, was denying any British involvement in the House of Commons, Auxiliaries were wearing burnt corks on their berets. One Auxiliary wrote home to his mother admitting to his part in "the burning and looting of Cork":

> We did it alright… I have never experienced such orgies of murder, arson and looting as I have witnessed during the past 16 days with the RIC Auxiliaries… Many who witnessed similar scenes in France and Flanders say that nothing they have experienced ever compared to the punishment meted out to Cork.[16]

The following month the British Labour Party issued a report on the Irish situation that stated quite bluntly that there were things being done "in the name of Britain which must make her name stink in the nostrils of the whole world". It condemned "the reign of terror in Ireland" and the way it was being used to hold the Irish in subjection to "an empire that is a friend of small nations".[17] The Labour Party could never get it quite right.

The British government found itself in an increasingly difficult position in 1921. It was trying to force devolution, limited self-government, on a people that had decisively rejected it in favour of independence. Coercion had so far failed to bring the Irish to "their senses", and to continue down that road to the imposition of a martial law regime was clearly incompatible with self-government of any kind. Executing elected representatives by firing squad would be extremely difficult politically in what was still part of the United Kingdom. Moreover, there was no guarantee that increased coercion would work. In these circumstances, much to Henry Wilson's disgust ("rank, filthy, cowardice")[18], a majority of the cabinet supported Lloyd George's decision to negotiate with Sinn Fein. A truce was agreed on 9 July 1921 and peace negotiations finally began on 11 October. At this point the Sinn Fein alliance began to break up as the hard-line Republicans stood by the cause of an Irish Republic, while the more moderate elements, who by now included Michael Collins, were prepared to pledge allegiance to the crown, and accept British military bases, partition and the Irish Free State. The Anglo-Irish Treaty that was finally agreed on 6 December 1921 was, as Lord Curzon put it, "an astonishing victory for the empire".[19]

The pro-treaty faction inevitably found themselves drawn into an alliance with the British against the hard-line Republicans, an alliance that was to be cemented by civil war. When fighting finally broke out between a reconstituted IRA and the Free State, the British stepped in to arm their new ally. Having failed to defeat the IRA themselves, the British had procured Irishmen to do it for them. In retrospect, the Republican resort to arms can be seen as a serious mistake, a doomed venture, but nevertheless the fact remains that they were protesting against a violation of the Irish people's right to self-determination. There can be no serious doubt that if the Irish people had been allowed a free vote without the threat of British military intervention in the general election of June 1922, they would have chosen a Republic.

One last point: while the Free State had accepted partition, they had been promised a Boundary Commission which would redraw the border between the North and the South on democratic principles. The expectation was that two counties and part of a third would inevitably have to come into the Free State. Michael Collins was seriously concerned with developments in the North where the Catholic minority was subjected to ferocious repression. Indeed, when Henry Wilson retired as chief of the Imperial General Staff and became an Ulster Unionist MP and security adviser to the Stormont government, Collins had him assassinated. But Collins died in the civil war

THE BLOOD NEVER DRIED

and the Free State government came out of it completely dependent on the British. The British promptly reneged on the boundary agreement, leaving a large Catholic minority to the tender mercies of the Ulster Unionists.[20]

The revolt in Egypt, 1919

Egypt was, as historian Anthony Clayton has pointed out, "the first of the Arab lands to challenge Britain with an armed uprising".[21] The rebellion was provoked by the British refusal to allow an Egyptian delegation headed by Saad Zaghlul, a former minister of justice, to travel to Paris to put Egypt's claim for independence to the Peace Conference. The refusal was regarded as particularly insulting as a delegation from Syria was making the journey. The nationalist Wafd party launched a popular campaign in support of the delegation and on 8 March 1919 the British responded by arresting Zaghlul and other leaders and deporting them to Malta. The following day:

> saw peaceful protest demonstrations by students, and by the 10th, all the capital's students, including those of al-Azhar, the great mosque and centre of Islamic learning, were on strike. On that day a large demonstration clashed with security forces, causing the first casualties of the revolution. The following days and weeks witnessed a veritable explosion of popular protest with almost daily demonstrations in the streets of Egypt's cities and bloody clashes with British military forces. This was accompanied throughout the country by attacks on British installations and personnel, the cutting of railway lines and other forms of popular revolutionary action.[22]

By 17 March the British had lost control of Upper Egypt. The revolt was not just a response to the nationalist demands raised by the Wafd. It was also fuelled by bitterness at how Egypt had been exploited during the war. In 1916 the British had introduced labour conscription, enlisting 1.5 million men, a third of all those aged between 17 and 35. They had also requisitioned buildings, crops and animals. The country was now run for the benefit of the British war effort in the Middle East. By 1918 poverty and hunger in the countryside were such that the Egyptian death rate exceeded the birth rate for the only time in the 20th century. While the war had brought "huge fortunes" to a handful of Egyptian landowners and businessmen, it also "brought misery to untold thousands of less fortunate Egyptians".[23]

The revolt took the British by surprise with much of the country passing out of their control. Communications were cut and in many towns and villages revolutionary committees took over. The rebels attempted to seize railway stations and cut the railway lines. On 23 March at Medinet troops drove off a crowd of 4,000 protesters attempting to storm the railway station, killing hundreds of people. That same day protesters stopped a train and hacked to death the seven soldiers and one British civilian found travelling on it. They were killed because they were the people "who seized our grain and camels, our money, who orphaned our children, who fired at al-Azhar and the mosque of Hussein".[24] By late March, however, the British were in a position to begin the reconquest of the country. Crowds were machine gunned and bombed from the air and heavily armed mobile columns were despatched to "pacify" the countryside, shooting anyone who resisted, burning villages and flogging suspects (in one village every man was publicly flogged). By the end of April the revolt had been put down with over 1,000 Egyptians killed, over 1,500 imprisoned and 57 hanged. Some 40 Britons were killed.

The revolt in the countryside was accompanied by widespread strikes. In Cairo the trams and the electric company were shut down. Printers, dockers, postal workers, transport workers and factory workers walked out. The railway workshops were shut down. On 21 April Lord Allenby, the High Commissioner, informed London that he was issuing a proclamation "ordering all back to work". He complained that British troops ordered into the railway workshops had refused. "Some trade union microbe has got into them" and they were refusing to obey orders because they considered it "strikebreaking". "I can't shoot all of them for mutiny", he wired.[25]

While the British succeeded in regaining control of the country, they were, nevertheless, forced into a humiliating political retreat. On 7 April Zaghlul was released and the Wafd delegation was allowed to go to Paris. Its demands for independence were ignored. Back in Egypt, however, protest continued. On 23 May 1921 it flared up into serious rioting in Alexandria with nationalist crowds fighting troops and police. Over 40 people were killed and many more injured. This outbreak was followed by clashes elsewhere, and the British feared another 1919. In December, Allenby had Zaghlul arrested once again

THE BLOOD NEVER DRIED

and this time deported him to the Seychelles. His arrest was accompanied by a massive show of force with tanks on the streets of Cairo and battleships at Alexandria and Port Said. There were still some clashes, but the British believed their precautionary measures had prevented another full-scale revolt.

The following year, in February 1922, the British finally conceded formal independence, but on terms that left Egypt a client state, still under British economic and financial control, and under military occupation. Protest and resistance continued. In September 1924 Zaghlul visited London for discussions with the Labour prime minister, Ramsay MacDonald. His hope for a Labour commitment to full independence for Egypt were, of course, disappointed. Soon after, on 19 November, the commander in chief of the Egyptian army, General Lee Stack, was assassinated by nationalist gunmen in broad daylight in Cairo. This was a dramatic challenge to British authority and Allenby responded with a show of strength. Troop reinforcements were rushed to the country, battleships were once again despatched to Alexandria and Port Said, and RAF aircraft made intimidating flights over Egyptian cities. Allenby presided over "a police reign of terror".[26] Once again the people were suitably cowed and Egypt, as Clayton, puts it, "returned to a state of sullen quiet".[27]

"Holding India by the sword"

The most serious post-war challenge to the British Empire came in India. Here the war had "meant misery and a fall in living standards for the majority of the Indian people", although inevitably some businessmen and industrialists had made "fabulous profits". This led to an explosion of trade union militancy and social unrest that the viceroy, Lord Chelmsford, was to describe as "a sort of epidemic strike fever". In March 1918 there was a textile strike in Ahmedabad and in January 1919 over 100,000 textile workers struck in Bombay with many other workers from clerks to dockers also coming out.[28] The strike movement assumed even more "formidable dimensions" in 1920-21 with 1.5 million workers taking part in over 200 strikes in the first half of 1920 alone. The tremendous growth in trade union membership and organisation culminated with the formation of the All-India Trades Union Congress (AITUC) in September 1920. In his inaugural address the organisation's first president, the veteran nationalist leader Lala Lajpat Rai, told the delegates that "we are passing through a revolutionary period".[29] There were also widespread food riots and peasant unrest in many parts of the country. This social turmoil coincided with, and was part of, a great national challenge to British rule, a challenge that was without precedent in the history of the Raj. According to one historian, by 1920-21 the British were facing their "worst moment…in the 90 years between the Mutiny and 1942". They found themselves "confronted by an opposition movement of a kind and extent they had never encountered before".[30]

The challenge took the British by surprise. A package of political reforms in 1918, the Montagu-Chelmsford reforms, had introduced limited self-government on a restricted franchise at the provincial level. This, it was hoped, would conciliate moderate Indian opinion. The reforms were accompanied, however, by the Rowlatt proposals that considerably strengthened police repressive powers (allowing up to two years imprisonment without trial). These were regarded as both an insult and a threat, and were to provoke massive opposition. The opposition to Rowlett was led by Mohandas Gandhi, a man a senior British official described as "honest, but a Bolshevik and for that reason very dangerous". But despite British opinion, he was certainly no "Bolshevik". While he had made a name for himself campaigning for civil rights, first in South Africa and more recently in India, he had also supported the empire during the Boer War, in the suppression of the Zulu revolt of 1906, and during the First World War. Indeed, he had helped recruit men into the Indian army as late as 1918. What Gandhi now proposed was a strategy of peaceful civil disobedience that involved turning the Indian National Congress from an elite organisation into a mass force. And this campaign was to be conducted in alliance with the Khilafat movement, the Muslim campaign in support of the Turkish Caliphate, which the British were in the process of dismantling in the Middle East.

A general strike was called in protest against Rowlatt for 30 March, but then postponed until 6 April. It went ahead in Delhi on the 30th and inevitably there were clashes with the police in which people, both Hindus and Muslims, were killed. The following day:

The funeral processions met at the scene of the firing and Hindus and Muslims embraced, declaring that their unity had been sealed in blood. Memorial services at the [mosque of] Jama Masjid were attended by an overflow crowd, not only of Muslims, but also of

THE BLOOD NEVER DRIED

Hindus. When Swami Shradhanand, an Arya Samaj [a Hindu reform movement] leader, not known for his friendliness to Muslims, arrived at the mosque, he was quickly propelled to the pulpit and asked to speak. It was an unprecedented display of communal harmony.[31]

On 6 April there were general strikes in most Indian towns and cities with widespread displays of Hindu-Muslim unity. The protests were generally peaceful, although there were some clashes, particularly in Punjab, where the governor, Michael O'Dwyer, was a strong proponent of repression. When Gandhi was arrested (he was soon released) to stop him travelling to Punjab, however, serious rioting broke out. In Ahmedabad the textile workers took to the streets, fighting with the police and burning down government buildings, offices and police stations (51 buildings were destroyed). By the time the police had regained control of the city, 28 people had been killed, including a British police sergeant. There was a two-day general strike in Bombay on 10 and 11 April that went off without violence, but in Calcutta on the 12th troops machine-gunned a crowd, killing nine people. Gandhi was appalled by the violence which he blamed on the people rather than the police. According to his doctrine, there should never be retaliation against police attack. Indeed, on 14 April he wrote to the viceroy to condemn events in Ahmedabad as "utter lawlessness bordering almost on Bolshevism". He expressed "the deepest humiliation and regret" that the people were not yet ready for non-violence, that he had "underrated the power of hatred and ill will".[32] This completely ignored the fact that deaths and injuries were overwhelmingly inflicted by the police and troops. And, of course, he had not yet heard of the massacre at Amritsar the previous day.

In Amritsar, in Punjab, the general strike on 6 April had been peaceful. When news arrived of Gandhi's arrest on the 10th, however, large crowds took to the streets and clashed with troops, who opened fire. After between 20 and 30 people had been killed, an outraged crowd set about destroying British property, killing five Britons (three bank managers, a railwayman and an army sergeant) in the process. A British schoolteacher, Marcella Sherwood, was badly beaten and only rescued by the parents of some of her schoolchildren. An uneasy calm returned to the city and the protesters decided to proceed with an anti-Rowlatt rally on the afternoon of 13 April at the Jallianwalla

Bagh, an enclosed space. The meeting was banned but they decided to defy it. General Reginald Dyer decided to make an example of them. He marched a detachment of Gurkhas to the rally and without any warning opened fire on the 20 to 25 thousand people peacefully listening to speeches. The troops continued firing for over ten minutes with Dyer only ordering a ceasefire when they were nearly out of ammunition. By the time they had finished the bodies were piled ten to 12 deep around the exits. Dyer made no attempt to help the wounded and dying. Indeed, the curfew came into effect soon after he ceased shooting so that the wounded and injured were left screaming, moaning and dying all through the night.

Dyer himself later estimated that he had probably killed two to three hundred people, although he admitted the figure might have been as high as four to five hundred. The official estimate was finally put at 329 people killed, of whom 42 were children, one a six week old baby, and 1,200 injured. This was certainly too low. According to Helen Fein, "a house-to-house census showed that 530 were reported killed" although even this was probably an underestimate as the city was full of people come in from the country for a fair. Dyer himself made it clear that regardless of the number, he was completely unrepentant and that if he had had more troops and more ammunition he would have killed many more. Indeed, he said that if he could have got an armoured car in position, he would have turned a machine gun on the protest as well. In his report of 25 August 1919 he wrote:

> I fired and continued to fire until the crowd dispersed, and I considered that this is the least amount of firing which would produce the necessary moral and widespread effect it was my duty to produce...It was no longer a question of merely dispersing the crowd, but one of producing a sufficient moral effect, from the military point of view, not only on those who were present, but more specially throughout the Punjab.

He had, as he quite openly admitted, carried out an exemplary massacre intended to terrorise the population.[33]

The punishment to be inflicted on Amritsar was not yet complete. Dyer ordered that any Indians wishing to go down the street on which Marcella Sherwood had been attacked had to crawl on their bellies. This was enforced at bayonet point. He also instigated a regime of public floggings, which were accompanied by unofficial reprisals of often considerable brutality. Elsewhere in Punjab, there was "violent, brutal repression" with shootings and floggings, villages bombed from the air and the imposition of collective punishments.[34]

The Amritsar massacre caused an outcry in Britain with even the Lloyd George government condemning Dyer's conduct. In India, however, the British regarded him as the hero who had saved them from another 1857. As far as the army was concerned, he had been thrown to the wolves, by a gang of cowardly politicians, for doing his duty.[35] Indian opinion, on the other hand, had learned that British control would never be given up voluntarily, but would have to be overthrown. Gandhi and his supporters prepared for a second round of civil disobedience in 1920.

The British faced another crisis in 1919. In May fighting broke out on the frontier when Afghan troops attempted to seize Peshawar and Quetta, raising the local tribes in revolt. The Afghans were driven back and British troops were despatched on punitive expeditions into Afghanistan. Jalalabad was heavily bombed and there was even an air raid on Kabul before peace was concluded in August. Fierce fighting continued against the frontier tribes well into 1921, with the British eventually suffering over 5,000 fatalities, and the area was still not pacified.[36]

Gandhi, meanwhile, gave notice to the British on 22 June 1920 that the movement of non-cooperation with the British was to be relaunched unless the British conceded self-government. As far as a growing number of Indians were concerned, the Amritsar massacre had deprived the British of any moral right to rule. The movement was relaunched on 1 August, although it only proceeded to gather momentum slowly. Gandhi was determined to avoid popular violence, and in the aftermath of Amritsar the British authorities too decided to try and avoid provocation. The military were not happy with this approach. On 15 July 1920 the commander in chief, General Henry Rawlinson, complained that:

Unless we, as a government, are prepared to act vigorously and take strong measures to combat the insidious propaganda of the extremists we are bound to have something very like rebellion in India before long... You may say what you like about not holding India by the sword, but you have held it by the sword for 100 years and when you give up the sword you will be turned out. You must keep the sword ready to hand and in case of trouble or rebellion use it relentlessly. Montagu [secretary of state for India] calls it terrorism, so it is and in dealing with natives of all classes you have to use terrorism whether you like it or not.

There is no doubt that the great majority of the British in India, soldiers, officials and civilians, agreed with Rawlinson on this. A few months later he noted in his journal that he "was determined to fight for the white community against any black sedition or rebellion", and, if necessary, "be the next Dyer".[37] If the nationalists could not be outmanoeuvred, there was always the sword.

The first phase of the non-cooperation movement involved the boycott of official bodies and institutions. Congress and Khilafat supporters withdrew from elected bodies, boycotted the courts, resigned from government employment, and boycotted schools and colleges. The movement was particularly successful in the educational field with thousands of students withdrawing from schools and colleges under government control. The next phase involved a boycott of imported cloth, primarily from Britain, and of alcohol. This involved turning the movement into a mass phenomenon with committees being established at village level to police the boycott. It had a tremendous impact, cutting the import of cloth by nearly half. In July 1921, at the All-India Khilafat Conference, Mohammad Ali, one of the leaders of the movement, and with his brother, Shaukat, a close ally of Gandhi's, stepped up the pressure when he called on Muslims not to serve in the army. He was promptly arrested. His appeal was repeated, often word for word, throughout the country by both Congress and Khilafat supporters, was adopted in resolutions at mass meetings and widely published. The movement gave a display of its strength on 17 November 1921, when the Prince of Wales arrived at Bombay to begin a tour of the country. He was greeted by a nationwide general strike and three days of rioting in Bombay itself. Everywhere the prince went, he "was greeted with empty streets and downed shutters".[38] The non-cooperation movement was becoming a rival government, supplanting the British, and moving towards the final challenge, a tax strike. As one historian has observed, they had the government "running scared".[39] Indeed, according to Sumit Sarkar, "between November 1921 and February

1922", the movement "very nearly brought the government to its knees". In December the viceroy, Lord Reading, was urging substantial concessions on London.[40]

The non-cooperation movement was accompanied by a great wave of industrial unrest. In 1921 there were 396 strikes involving over 600,000 workers totalling nearly 7 million working days. While many Congress members were involved with the unions, Gandhi himself was noticeably unsympathetic, and was increasingly looking to Indian business for support. Alongside the industrial unrest, in many parts of the country peasant movements were growing in strength, challenging the power of both the landlords and the British. This rural unrest burst into open rebellion in Malabar in August 1921, when Muslim peasants, the Moplah, rose against their landlords (mainly Hindus) and the British. In a number of districts "Khilafat republics" were established and by September the British commander, Major General Burnett-Stuart, could report that "the situation is now clearly actual war...and prolonged rebellion".[41] He found himself confronted by some 10,000 armed guerrillas, many of them former soldiers, fighting over jungle terrain that lent itself to guerrilla warfare. The result was portrayed by the British as a sectarian affair, as a Muslim attack on Hindus, and although there were some sectarian excesses, by and large the rebels avoided them. Indeed, there were Hindus actually fighting with some rebel bands. The British proceeded to crush the rebellion. As Sarkar puts it, once they were confronted with "a really formidable threat", just as in 1857 and 1919, "the mask of British liberalism fell off completely".[42] According to Burnett-Stuart, it was likely that the war would have to continue in some districts "until every Moplah is either exterminated or arrested."[43] By the time the revolt was finally crushed in February 1922, the British had, according to official figures, killed 2,337 and detained over 45,000. Burnett-Stuart himself thought the official figure too low and gave as his own estimate for rebel fatalities, three to four thousand. His own losses were 43 men killed. There was one particular atrocity that outraged Indian opinion in November 1921. A hundred prisoners (including three Hindus) were loaded into a railway wagon for transportation. When it was opened 56 of them were dead from asphyxiation and heat exhaustion, and another 24 died subsequently.

The non-cooperation movement's increasing militancy and popular involvement caused Gandhi serious concern. Its potential for radicalisation and for spilling over into violent struggle led him to decide to call the whole movement off. The occasion was provided by a clash between police and peasants at Chauri Chaura in Uttar Pradesh. After the police had beaten one of the peasant leaders and opened fire on demonstrators, a crowd, chanting "Long Live Mahatma ['Great-Souled'] Gandhi", burned down the police station and killed 23 policemen.[44] Gandhi responded by calling the movement off on 12 February. Sarkar makes the important point that while "there was ample combustible material in the India of 1919-22, perhaps even at times an objectively revolutionary situation", Gandhi rejected the implications of this, and there was "nothing at all in the way of an alternative revolutionary leadership".[45] The movement that had seriously shaken British rule collapsed almost overnight. When at last the British moved to arrest Gandhi on 10 March 1922 and sentence him to six years in prison, there were no protests.

War in Iraq
On 22 August 1920 T E Lawrence ("Lawrence of Arabia") published an article in the *Sunday Times* on the war in what was to become Iraq:

> The people of England have been led in Mesopotamia into a trap from which it will be hard to escape with dignity and honour. They have been tricked into it by a steady withholding of information. The Baghdad communiqués are belated, insincere, incomplete. Things have been far worse than we have been told, our administration more bloody and inefficient than the public knows. It is a disgrace to our imperial record, and may soon be too inflamed for any ordinary cure. We today are not far from a disaster.[46]

The similarities with the later 2003 Iraq war are, of course, striking and suggest an inability to learn from history that marks out the architects of that later conflict as incompetent to the point of criminality. We shall return to this discussion in Chapter 12. For the moment, how did the British find themselves in the position Lawrence describes and how did they remedy it?

Lawrence was the advocate of a policy of indirect rule in Iraq. He urged the installation of a monarch from the Hashemite dynasty under British protection. This would be a client regime, running the country in Britain's interests and under British supervision, but nevertheless it

THE BLOOD NEVER DRIED

would take the edge off Arab national sentiment. Having been promised independence by the British during the war, the imposition of direct rule was bound to provoke Arab resistance. A policy of direct rule on the Indian model prevailed, however. The first British high commissioner, Percy Cox, was convinced that "the people of Mesopotamia had come to accept the fact of our occupation and were resigned to the prospect of a permanent British administration".[47] In May 1918 Cox was transferred to Iran and Colonel Arnold Wilson succeeded him as high commissioner. He proceeded to "Indianise" the administration in the face of growing Arab hostility. So the British abolished the various representative institutions that had existed under the Turkish Empire, filled the administration with British officials and in 1919 also refused permission for an Arab delegation to travel to Paris to petition the Peace Conference for independence. In April 1920 British control over Iraq was confirmed by the League of Nations. There were protest meetings and demonstrations against this decision in Baghdad, but the British suppressed the opposition. The ground had been prepared for revolution.

There had already been serious clashes in Kurdistan in 1919 where Shaykh Mahmud Barzini had raised the standard of a Free Kurdistan.[48] British forces had crushed the revolt. Now a much more serious outbreak took place on the Upper Euphrates. The revolt began in June 1920 with a British force besieged by some 4,000 rebels in the town of Rumaitha. The first relief column was ambushed and driven off with heavy losses (48 killed and 160 wounded). It was not until 20 July that a much stronger column broke the siege. By now much of the country had risen with an estimated 130,000 rebels in arms, some 60,000 of them equipped with firearms. The British found themselves embroiled in what Mark Jacobson has described as "the largest British-led military campaign of the entire inter-war period".[49]

The rebels waged a mobile guerrilla war that, at least initially, the British had no answer to. One British officer explained that "the difficulty in coping with Arabs is the extraordinary manner they seem to appear from nowhere and their mobility". He wrote from experience having been with the "Manchester Column" at the end of July, when it was attacked on the road to Kifl. The column was nearly overrun and only fought its way clear with heavy casualties. This was the worst British disaster of the revolt. Of the 1,100 men with the column, some 400 were killed or missing, including 280 soldiers of the Manchester Regiment. The rebels took 79 British and 81 Indian soldiers prisoner. They were held at Najaf and were treated considerably better than the British treated rebel prisoners. The column also lost almost all of its transport (130 out of 150 carts) and an 18 pounder gun.[50] A few days later, on 30 July, the commander in chief, General Haldane, cabled London that "rebellion has spread almost to Baghdad, where my position is by no means secure".[51] As the high commissioner observed, "Troubles now come upon us thick and fast".[52]

Only the arrival of substantial reinforcements turned the tide and allowed Haldane to begin the reconquest of the country. The railways were protected by an extensive system of blockhouses, punitive columns were despatched throughout the countryside, burning villages, shooting rebels and seizing livestock, and rebel strongholds and concentrations were shelled and bombed from the air. The British used "gas shells in quantity…with 'excellent moral effect'".[53] By the end of October organised resistance had been finally crushed with the surrender of Najaf and Karbala. Mopping up operations continued into the next year.

The revolt cost the British 426 soldiers killed, 1,228 wounded and 615 missing. Rebel fatalities were officially 8,450, but a figure of over 10,000 is more realistic. While defeated, it was nevertheless successful in one respect. It brought to an end the British direct rule regime. Instead the Hashemite, Faisal, was installed as king, after a rigged referendum, in August 1921. The British controlled the country by means of this client regime until 1958.

One other consequence of the revolt was the embrace of air power by the British as an economical means of colonial policing. Bombing had played an important part in the suppression of the revolt with the RAF dropping 100 tons of bombs. The RAF could destroy villages with impunity whereas the more traditional punitive column involved hundreds of soldiers taking casualties to accomplish the same end. Wing Commander Arthur Harris made the point that the Arabs and Kurds "now know what real bombing means in casualties and damage. Within forty-five minutes a full-size village can be practically wiped out and a third of its inhabitants killed or injured".[54] He was, of course, to put his ideas into effect most murderously as chief of Bomber Command during the Second World War.

British ambitions in the Caucasus and Transcaspia were frustrated

THE BLOOD NEVER DRIED

by the Bolsheviks, but there was more success in Persia. Before the war British influence had been shared with Tsarist Russia and when the war broke out the two great powers proceeded to occupy the country. The Russian Revolution left the British dominant throughout the whole of Persia, although they faced resistance from the nationalist Jangali movement led by Kuchek Khan.[55] In July 1918 the Jangalis had attacked British troops occupying the strategic town of Resht. They captured half the town and burned down the British consulate, but "after several days of bloody streetfighting, the British troops backed up by aerial bombardment managed to drive the Jangalis out".[56] Subsequently the Bolsheviks intervened in Persia, allying themselves with Kuchek Khan. By June 1920 the Jangalis had taken control of Gilan province and proclaimed the Iranian Soviet Socialist Republic. By now the British were seriously concerned and Lord Milner told the cabinet that if Persia were lost "our whole position in the East would be gravely imperilled".[57] The British wanted a strong but subservient government in Tehran. In February 1921 they supported a coup carried out by the Cossack brigade that placed power in the hands of Reza Khan. Soon after both Britain and the Soviet Union withdrew their troops from the country. By the end of July Reza Khan had crushed the Jangalis and proceeded to consolidate his position as the country's dictator. In October 1925 he deposed the Qajar dynasty, and once again with British support, proclaimed himself Shah. As he assured British officials, "he would do with Persian hands that which the British wished to do with British hands".[58] Together with the British, Reza Khan was to bleed his country dry.[59]

The Chinese Revolution, 30 May 1925

At the end of the First World War, Britain was still the dominant imperial power in China, although its position was under challenge by both the Japanese and the United States. In the 1920s British investments in China were valued at some £100 million, only 5 percent of British overseas investments, but 35 percent of the total foreign investment in China. Shanghai, the fourth largest port in the world, was the fulcrum of the British position. In 1925 there were some 6,000 Britons resident in the city, and it was effectively under the control of the British consul-general, Sidney Barton. Foreigners had an extremely privileged position, so that, for example, the international settlement that occupied nine square miles of the city had a municipal council elected by foreigners, while the 900,000 Chinese who lived in the area had no representation at all.[60] These privileges, derived from the unequal treaties imposed on China since the Opium Wars, were coming under increasing challenge from the nationalist Kuomintang movement and from the Chinese Communist Party.

The 1920s saw increasing working class unrest in much of China. In Shanghai the Japanese-owned textile mills were the scene of often violent clashes between workers and management. On 15 May 1925 a worker, Ku Cheng-Lung, at the Nagai Wata mill was killed by a Japanese foreman. The workers appealed to the students for support and on 30 May there were demonstrations in the city calling for an anti-Japanese boycott. Protesters clashed with the police and some arrests were made. A crowd of about 2,000 protesters assembled outside the police station on the Nanking Road, demanding their release. When they attempted to force their way into the station, Inspector Edward Everson ordered his Chinese and Sikh constables to open fire. They shot 12 people dead. According to another British policeman, Maurice Tinkler, one of the "swines" had bared his chest in defiance and consequently "attracted so much attention he was riddled". Tinkler cheerfully admitted that he was "longing for the opportunity to kill a bunch but have had no chance of firing yet".[61] The shootings provoked a general strike in the city, with the Communists giving the lead, on 1 June. By the 10th there were some 130,000 workers on strike including mill workers, transport workers, dockers, seamen, shop workers and many of the Chinese police. Thousands of students joined in the strike. Protest quickly spread beyond Shanghai. There were "few towns of any size which did not respond in some way…and in Hosan, Hunan and Kuantung peasants also entered what was no longer referred to as the May 30 incident, but the May 30 Movement".[62] On 19 June general strikes were called in Canton and Hong Kong. When demonstrators approached the Shameen concession area of Canton, on 23 June, they were machine gunned by British troops, with over 50 people killed. This massacre gave the "historic" Hong Kong strike increased impetus:

> The port went almost entirely dead; internal transportation was maintained at a barest minimum with great difficulty; hospitals faced the real possibility of having to close down; the food supply was critically threatened; banks ran the risk of collapse; and expatriate

THE BLOOD NEVER DRIED

families were unceremoniously stripped of domestic help… The strike, to be later submerged in a boycott, was to last 16 months.[63]

The boycott was not called off until 10 October 1926, by which time enormous economic damage had been inflicted on British interests. The May 30 Movement posed a serious challenge to the British position in China. Even though eventually beaten down both in Shanghai and in Hong Kong, it marked the beginning of the Chinese Revolution.

The Palestine revolt

BRITISH INTEREST in Palestine was primarily strategic. The country was of little economic interest, but was seen to be of considerable importance to the defence of the British position in Egypt and, once Turkey was finally defeated in the First World War, bolstering British domination of the Middle East. In October 1918 Leo Amery, a key member of prime minister Lloyd George's secretariat, argued that "strategically Palestine and Egypt go together", that Palestine was "a necessary buffer to the Suez Canal" and "geographically practically the centre of the British Empire".[1] This strategic interest intersected with the ambitions of the Zionist movement that hoped to establish a Jewish state in Palestine and was looking for an imperial sponsor.

As far as the British were concerned, this Zionist connection came to be seen as a way of strengthening the British claim to Palestine. If Britain undertook to sponsor Zionism, this would effectively see off any French claims to the country.[2] Moreover, a Zionist settlement would introduce a loyal and dependent population, a sort of Jewish Ulster, into the Middle East. Even though the settlers would not be British in origin, they would owe their allegiance to the British Empire. In fact, far from strengthening the British position, the Zionist settlement was to seriously undermine it.

Zionism and Imperialism

Zionism has always looked to the imperial powers for the realisation of its ambitions.[3] This derives both from the weakness of a settlement that would always require an imperial protector to defend it from the "natives" and from the position that the Middle East occupied in the struggle between rival empires. Moreover, the great majority of the world's Jews have never shown any desire to actually live in Palestine. The Ottoman Empire had seemed a possible sponsor before the First World War and it is worth remembering that both of Israel's first two prime ministers, David Ben Gurion and Moshe Sharett, had worn the Turkish fez in their youth. Ben Gurion had studied law in Istanbul in 1913-14 and had ambitions to be elected to the Turkish parliament, while Sharett served as a volunteer officer in the Ottoman army throughout the War.[4]

While the settlers on the ground inevitably looked to the Turkish government for support and protection, the international Zionist movement was concerned to persuade European governments to pressure the Turks into being more sympathetic. This involved developing a relationship not only with the rival European empires, but also with openly anti-Semitic governments and politicians. Indeed, according to one historian, Theodore Herzl, the founder of modern Zionism:

> regarded the anti-Semites as his most dependable friends and allies. Rather than attack and denounce anti-Semitism, Herzl declared that 'the anti-Semites will be our most dependable friends, the anti-Semitic countries our allies'.[5]

The Zionists, at this time, argued that there was no place for Jews in countries like Russia, Germany, France, Britain or the United States, and this sentiment was reciprocated by anti-Semites in those countries. They could cooperate on the basis of this shared understanding.

With regard to Britain, Herzl had tried to interest both Joseph Chamberlain, the colonial secretary, and the colonialist Cecil Rhodes in settlement projects. Most famously, Chamberlain had offered land in East Africa, what is usually referred to as the "Uganda" proposal, although the settlement would have been in Kenya. This was more a way of attaching Zionism to the British Empire rather than a serious alternative to Palestine. What it demonstrates quite clearly, however, is the extent to which Zionism was a European settler project, a child of Western imperialism, that showed no real concern for the inhabitants of the territory to be settled.[6] This was to be amply demonstrated over succeeding years. What was to be distinctive about Zionism was its promiscuity as regards choice of imperial sponsor.

The British decision to embrace Zionism was taken in response to the situation that confronted the empire in 1917. An agreement had already been concluded with the French, the Sykes-Picot Agreement, on the division of the Ottoman Empire, and at the same time the Arabs had, been promised self-government, in the Husayn-McMahon Correspondence. The incompatibility of these two separate undertakings was to be compounded by the Balfour Declaration of 2 November 1917 that promised the Zionists a "national home" in Palestine. This was seen as a way of outmanoeuvring the French so as to ensure that Palestine fell into British hands. There was also a concern that Germany was about to announce its support for the Zionist project. Indeed, so far as most Zionists were concerned at the time, Germany was the more sympathetic country because Britain was allied with Tsarist Russia, the land of the pogrom. Indeed, when the Germans went to war in 1914, they proclaimed themselves the liberators of Polish and Russian Jewry. Moreover, the Russian government responded by treating its Jewish subjects as the "enemy within", deporting from its Western territories over 3,000,000 million Jews, in the most appalling circumstances and with considerable loss of life.[7]

Lloyd George was to later emphasise the extent to which the Germans were "engaged actively in courting favour" with the Zionists. He wrote of how:

> The German General Staff...urged, early in 1916, the advantages of promising Jewish restoration to Palestine...at any moment the Allies might have been forestalled in offering this *supreme bid* [author's emphasis]. In fact in September 1917 the German government was making very serious efforts to capture the Zionist movement.

He put their failure down to the fact that "fortunately the Turk was too stupid to understand". What was at stake was the support of "Jewish sentiment...throughout the world" which the Zionists promised to deliver to their benefactor. Particularly important was the belief that, by embracing Zionism, Britain would rally "Russian Jewry to the cause of the Entente".[8] The reality was, however, that Zionist promises of delivering support were empty. The movement just did not have the influence that its spokesmen claimed. Indeed, as one historian has pointed out, Chaim Weizmann, the man with whom the British negotiated, had "simply elected himself—with

THE BLOOD NEVER DRIED

authority from no one—as a representative of the Jewish people".[9]

Clearly, a number of factors were involved in the making of the Balfour Declaration, but what pulled them all together was imperial self-interest. Accordingly, Arthur Balfour, the foreign secretary, sent his notorious letter, promising an Arab country to Zionist settlers, to Lord Rothschild for communication to the Zionist Federation:

> His Majesty's Government view with favour the establishment in Palestine of a national home for the Jewish people, and will use their best endeavours to facilitate the achievement of this object, it being clearly understood that nothing shall be done which may prejudice the civil and religious rights of the existing non-Jewish communities in Palestine, or the rights and political status enjoyed by Jews in any other country.[10]

The Palestinian Arabs, Christian and Muslim, despite being an overwhelming majority of the population (93 percent), found themselves relegated to the status of "existing non-Jewish communities" and their "civil rights" did not include being consulted about their country being given away.

The mandate

Britain was awarded control over Palestine by the League of Nations in 1922 with the Balfour Declaration incorporated into the mandate. Moreover, the first high commissioner, Herbert Samuel, was not only a senior Liberal politician and a former home secretary, but also a Jew and a Zionist (the two were and are not interchangeable) and had only recently acted as an adviser to the Zionist movement.[11] As someone whose ancestors "had dwelt in this very land for a thousand years" and who now "after another two thousand years was charged with the special duty of preparing for the return that had been longed for through all that time", he regarded his appointment as a "high privilege". The British government, he later wrote, not only knew "of my Zionist sympathies", but had appointed him "largely because of them".[12]

As a good Liberal, Samuel was, as Sahar Huneidi puts it, to make "pacifying statements about Zionist and British intentions", but in practice, "he went ahead and firmly laid down the foundations of a fully-fledged Jewish state". From the moment he took office, he introduced ordinances "vital to the Zionists", allowing Jewish immigration, facilitating land transfers and privileging the settlers. Hebrew was recognised as an official language along with English and Arabic. The Zionist settlement was from the beginning allowed to function as a state within a state, even to the extent of establishing its own militia, the Haganah. The British treated the Zionists' Jewish Agency, as if it was a government in waiting. As for the Arabs, they found themselves with "no voice or say in the government of the country". One British official, Ernest Richmond, wrote home that the Arabs were starting:

> To regard the government as Jewish camouflaged as English. They will not accept Jewish rule. We deny them all the representative institutions which they enjoyed under the Turks… The country is in a ferment.[13]

This ferment was to seriously test the British commitment to the Zionist project.

Palestinian hostility to Zionism manifested itself even before the First World War. In 1882 there had been only 24,000 Jews in Palestine, but by 1914 there were 85,000. The five Jewish settlements of 1882 had increased to 47 by 1914 and Jewish landholding from 25,000 dunams to over 420,000. Land was purchased from absentee landlords and the existing Arab tenants, who had often farmed the land for generations, were evicted to make way for European settlers. The Zionist purchase of land in the Plain of Esdraelon resulted in the eviction of 8,000 Arabs and the destruction of 22 villages.[14] Inevitably this caused conflict, often violent. The first violent clashes had taken place as early as 1886 when Palestinians attacked the Zionist settlement at Petah Tikva, "inflicting considerable damage and killing one Jewish settler". The Arab farmers felt "alienated from the land that they had cultivated for centuries" and were determined to resist. There were many such clashes in the years before the Balfour Declaration.[15]

Once Palestine came under British rule, hostility to Zionist settlement was joined by resentment at the way the British had reneged on promises of self-government made during the war. Indeed, as far as Palestine was concerned, self-government was ruled out until there was a Zionist majority. As Balfour had put it in a letter to Lloyd George, "In the case of Palestine we deliberately and rightly decline to accept the principle of self-determination"; after all, "if the present inhabitants were consulted they would unquestionably give an anti-Jewish verdict".[16] While privately acknowledged, this policy was never made explicit for fear of the explosion of Palestinian anger it would provoke.

The first serious clashes under the mandate took place in April 1920 and May 1921. On the first occasion there was serious rioting in Jerusalem that left five Jews and four Arabs dead. The subsequent British Commission of Inquiry "listed as the causes of unrest in the country: British promises to Arabs during the war; the conflict between these promises and the Balfour Declaration; fear of Jewish domination; Zionist aggressiveness; and foreign propaganda". It described Zionist attitudes and behaviour as "arrogant, insolent and provocative... If not carefully checked they may easily precipitate a catastrophe, the end of which is difficult to forecast".[17] The following year a much more serious outbreak took place after clashes between Zionists and Communists, all Jews, in Jaffa, on May Day. This precipitated attacks on the settlers that spread to other towns and were only suppressed by the police after 47 Jews and 48 Arabs had been killed.

What prevented the apparently inevitable progress to a full-scale Palestinian rebellion at this time? Certainly the ferocity of Arab hostility took the British authorities by surprise, and led to a pulling back from their Zionist commitment. Even the high commissioner Herbert Samuel, for example, found himself bitterly criticised by the Zionist leadership for showing too much concern for Arab sensibilities. This in turn led the Palestinian notables, the rural and urban upper class, to believe that the British were susceptible to pressure, so that a resort to violence would be unnecessary. Decisive, however, was the fact that in the 1920s the Zionist project came close to foundering altogether because European Jews showed no inclination to emigrate to Palestine.

The faltering of Jewish immigration took the edge off Palestinian hostility and indeed suggested that the Zionist settlement, the Yishuv, would never become strong enough to take over the whole country. A serious economic crisis hit the settlement in 1926 and the following year, while 3,000 immigrants arrived, 5,000 left.[18] What transformed the situation was the rise of extreme anti-Semitism in Europe, in particular the coming to power of the Nazis in Germany.

The 1920s closed with a further outbreak of violence in August 1929 that was deliberately provoked by the "Revisionist" wing of the Zionist movement, the fascist sympathisers of Vladimir Jabotinsky.[19]

Jabotinsky's supporters used a dispute concerning the Wailing Wall in Jerusalem as an occasion for an aggressive demonstration. The resulting week of violence saw considerable damage inflicted on the Yishuv, with six settlements virtually destroyed and 133 Jews killed. Officially 117 Palestinians were killed in the fighting, but the real figure "was probably higher because many of those killed and injured were not brought to hospital".[20] The Arab fatalities were in the main inflicted by British police and troops. Indeed, what particularly disturbed the authorities was the anti-British character to the outbreak with serious clashes taking place in purely Arab towns such as Nablus, Jenin, Acre and Gaza.

The road to revolt

The Palestinians' situation was to deteriorate during the 1930s. The rise of Nazism and the encouragement this gave to anti-Semites throughout Europe saved the Zionist project. Jewish immigration increased dramatically. The figures speak for themselves:

Year	Number of immigrants
1929	5,249
1930	4,944
1931	4,075
1932	12,553
1933	33,337
1934	45,267
1935	66,472
1936	29,595
1937	10,629
1938	14,675
1939	31,195
1940	10,643

According to Yehoshua Porath, 1935 was the "turning point in the struggle of the Palestinian Arabs" with immigration over 66,000 and the Zionists purchasing "almost 73,000 dunams" of land.[21] Nevill Barbour makes the point that the corresponding figure for immigration into Britain just in 1935 would have been 2,000,000, while the corresponding figure for the whole period from the end of the First World War until the end of the Second World War would have been

THE BLOOD NEVER DRIED

20,000,000.[22] At the same time as this massive immigration into Palestine was taking place, both Britain and the United States were severely restricting Jewish immigration. In 1935, for example, the United States only allowed in 4,837 Jewish immigrants. If we take the four years from 1932 until 1935, whereas 144,093 immigrants arrived in Palestine, the figure for the United States was only 14,118.[23] Moreover, whereas those Jews who actually made it to the United States or Britain arrived as refugees, in Palestine they came as colonists, determined to take the country over and displace its inhabitants. George Antonius, one of the leading Arab intellectuals of the day, made the still pertinent point in 1938 that:

> The treatment meted out to the Jews in Germany and other European countries is a disgrace to its authors and to modern civilisation; but posterity will not exonerate any country that fails to bear its proper share of the sacrifices needed to alleviate suffering and distress. To place the burden upon Arab Palestine is a miserable evasion of the duty that lies upon the whole civilised world. It is also morally outrageous. No code of morals can justify the persecution of one people in an attempt to relieve the persecution of another. The cure for the eviction of Jews from Germany is not to be sought in the eviction of Arabs from their homeland; and the relief of Jewish distress may not be accomplished at the cost of inflicting a corresponding distress upon an innocent and peaceful population.[24]

One other point worth making here is the extent to which the Zionist movement actually collaborated with the Nazis in the 1930s, in particular with the SS. To be blunt, they found they had a shared interest in the eviction of Jews from Germany. Reinhard Heydrich no less, later to be the architect of the Holocaust, in September 1935 proclaimed his solidarity with Zionism in the SS newspaper, *Das Schwarze Korps*. The Nazis, he made clear, were "in complete agreement with the great spiritual movement within Jewry itself, the so-called Zionism, with its recognition of the solidarity of Jewry throughout the world, and the rejection of all assimilationist ideas". Adolf Eichmann, a key figure in the destruction of Europe's Jews, actually visited Palestine in 1937 at the invitation of the Zionists. The Gestapo worked closely with Mossad, the Zionist agency handling illegal immigration. In 1939 Heydrich was demanding that Mossad should be sending off "400 Jews per week...from Berlin alone". This cooperation extended to the SS providing the Haganah with smuggled arms.[25] The moral bankruptcy of the Zionist movement is nowhere better demonstrated than in Ben Gurion's response to the possibility of thousands of Jewish children being admitted into Britain after the Kristallnacht pogrom in Germany. On 7 December 1938 he told a meeting of Zionist leaders:

> If I knew that it would be possible to save all the children in Germany by bringing them over to England, and only half of them by transporting them to Eretz Yisrael, then I would opt for the second alternative. For we must weigh not only the life of those children, but also the history of the people of Israel.[26]

With the Nazis, of course, there was to be no such choice.

Between 1920 and 1939 the Zionists purchased more than 846,000 dunams of land, which brought the amount of Jewish-owned land to 1,496,000 dunams. While this was only 5 percent of the country's total land area, it was a fifth of the arable land. According to Pamela Ann Smith, what this meant was that in 1935 each Jewish colonist had an average of 28.1 dunams, while each Palestinian had only 9.4 dunams. This transfer of land into Zionist hands inevitably resulted in increased poverty and landlessness for the Arab population. Moreover, with the explosion in Jewish immigration came an influx of Jewish capital that led "to an excessively high rate of inflation when agricultural wages were severely depressed".[27] And, of course, the Arabs were not just evicted from their land, but were also confronted by the Jewish-labour only policy of the Histadrut, the Zionist trade union movement. Employers who took on Arab workers were picketed, often violently, in an attempt to drive them out. Even when they were employed Arab workers were paid considerably less than Jewish workers.[28] For many Arab families, the shanty slums that grew up around the towns and cities became home. Surviving in the most appalling conditions, living in hovels, communities of the dispossessed sprang up. According to one commentator, in 1935 in Haifa alone, there were 11,000 families living in these new slums.[29] These people, the rural and the urban dispossessed, were to be the backbone of the coming revolt.

The growing unrest also had a political dimension. The dramatic increase in Jewish immigration confronted the Palestinian leadership with the prospect that a Zionist majority was not too far off. This was at a time when, elsewhere in the Middle East, British and French imperialism was having to make important concessions to Arab nationalism. In Egypt, Iraq and Syria the British and the French had been forced to concede varying degrees of self-government in the face of Arab protest. In Syria a general strike that had lasted for seven weeks had forced the French to retreat. Only in Palestine were there to be no concessions. British commitment to the Zionists meant that there would be no self-government until there was a Zionist majority. Reluctantly and half-heartedly, the Palestinian leadership, that had hitherto placed its reliance on the British, recognised that a stand would have to be made.

On 27 October 1933 a demonstration against Jewish immigration was dispersed by police gunfire that left 15 protesters dead. A general strike was called that was accompanied by demonstrations and protests that left another ten people dead. The authorities rode out the disturbances, apparently oblivious to the deteriorating situation. And all the time the settlers became increasingly arrogant and aggressive in the belief that the future belonged to them. The Yishuv was increasing in wealth and numbers and, courtesy of the Nazis, was taking steps to arm itself. This became common knowledge in October 1935, when a secret shipment that included 254 Mauser pistols and 50,000 rounds of ammunition was discovered in Jaffa. Arab opinion was outraged.[30]

Even while the notables, led by the Mufti, Mohamad Amin al-Husayni, still hoped for British intervention on their behalf, others were deciding to resort to arms. A Syrian preacher, Izz al-Din al-Qassam, whose following was among the dispossessed, was organising an underground network. His intention was to launch a revolutionary war. He took to the hills around Jenin with a guerrilla band, but it was wiped out by the British and he was killed in November 1935. His death, according to the Mufti's biographer, "sent a wave of grief and rage over Palestine. He became a symbol of martyrdom and self-sacrifice, embodying for her people a selflessness conspicuously absent among their leaders".[31] His funeral was "a great national demonstration against the government".[32] The Mufti and the rest of the Palestinian leadership were noticeably absent. Events were escaping from their grasp.

Ben Gurion later paid a begrudging tribute to the dead Islamic revolutionary. In July 1938, he told a Zionist audience:

From the time of Sheikh Izz al-Din al-Qassam it was clear to me that we were facing a new phenomenon among the Arabs…not a matter of a political career or money. Sheikh Al Qassam was a zealot ready to sacrifice his life for an ideal. Today we have not one, but hundreds, perhaps thousands like him. Behind them is the Arab people.[33]

The Great Revolt, 1

According to Rosemary Sayigh, the Palestinian Revolt "was the most sustained phase of the anti-imperialist struggle in the Arab world before the Algerian War of Independence".[34] What is astonishing is how little it figures in British history books. A revolt that was sustained from 1936 to 1939, that for a while saw much of Palestine in rebel hands, and whose defeat was a vital preparation for the mass expulsion of the Palestinians from their land in 1948, has been pretty much ignored. And indeed, much the same was true at the time. The British left, for example, was vitally concerned with the civil war in Spain, but virtually ignored the great popular rebellion against British imperialism in Palestine, a rebellion that was put down with considerable brutality.[35] What will be argued here is that the revolt was a pivotal moment in the history of the Middle East and that the British response is one of the most shameful episodes in the history of the empire.

While the outbreak was inevitable, given the accumulation of Palestinian grievances, what finally precipitated the revolt was an attack by Arab guerrillas, almost certainly followers of al-Qassam, on 17 April 1936. A bus was stopped near Nablus and two Jewish passengers were killed. Two days later Revisionist gunmen killed two Arab shepherds in reprisal. These sparks were enough to ignite a massive conflagration. On 19 April there was serious rioting in Jaffa in which nine Jews were killed. The following day a general strike was called and quickly spread throughout Palestine with local committees being formed to supervise the stoppage. This was very much a spontaneous affair. It was the work of an emerging radical leadership at local level that was acting independently of the traditional notables. The general strike was called, for example, without the Mufti's involvement. According to his biographer, the Mufti was still trying to serve "two masters, the British and the Palestinians, and was now being forced to choose". On 25 April a Committee of Ten, soon to become the Arab Higher Committee (AHC), involving all the Arab political factions, was formed. The Mufti became its president. The

AHC was very much "the child of the spontaneous revolt" rather than its father as it appears in some accounts, and at least initially, "it did not lead the revolt so much as be led by it". Leadership remained in the hands of the local committees, "controlled by young radicals".[36] According to George Antonius, far from the revolt "being engineered by the leaders", it was, in fact, in a very marked way a challenge to their authority and an indictment of their methods.[37]

The general strike was to last for 175 days, the longest in history. It was inevitably accompanied by considerable violence and in the countryside armed bands were formed that clashed with the British and the Zionists. The movement had some weaknesses. In Haifa, Arab dockers soon returned to work for fear of their jobs being taken by Zionist scabs. The Histadrut was everywhere involved in providing "highly motivated strike-breakers".[38] More important, the AHC did not call out Arab civil servants, but instead demanded that they donate part of their salaries. This was a serious mistake. If they had come out on strike, the administration would have been brought "to an almost total standstill".[39] The British responded to this challenge with repression that increased in ferocity as the strike went on.

When the British brought in troops to restore order in the towns and cities in late May, they found themselves faced by barricades, stoned by hostile crowds and shot at by snipers. In Gaza resistance was so fierce that tanks and armoured cars had to be sent into the city. The situation was most serious in Jaffa. Here the high commissioner, Arthur Wauchope, confessed that the old city of narrow streets and alleyways "formed a hostile stronghold into which government forces dare not penetrate".[40] The British responded by blowing up 237 houses, ostensibly on public health grounds, leaving thousands of people homeless. As John Marlowe observed, most were forced to live "in insanitary hovels on the outskirts of Jaffa, built mainly from old petrol tins. So much for the administration's concern for sanitation".[41] With the armed reoccupation of the towns and cities, the revolt's centre of gravity shifted to the countryside where the armed bands were in control. Volunteers came from other Arab countries to bolster the armed struggle. The Syrian revolutionary, Fawzi al-Qawuqji established a revolutionary command in an attempt to give the movement direction and control.

The British responded to what was becoming a guerrilla war with mass arrests, shootings, torture and the blowing up of houses. By the time the general strike was finally called off on 10 October 1936, 37 British troops and police had been killed, 80 Jewish settlers and over a thousand Palestinians. The scale and ferocity of the revolt were such that there can be no real doubt that, but for their Zionist commitment, the British would have made substantial concessions to the Palestinians to bring the conflict to an end. Not only was the revolt proving extremely costly, but it was also compromising Britain's relations with the rest of the Arab world. The British desperately needed some way out that could satisfy both their Zionist commitment and placate the Palestinians. To this end, the British government appointed the Peel Commission.

While the AHC demanded independence for Palestine, the Peel Commission was to recommend the partition of the country. Its report, published on 7 July 1937, proposed that Palestine and neighbouring Transjordan be divided into a Jewish state, an Arab state and a British enclave. The Zionists were to receive 40 percent of Palestine consisting of the coastal plain, though not the port cities of Jaffa, Haifa and Acre, which were to remain under British control, and most of Galilee, with its hundreds of Arab villages. The British were to control a strategic corridor from Jaffa to Jerusalem. The rest of Palestine and Transjordan would become an Arab state ruled by King Abdullah. The proposed Zionist state would have a population of 258,000 Jews and 225,000 Arabs, while the proposed Arab state would have a Jewish minority of only 1,250.[42] For those Arabs unfortunate enough to find themselves in the new Jewish state, forced removal was, given the Zionists' track record, a certain fate. Ben Gurion made the position absolutely clear: "I am for compulsory transfer; I don't see anything immoral in it".[43] Nevertheless, while the commission promised the establishment of a Jewish state, there was considerable argument within the Zionist movement about whether its proposals were acceptable. The Revisionists, for whom any Jewish state that did not encompass the whole of Palestine, together with Transjordan, part of Syria and much of Lebanon, was a betrayal, inevitably rejected the proposals out of hand. The Jewish Agency, however, while sharing most of the Revisionists' territorial ambitions, took a more pragmatic view. Partition was acceptable because it would establish a Jewish state now. The seizure of more territory would become possible as the Jewish state became strong enough to wage wars of conquest. The AHC rejected the proposals as totally unacceptable. The revolt flared up again.

THE BLOOD NEVER DRIED

Before we consider the second phase of the Great Revolt, it is worth briefly examining the attitude of the British Labour Party to the struggle in Palestine. The Labour Party had endorsed Zionism even before the Balfour Declaration. In 1922, Ramsay MacDonald, the party leader, had published an enthusiastic appreciation of the Zionist project, *A Socialist in Palestine*, and remained a consistent supporter of the cause for the rest of his life. In 1930, when Labour was in power the colonial secretary, Sidney Webb, proposed a retreat from the Balfour commitment in deference to Arab objections. He was repudiated by the now prime minister, MacDonald, after frantic Zionist lobbying.

With the outbreak of the Great Revolt, Labour took its stand with the Zionist settlers, condemning the general strike and armed insurrection as "fascist" and urging the government to stand firm. Initially Labour opposed the Peel Commission's partition proposals as a betrayal of Zionism, but once the Jewish Agency indicated its acceptance, inevitably the party endorsed their stand. Herbert Morrison, one of the party's leaders, was not alone in his enthusiastic celebration of Zionist colonisation: "The Jews have proved to be first class colonisers, to have the real good, old empire qualities, to be really first class colonial pioneers". This Labour support for Zionism was to continue into the Second World War. In 1944 the party was actually to propose the removal of the Arab population from Palestine "on humane grounds... Let the Arabs be encouraged to move out, as the Jews move in".[44] The Palestinians had nothing to gain from looking towards the Labour Party.

The Great Revolt, 2

On 26 September 1937 Palestinian revolutionaries assassinated the district commissioner of Galilee, Lewis Andrews, and his police bodyguard in Nazareth. This attack was condemned by the AHC, but the British seized on it as an opportunity to arrest as much of the Arab leadership as possible. The Mufti, however, managed to escape to Syria. Andrews' successor in Galilee, Alec Kirkbride, regarded the arrests as a mistake as they left "no Arabs of influence with whom I could deal and the masses were completely out of control". On taking up his post, it was made clear to him by his Arab subjects that he "would be killed at the first opportunity as would anyone else who followed next".[45] The response to the arrests was a revival of the guerrilla war in the countryside, but at a level of intensity far greater than in 1936. Moreover, the struggle increasingly took on a class dimension with "the poor peasantry…asserting themselves against the landowning elite". For a brief period, according to Ann Lesch, the people challenged the political dominance of this elite.[46]

The revolt increased in strength through the winter of 1937 and into 1938, achieving its greatest successes that summer and autumn. Much of the countryside was in rebel hands, with revolutionary courts set up and a revolutionary administration beginning to emerge at a local level. At the height of the revolt there were between 10,000 and 15,000 rebel fighters in arms. As their hold on the countryside tightened, the rebels moved down into the cities, occupying Jaffa, Beersheba, Gaza, Jericho, Bethlehem, Ramallah and other centres. In October 1938 they took over the Old City of Jerusalem, driving out the police. The rebels proclaimed a moratorium on all debts, something very popular with the poor, and proscribed the Turkish fez, insisting that the kaffiyah headdress of the Arab revolutionaries be worn in the cities.

For the British, the situation was dire. Hugh Foot, an assistant district commissioner, later remembered that they were confronting:

> a full-scale rebellion… All ordinary administration ceased. Every morning I looked through a list of disorders and destruction— telephones cut, bridges damaged, trains derailed, convoys ambushed, fighting in the hills. For two years I never moved without a gun in my hand—we soon learned that it was useless to have a gun in the holster.[47]

Another official, Edward Keith-Roach, district commissioner for Jerusalem, remembered how:

> On three occasions I missed death from bombs by a few inches, and Arabs were caught with revolvers in my garden a couple of times… Scores of my acquaintances met their death by bullet or bomb, and one never knew who would be the next victim… Police and military were attacked 1,000 times and Jewish settlements over 600. The telephone was sabotaged on 700 occasions and the railways and roads on 340. The Iraqi Petroleum Company pipeline was damaged at an average rate of twice a week.[48]

THE BLOOD NEVER DRIED

At the end of November 1938 the commander in chief, General Richard Haining, reported "a very deep-seated rebellious spirit throughout the whole Arab population, spurred on by the call of a Holy War". The rebels, he went on, have "such a hold over the mass of the population that it is not untrue to say that every Arab in the country is a potential enemy of the government".[49] One of his divisional commanders reported that "the country was in a state of extreme unrest bordering on anarchy".[50] With the international situation threatening war with Germany in 1938, the British could not reinforce their forces in Palestine. Once Chamberlain's government concluded the Munich Agreement with Hitler in September, however, reinforcements could be rushed in. The reconquest of the country could now begin. The British set about regaining control of the cities, with Jerusalem being cleared first. Once this was achieved, the "pacification" of the countryside could begin. This was to be accomplished with considerable brutality.

The routine brutality of colonial rule is brought out in David Smiley's account of his experiences as a young officer in Palestine. He was invited to accompany a police patrol on a raid. They burst into a house, seizing three suspects. The women and children were sent out while the prisoners were interrogated:

The first man was seized by two Arab policemen and held upside down while his feet were placed between a rifle and its sling. He was then kept in this position while policemen took it in turns to beat the soles of his feet with a leather belt with short pauses for questioning. After a time, he agreed to talk, and the beating ceased. The second man talked after the application of a lighted cigarette to his testicles, but the third seemed to be the leader and was more truculent. In a flash, the Arab sergeant flew at him and hit him in the face until both his eyes were closed, blood was flowing and a number of teeth were spewed out onto the floor. He then agreed to talk.

The young Smiley was, he admits, "somewhat shocked" by all this, and complained, quite correctly, that these were the methods of the Gestapo. He was assured "that force was the only language these Arabs understood" and that one never had to torture prisoners oneself, but ordered the Arab police to do it.[51]

This particular episode is worth recounting for two reasons. First, it is a graphic illustration of the nature of British rule in Palestine. Second, in more general terms, the reality of colonial rule is that it always rests on the shoulders of a policeman or soldier beating a suspect or applying a cigarette to their testicles. This is something that the apologists for the empire, whether they be politicians, academics or journalists, are seldom prepared to confront.

The letters home of another British policeman, Sydney Burr, provide further insight into the reality of British rule. He complained of the leniency of the courts, but happily this was not too much of a problem because "any Johnny Arab who is caught by us in suspicious circumstances is shot out of hand". After a bomb attack, he described how the police had "descended on the sook [market] and thrashed every Arab we saw, smashed all shops and cafes and created havoc and bloodshed". Most disturbing, perhaps, was his revelation concerning road accidents: "Most accidents out here are caused by police as running over an Arab is the same as a dog in England except we do not report it".[52] Charles Tegart, a man with considerable experience of policing the "natives'"in India, was bought in to advise the British administration. One of his innovations was the establishment of "Arab Investigation Centres" where "the gentle art of the third degree" was practised on Arab suspects "until they spilled the beans".[53] Indeed, the phrase "duffing up" actually comes from the interrogatory exploits of one particular police man, Douglas Duff.[54]

From late 1938 into 1939 the Great Revolt was relentlessly ground down. Villages were bombed (Arthur Harris of Second World War fame, the RAF Air Commodore in Palestine, advocated "one 250 lb or 500 lb bomb in each village that speaks out of turn").[55] While the fascist bombing of Guernica in Spain caused outrage in Britain, British aircraft were bombing Palestinian villages with hardly a murmur. In 1938 one RAF squadron alone dropped 768 20 lb and 29 112 lb bombs and fired over 62,000 rounds in operations against rebel targets.[56] Thousands of Palestinians were interned without trial, harsh collective punishments were imposed on whole communities, routine use was made of Arab hostages as human shields, and ID cards were introduced. Collective punishments were often drastic. After the shooting of an assistant district commissioner in Jenin in August 1938, much of the town was blown up as a reprisal. Early the following year an army vehicle was blown up by a mine, killing one soldier and wounding two

THE BLOOD NEVER DRIED

others. In reprisal much of the village of Kafr Yasif was burned down. When neighbouring villagers came to help put out the fires, they were machine-gunned, and nine of them were killed.[57] One last episode is worth mentioning, the screening of the inhabitants of the village of Halhul in the summer of 1939. Suspects were kept in the open for five days with hardly any water as a punishment. At the end of the five days many of them had collapsed and five were dead.[58] The British also hanged 112 Palestinian freedom fighters.

The British were, of course, able to call on the assistance of the Zionists in their efforts to crush the revolt. The Jewish Agency was eager to cooperate, providing strike-breakers through the Histadrut and thousands of volunteer police through the Haganah. Most important was the establishment of the Special Night Squads by Orde Wingate, a British officer, who "went out to beat the Arab gangs at their own game. His methods were extreme and cruel".[59] The Special Night Squads, Jewish volunteers under British officers, were what today would be called "death squads", torturing and summarily executing prisoners and suspects. While the Jewish Agency cooperated with the British, the Revisionists through their underground militia, the Irgun, carried out a series of terrorist bombings of Palestinian civilian targets. On 6 July 1938 a bomb killed 21 Arabs in a market in Haifa; on 15 July ten Arabs were killed by a bomb in Jerusalem; on 25 July, another market bombing in Haifa killed 39 Arabs; and on 26 August a bomb in Jaffa killed 24 Arabs.[60] The Palestinians staged a week-long general strike in protest against these attacks.

Defeat and aftermath

The British had successfully defeated the Great Revolt by the spring of 1939, although military and police operations continued throughout the rest of the year and into 1940. By the end of the conflict some 5,000 rebels had been killed. But while the revolt was militarily defeated, the increasing danger of war with Nazi Germany forced the British into major concessions to the Palestinians. The prospect of war increased Palestine's strategic importance and made the maintenance of good relations with the Arab states throughout the Middle East an absolute priority. To this end, in May 1939, the Chamberlain government issued a White Paper that in effect repudiated the Balfour Declaration. For the next five years Jewish immigration was to be limited to 75,000 people and after that could only be resumed with Palestinian agreement. In the House of Commons the Labour Party and a handful of Conservatives led by Winston Churchill voted against this "betrayal" of the Zionist cause. The retreat was considered necessary, however, to safeguard the empire's position in the Middle East. The Zionists were, of course, outraged, but in fact this was to be only a temporary setback. The reality of the situation was that the Yishuv had increased in strength considerably during the revolt, while the Palestinians had been weakened. Although still dependent on the British for the time being, the Jewish Agency, with Ben Gurion leading the way, began looking for a more reliable imperial sponsor that would not feel the same need to appease the Arabs. Ben Gurion increasingly looked to the United States.

During the Second World War the Jewish Agency followed a policy of cooperating with the British against the Nazis while, at the same time, fighting to overthrow Chamberlain's White Paper. The Revisionists split with one faction opting to cooperate with the British, while another faction actually attempted to ally itself with the Nazis. By now, of course, the Nazis were moving in the direction of the mass murder of Europe's Jews and their earlier cooperation was soon forgotten. The Mufti, however, did ally himself with Nazi Germany, hoping for a British defeat in the Middle East. This did the Palestinian cause considerable damage, although there is no evidence that he was complicit in the Holocaust. As for the Zionists, by the end of the war they felt themselves strong enough to break with the British Empire and in October 1945 launched a guerrilla campaign to drive the British out of Palestine. This war continued until the British finally evacuated the country at the end of June 1948. With the support of both the United States and the Soviet Union, the Zionists proceeded to establish the state of Israel, driving out some 700,000 Palestinians in the process. While the Americans provided diplomatic support, the Russians actually armed the new state.[61] Both countries saw their support for Israel as a way of weakening the British Empire. And, indeed, the British had suffered the first major blow to their position in the Middle East at the hands of people they had invited in.

Quit India

O N 2 March 1930 the viceroy of India, Lord Irwin, received an ulti-matum in the form of a polite letter from Gandhi. The letter was delivered by Reg Reynolds, a young left wing British Quaker.[1] In the letter Gandhi condemned British rule as "a curse" that "has impoverished the dumb millions by a system of progressive exploita-tion and by a ruinously expensive military and civil administration… It has reduced us politically to serfdom." The viceroy, Gandhi pointed out, received a salary that was considerably "over five thousand times India's average income" and he urged him, in vain one suspects, "to ponder this phenomenon". All this had to end. British violence, Gandhi promised, was going to be defeated by Indian non-violence. The Gandhian method was to be put to the test.[2]

Gandhi's strategy was to launch a campaign of civil disobedience once Irwin had rejected the Congress demands. The issue he had decided to organise around was not the Congress demand for com-plete independence, however, but the repeal of the salt laws. This was something immediate and tangible, but, at the same time, also a "symbol of imperial exploitation to which all Indians could respond".[3] The result was a masterpiece of political mobilisation.

The British enforced a monopoly on the sale and production of salt, even though in the coastal areas it was freely available. On 12 March Gandhi, together with 78 volunteers, began a march through Gujerat to the sea at Dandi with the declared intention of breaking the salt laws. The march took 25 days to cover 240 miles with Gandhi speaking to often huge crowds along the way (20,000 at Nadiad,

10,000 at Anand, 15,000 at Broach and 30,000 at Surat). His progress inspired Congress supporters and by the time he broke the salt laws at Dandi on 6 April 5 million people, at rallies and demonstrations throughout the country, joined him in his defiance.

One particular episode best demonstrates the British response to the Congress campaign of civil disobedience. On 5 May Gandhi informed the authorities that he would be leading a protest at Dharasana salt works later in the month. That same day he was interned under a regulation dating from 1827. The protest went ahead without him on 21 May when some 2,000 Congress supporters confronted the police at the salt works. A horrified American journalist, Webb Miller, reported that in "18 years of my reporting in 20 countries, during which I witnessed innumerable civil disturbances, riots, street fights and rebellions, I have never witnessed such harrowing scenes as at Dharasana". He described how:

> In complete silence the Gandhi men drew up and halted a hundred yards from the stockade. A picked column advanced from the crowd, waded the ditches and approached the barbed wire stockade...at a word of command, scores of native policemen rushed upon the advancing marchers and rained blows on their heads with their steel-shod lathis [long bamboo sticks]. Not one of the marchers even raised an arm to fend off blows. They went down like ninepins. From where I stood I heard the sickening whack of the clubs on unprotected skulls... Those struck down fell sprawling, unconscious or writhing with fractured skulls or broken shoulders.

And after the first column had been beaten down, another advanced and once again the police "rushed out and methodically and mechanically beat down the second column". This went on for hours until some 300 or more protesters had been beaten, many seriously injured and two killed. At no time did they offer any resistance.[4] Irwin wrote to the king, "Your Majesty can hardly fail to have read with amusement the accounts of the several battles for the Salt Depot at Dharasana".[5]

While the spectacle of the police savagely beating unresisting demonstrators rallied support for Congress, the fact was that most of those who took to the streets were not prepared to stand by and be beaten. In many places, when the police attacked the people resisted. In Peshawar in the North West Frontier Province, armoured cars were driven through the streets to disperse crowds protesting against the arrest of one of Gandhi's Muslim allies, Abdul Ghaffar Khan, on 23 April. People were run over and killed. In response the crowds turned on the British, setting fire to one of the armoured cars and forcing the troops to evacuate the city. According to the official report of the episode, 30 demonstrators had been killed, but unofficial estimates were that there were "two to three hundred killed and many more wounded". During the fighting, a platoon of the Garwhal Rifles, a Hindu unit, refused to open fire on the Muslim crowds. It was subsequently disbanded and at the court martial of the mutineers, one man was transported for life, one received 15 years in prison and another 15 received between three and ten years. One of the prisoners told the court, "We will not shoot unarmed brethren... You may blow us from your guns, if you like." The British did not reoccupy Peshawar until 4 May after a massive show of strength. There followed "a reign of terror" that saw sporadic clashes spreading throughout the province.[6]

Elsewhere, in the city of Sholapur, news of Gandhi's arrest provoked a general strike on 7 May. In clashes the following day, the police killed 25 protesters. After days of street fighting the police withdrew, leaving the city "in the hands of revolutionary councils". Order was not restored until 16 May when a brutal martial law regime was introduced, accompanied by "the merciless flogging of the workers".[7] A man was imprisoned for seven years for "carrying the Congress flag".[8] The leaders of the Sholapur uprising—Mallappa Dhansetti, Qurban Hussain, Shrikrishna Sarda, and Jagannath Shinde—were all put on trial for their lives. They were hanged on 12 July 1931.[9] And there were bloody clashes in many other places as the police were let loose to beat the opposition into submission. There were, in the words of one historian, "horrifying acts of police brutality."[10]

By the time Gandhi called off the first phase of the civil disobedience campaign in March 1931 there were, according to the authorities, over 60,000 protesters in prison, although Congress estimates put the figure at over 90,000. Among them was one of Gandhi's lieutenants, Jawaharlal Nehru. At his trial on 24 October 1930, only days after his release for an earlier offence, he made the Congress position clear:

We have no quarrel with the English people, much less with the English worker. Like us he has himself been the victim of imperialism, and it is against this imperialism that we fight. With it there can be no compromise. To this imperialism or to England we owe no allegiance and the flag of England in India is an insult to every Indian. The British government today is an enemy government for us, a foreign usurping power holding on to India with the help of their army of occupation. My allegiance is to the Indian people only and to no king or foreign government.

He was sentenced to two and a half years in prison.[11]

India and the Labour Party

What will perhaps be surprising to most readers is that during the first phase of the civil disobedience movement from 1929 until 1931 there was a Labour government in power in Britain. The beatings at Dharasana, the shootings at Peshawar, the floggings and hangings at Sholapur, the mass arrests, and much else were all presided over by a Labour prime minister, Ramsay MacDonald and his secretary of state, William Wedgwood Benn. The government, it is worth noting, was also complicit in a sustained attack on trade unionism in India, an attack that Sumit Sarkar has described as "a massive capitalist and government counter-offensive" against workers' rights.[12] This had involved the arrest on 20 March 1929, before Labour took office, of 31 trade union and socialist leaders and activists, including three British Communists. Their trial at Meerut lasted for nearly four years, and despite representations from the Labour left, most notably Fenner Brockway, Wedgwood Benn refused to intervene and have them released.[13] This involvement in colonial repression has been largely written out of the Labour Party's record. Indeed one is hard pressed to find any mention of it at all in most histories of the party. While MacDonald is often maligned, it is for his defection to the Conservatives in 1931, rather than for his government's forgotten record in India.[14] But while readers today might be surprised by the Labour government's conduct in India, especially in view of the widely held belief that Labour "gave" India independence in 1947, the same was not true of Indian nationalists at the time.

Nehru, for example, had no illusions regarding the British Labour Party. In June 1929 he warned that while one knew where one was when the Conservatives were in power in London, "with Labour there is so much empty and pious talk that some minds are apt to be confused". It was quite possible that the Labour government "may adopt an aggressive anti-Indian attitude". What the movement had to remember, he insisted, was that "India's prospect depends not on any government in power in England, but only on the organised strength of the Indian people".[15] In his *Autobiography* Nehru remembered being warned by the veteran Congress leader Lala Lajpat Rai, only days before his death on 17 November 1928, that:

> We should expect nothing from the British Labour Party. The warning was not necessary so far as I was concerned, for I was not an admirer of the official leadership of British Labour; the only thing that could surprise me in regard to it would have been to find it supporting the struggle for India's freedom, or doing anything effectively anti-imperialistic or likely to lead to socialism.[16]

The circumstances of the death of Lajpat Rai are perhaps instructive in this regard. A one time admirer of the British Labour Party and a friend of Keir Hardie's, he was becoming increasingly disillusioned and in December 1927 had published bitterly critical articles attacking the Labour Party's political trajectory ("English Socialism a huge mockery" and "Labour Party under Imperialist MacDonald").[17] Lajpat Rai's disillusion stemmed from MacDonald's decision to support the Simon Commission that the Conservative government set up to report on Indian constitutional arrangements in 1927. This was to be an all-British body without any Indian members. As far as all shades of Indian opinion were concerned this was a racist insult and there was a general determination to boycott the commission. Despite this, MacDonald appointed two Labour MPs to serve as members, Clement Attlee and Vernon Hartshorn. When the commission eventually arrived in India on 3 February 1928, it was greeted by a general strike. Everywhere that Simon and his colleagues went, they were met by militant demonstrations demanding they "go home". The commission demanded that the police take action against the protesters. On 30 October 1928 Lajpat Rai led a peaceful demonstration in Lahore that was attacked by the police. He was personally beaten by a British police officer and never recovered from his injuries, dying just over two weeks later.

This episode was, as Nehru put it, "little short of monstrous": "even the greatest of our leaders, the foremost and most popular man in the Punjab", could be beaten and killed with impunity. It was a "national humiliation".[18] There is, of course, something richly symbolic about Clement Attlee deciding the fate of India with his Conservative parliamentary colleagues, while outside Lajpat Rai, a veteran 63 year old Congress leader, the first president of the All-Indian Trade Union Congress, a friend of Keir Hardie's, was beaten to death by a British policeman.[19] The Simon Commission, of course, expressed its regret.

The Labour government's repression of the national movement in India in 1929-31 was not some sort of aberration. While there always were and still are anti-imperialists within the Labour Party, Labour governments invariably sought to defend the empire, and even when they promised reform, this was always advocated as a way of making the empire stronger. Their main difference with the mainstream of the Conservative Party was a rhetorical one, with the Labour leadership advocating what can perhaps best be described as an "ethical imperialism". Indeed, as early as 1901, writing in the *International Journal of Ethics* no less, MacDonald had typically argued that:

So far as the underlying spirit of imperialism is a frank acceptance of national duty exercised beyond the nation's political frontiers, so far as it is a claim that a righteous nation is by its nature restless to embark upon crusades of righteousness wherever the world appeals for help, the spirit of Imperialism cannot be condemned...the compulsion to expand and assume world responsibility is worthy at its origins.[20]

In his 1907 book, *Labour and the Empire*, MacDonald espoused a "socialist imperialism". The empire, he argued, was a historical fact, and Labour no more wanted to get rid of it than they wanted to restore the Stuarts. Indeed, the Labour Party felt "the pride of race", but nevertheless:

Its imperialism is...not of the aggressive or the bragging order; it does not believe in the subjection of other nationalities; it takes no pride in the government of other peoples. To its subject-races, it desires to occupy the position of friend.[21]

THE BLOOD NEVER DRIED

As for India, he argued in 1910 that, while the future belonged to nationalism, "if we are wise the day when it goes so far as to threaten us with expulsion is so remote that we need not hardly think of it at all".[22] Others were more crude. When MacDonald formed his first Labour government in January 1924, he appointed J H Thomas as colonial secretary. Thomas famously introduced himself to his officials with the remark that "I am here to see that there is no mucking about with the British Empire".[23] To be fair to Thomas, it has to be said that as both a trade union leader and Labour politician he had always done his best to see that there was no mucking about with British capitalism either. His enthusiasm for the empire knew no bounds, however: "We love our empire. We are proud of the greatness of our empire".[24]

Towards "Quit India"
For the second time Gandhi called off a movement that was gathering in strength. In March 1931 he concluded the Gandhi-Irwin Pact with the viceroy, much to the dismay of his followers. The pact, as one of Irwin's biographers puts it, "gave Irwin all he wanted at the cost of nothing more than he could afford".[25] In effect Gandhi called off the civil disobedience campaign in return for what could have been had before it was launched. Congress, as Sumit Sarker puts it, "had spiked its own guns…and had missed the psychological moment for an all-out no-revenue and no-rent movement".[26] Why did Gandhi once again propose retreat? A major factor was that Congress's capitalist backers were becoming increasingly alarmed by the direction the struggle was taking and were putting pressure on Gandhi to do a deal.[27] Irwin, moreover, was well aware of this from intelligence reports. Even so, while the Conservative front bench was supportive of Irwin's tactics (he was, after all, a staunch Tory), the fact that he had even met Gandhi provoked outrage from the Conservative right wing. Winston Churchill led the way: "It is alarming and also nauseating to see Mr Gandhi, a seditious Middle Temple lawyer, now posing as a fakir of a type well-known in the East, striding half-naked up the steps of the vice-regal palace…to parley on equal terms with the representative of the King-Emperor".[28] This combination of racism and ignorance (a fakir was a Muslim ascetic) was to characterise Churchill's attitude to India and Indians. What he, in effect, proposed was the destruction of Congress by whatever repression was necessary. India should be held

by the sword. Both the Labour and Conservative front benches, however, favoured a combination of repression *and* manoeuvre. And Irwin had certainly outmanoeuvred Gandhi.

The Labour government collapsed under the weight of the Great Depression in August 1931 with MacDonald, Thomas and a handful of others joining a Conservative-dominated National Government. MacDonald stayed on as prime minister. Irwin, meanwhile, had already been replaced as viceroy by Lord Willingdon.[29] By the end of the year it had become apparent, even to Gandhi, that he had been outmanoeuvred, and he proposed a return to civil disobedience. The problem was that the state machine was geared up for repression and had in fact continued cracking heads and throwing people into prison throughout the so-called truce that Gandhi had negotiated, whereas the mass movement was demoralised by retreat. On 4 January 1932 Gandhi was once again arrested and a massive crackdown was launched. Between January 1932 and March 1933 some 120,000 people were arrested. As Willingdon cheerfully confessed, he was "becoming a sort of Mussolini in India".[30] Despite tremendous heroism the movement went down to defeat.

In the aftermath of defeat Congress moved to the right. This process was aided and abetted by the Government of India Act of 1935, which was very much part of the British policy of manoeuvre. This act proposed the establishment of an All-India Federation made up of the British-ruled provinces and the princely states (these covered 712,000 square miles and had a total population of 81 million). It was constructed so as to deny Congress any chance of ever securing a majority and to leave effective power in the hands of the viceroy.[31] At a provincial level, however, elected ministries would exercise limited but real powers. What the British hoped was to foster provincialism as a way of weakening the Congress and bringing more "responsible" politicians to the fore. In the 1937 elections Congress won 716 out of 1,585 provincial seats, with a clear majority in five provinces. Nehru and the left opposed taking office, but they were swept aside. In the event, Congress administrations were formed in seven provinces. British strategy seemed to be working and, given time, there might have emerged out of Congress "responsible" leaders with whom the British could have worked. The Second World War was to effectively close off this prospect, as we shall see.

One indication that British strategy was realistic is the way in

THE BLOOD NEVER DRIED

which Congress administrations came to clash with working class and peasant protest and showed a willingness to make use of the police against their own supporters. As one historian has observed, Congress administrations "showed few inhibitions about taking repressive action, and sometimes a suspiciously greater willingness to force strikers back to their machines under the muzzle of a gun...than the preceding colonial regimes".[32] In 1938 the Congress administration in Bombay passed a Trades Disputes Act intended to curb the unions by imposing compulsory arbitration, making illegal strikes punishable by six months imprisonment and encouraging company unions. The British governor, Lumley, described the measure as "admirable".[33] On 7 November there was a general strike in protest against the act and the police opened fire on the demonstrators, killing one and wounding 11. The Bombay administration "was determined to curb labour unrest at any cost".[34]

How did the left respond to these developments? Within the leadership of the Congress, the two spokesmen of the left were Jawaharlal Nehru and Subhas Chandra Bose. To a considerable extent, their respective stances were to be determined by international developments. Nehru attempted to align Congress with the Spanish Republic, fighting against Franco, and the Chinese Republic, fighting the Japanese. He supported the Palestinian Revolt, but also urged that Jewish refugees be welcomed in India. Nehru made anti-fascist "Popular Frontism" his touchstone. Much less satisfactory was his domestic stance, where he continually compromised with the Congress right wing, even to the extent of endorsing the Bombay Trades Disputes Act. Bose took a radically different stance internationally, regarding the rise of fascism as something that Congress should take advantage of. Britain's difficulty would be India's opportunity, a stance that during the Second World War would lead him into an alliance, first with Nazi Germany, and later with Imperial Japan. His domestic stance was more combative than Nehru's and Gandhi was to force his resignation as Congress president in April 1939. Nehru refused to support Bose in this conflict, because, as far as he was concerned, in the end, with whatever reservations, the movement had to follow Gandhi.

While attention has generally focused on disputes within the Congress leadership, this has led to the neglect of important rank and file developments. As early as May 1934 some 100 delegates had come together to found the Congress Socialist Party (CSP), a loose organisation that worked within Congress. The CSP had politics that were similar in many ways to those of the British Independent Labour Party (ILP).[35] Although the CSP was never in a position to mount any serious challenge to the dominant right wing in the Congress, it was to play an important part in the Quit India Revolt.[36] Mention must also be made of the Communist Party of India (CPI), an organisation that included in its ranks many fine militants and activists, but that followed whatever line emanated from Moscow. When the Second World War eventually broke out, the CPI called for militant opposition to India's participation because the Soviet Union was allied with Nazi Germany. By the time Congress launched the Quit India movement in August 1942, the CPI was calling for equally militant support for India's participation in the war, because the Soviet Union was now allied with Britain.

What was decisive in defeating the British strategy of co-opting at least elements of Congress was the outbreak of war in September 1939. The viceroy Lord Linlithgow's decision to associate India with the British declaration of war without consulting Indian opinion provoked an immediate crisis. While Congress was opposed to fascism, and Nehru, in particular, had a considerably better record of anti-fascism than any member of the British government, the manner in which India was committed to the war showed that for the British this was an imperialist war, not an anti-fascist war. The All-India Congress Committee made its position clear:

> If the war is to defend the status quo of imperialist possessions and colonies, of vested interest and privilege, then India can have nothing to do with it. If, however, the issue is democracy and world order based on democracy, then India is intensely interested in it… If Great Britain fights for the maintenance and extension of democracy, then she must necessarily end imperialism in her own possessions and establish full democracy in India, and the Indian people must have the right to self-determination… A free democratic India will gladly associate herself with other free nations for mutual defence against aggression and for economic co-operation.[37]

The Congress leadership called on all the Congress provincial administrations to resign in protest against the war. Much to the

THE BLOOD NEVER DRIED

surprise of the British, they did. The British authorities began to prepare for a return to repression, while the Congress leadership began to prepare for a return to civil disobedience.

Quit India

By the summer of 1940 the viceroy and his administration had got ready to deal Congress what they hoped would be a crushing blow. A "Revolutionary Movement Ordinance" had been prepared, proscribing the organisation. The official in charge of security, Reginald Maxwell, was insisting that the intention was "not merely to reduce Congress to a condition in which they will be prepared to make terms but to crush Congress finally as an organisation".[38] The opportunity to strike did not present itself, however. The government in London, even once Churchill had become prime minister, was not prepared to move against Congress without sufficient cause. In the interim Linlithgow did his best to undermine Congress by encouraging communalist parties, in particular the Muslim League. For its part, the Congress leadership proceeded cautiously along the road to confrontation. In October 1940 Gandhi launched a campaign of individual "satyagraha" or civil disobedience whereby nominated individuals broke the law in symbolic demonstrations against the war. This campaign was continued until December 1941, by which time over 26,000 people had been imprisoned. The government had no difficulty in coping with this protest. The Communist Party was particularly scornful of such ineffective opposition to what they were denouncing as an imperialist war right up until the Nazi invasion of the Soviet Union in June 1941. In January 1941 the Communist underground helped the dissident Congress leader, Subhas Chandra Bose, slip out of the country on his way to Berlin via Moscow.[39] Here Bose was to recruit some 4,000 Indian prisoners of war into an Indian Legion before transferring his allegiance to Japan.[40]

The entry of Japan into the War on 7 December 1941 forced the pace of developments in India. First of all, the Japanese dealt a succession of massive, humiliating blows to the British Empire, blows from which it was to never really recover. And second, the British found themselves allied to the United States and under pressure to conciliate Indian nationalism. In March 1942 Churchill despatched Stafford Cripps, one of the leaders of the Labour left, to India as an emissary, charged with reaching an agreement with Congress. What

Cripps offered was a Balkanised India, that while formally independent would still dominated by the British. Even so, the breaking point came over who was to control the Indian army. Cripps promised an Indian minister of defence, but was forced to renege on this by Churchill and Linlithgow. The talks broke down, leaving the Congress leadership feeling betrayed and embittered. Only mass action would move the British. As for Churchill, the talks had successfully pacified the Americans and consequently had served their purpose. They were never intended to be successful.[41]

What Gandhi now proposed was a new campaign of mass civil disobedience, similar to but more militant than that of the early 1930s, and to be carried through to success. Meeting in Bombay, the All-India Congress Committee passed the so-called "Quit India" resolution that served notice not just on the British in India but proclaimed that "Burma, Malaya, Indo-China, the Dutch Indies, Iran and Iraq must also attain their complete freedom".[42] Only 13 of the 250 committee members voted against. No preparations had yet been made for the campaign, but the rhetoric used by the leadership made it clear that this was to be, in Gandhi's words, a "Do or Die" movement. In the event, its conduct was taken out of their hands. On 9 August the Congress leadership was arrested as over 500 people were picked up in the first police sweep. They were taken completely by surprise.[43] The decision to strike was sanctioned, not by Churchill, who was out of the country, but by the deputy prime minister, Clement Attlee.[44] Indeed, the attack on Congress was actually "supervised at a distance by Attlee".[45] The leadership of the Labour Party wholeheartedly supported the repression, although many party members and some MPs were appalled. What took the British completely by surprise was the popular response to the crackdown. The arrests provoked strikes, demonstrations and protests across India:

> Bombay exploded first. On the very first day, crowds started throwing stones and soda water bottles at trains, buses and cars and at the police. Some buses were also burnt. Post offices were attacked and looted. The police opened fire on 16 occasions, killing eight persons and injuring 44. Similar incidents occurred in Poona, Ahmedbad and in some suburban areas of Bombay. All these places observed hartals [general strikes]. Mills and factories were closed. The following day the crowds became more determined. On that day police opened

fire on 26 occasions, killing 16 and injuring 57... From 11 August disturbances spread to nearby areas like Kaira, Thana, Broach, Panch Mahals, Godhra, Surat, Ahmednagar, East Khandesh, Nasik, Satara, Belgaum, Dharwar, Ratnagiri, West Khandesh, Sholapur...[46]

The country was in the grip of a spontaneous movement of protest that the British responded to with shootings, beatings and mass arrests. One aspect of the repression did cause Labour cabinet members some disquiet: Amery complained to Linlithgow of their "sentimental feelings...against whipping" and advised that while this could continue "care should be taken to avoid publicity".[47]

There were widespread strikes in support of Congress. At Jamshedpur 30,000 workers at the Tata iron and steel works walked out for 13 days, causing the government considerable concern. In Delhi textile workers were out for 29 days. There were strikes at the Imperial Tobacco factories in Calcutta, Bombay, Bangalore and Saharanpur. The Hindustan Aircraft workers walked out in Bangalore. In Ahmedabad some 100,000 textile workers struck for nearly four months. There were strikes, complete or partial, in many other workplaces. Nevertheless, it is clear that the strike movement was disjointed and patchy, and never looked like developing into an all-India general strike. Part of the responsibility for this lies with the Communist Party which did its best to persuade workers to stay at work.[48]

Although taken by surprise, Linlithgow, at least initially, thought that he had the outbreak contained. On 11 August he reported to Amery that the "situation was not too bad", that Bombay was "the main storm centre" and that there was only "sporadic disorder elsewhere". The following day he wrote that "we are doing very well" and, while he expected more trouble over the next few days, "I am not in the least degree worried by the prospect." On the 15th alarm was beginning to set in and he informed Amery that "I have authorised machine-gunning from air of saboteurs". Two days later he told Amery that he was having to put down "a revolutionary movement... Of its seriousness and its total disregard for non-violence there can be no question." By now the movement had spread outside the cities and had a serious grip on much of the countryside, especially in Bihar and the eastern United Provinces. On 31 August Linlithgow wrote to Churchill that he was "engaged here in meeting by far the most serious rebellion since that of 1857, the gravity and extent of which we have so far concealed from the world for reasons of military security". Much of the countryside was still in the grip of "rampant" violence and he feared that September might see "a formidable attempt to renew this widespread sabotage of our war effort".[49]

While the disturbances in the cities had indeed been largely suppressed by the middle of August, the revolt had spread into the countryside where huge areas had been lost to government control and all communications severed. Large militant crowds marched to wreck or burn down police outposts, government buildings, post offices and railway stations. They blocked roads, tore up the railway tracks, demolished bridges and cut telegraph lines. The district officer in Darbhanga, R N Lines, described how in his area, the peasantry:

> Cut all the roads and railways. The roads were cut where they were carried over embankments several feet high, trees felled across them, masonry bridges demolished, pontoons of the pontoon bridge on the main road sunk; railways lines torn up, 40 foot spans of the bridges removed and dropped into the rivers, the delicate and at that time irreplaceable electrical signalling apparatus at all stations destroyed; telephone and telegraph wires everywhere cut, rolled up and carried off home... Police stations and government offices in outlying places were occupied.[50]

In Jamshedpur the police themselves went on strike and 33 of them were arrested by British troops. On a number of occasions crowds stormed the jails, at Ara releasing 700 prisoners, and at Hajipur 1,000. At Bhagalpur Central jail prisoners rioted and police were called in to restore order: 28 prisoners were killed and over 80 injured. Protesters hijacked trains and, as an outraged Lines complained, indulged "in ticketless travel en masse". Thousands of students were involved in the movement. At Benares Hindu University students took over the campus and proclaimed it liberated territory until British troops moved in on 19 August.[51]

At Madhuban the district magistrate, R H Niblett, was confronted by a crowd of 5,000 protesters accompanied by two elephants. They were only armed with spears, lathis and stones, however, and his policemen drove them off, killing 30 people according to the official estimate and unofficially perhaps as many as 300. The viceroy complimented him on his report of the episode, which read "like a tale of

1857".[52] Elsewhere the rebels were more successful. The government's own figures show that in the course of the revolt 208 police outposts together with 957 government buildings were destroyed or severely damaged. There were 332 railway stations destroyed or severely damaged, the track was cut 411 times and there were 66 derailments. The rebels destroyed or damaged 945 post offices and there were over 12,000 incidents of damage to the telegraph system.[53] Moreover, in a number of areas revolutionary governments were established, most notably in Contai, Tamluk, Ballin and Satara.[54]

This was a massive popular uprising, centred in Bihar and the eastern United Provinces, but with outbreaks in many other places as well. The British deployed over 30,000 troops to crush it. One district magistrate, N B Bonarjee, wrote of districts having "to be reconquered" and of what were "almost pitched battles taking place".[55] The confrontations were terribly one-sided, however, with rebel crowds without firearms battling against heavily armed troops supported where necessary by air attack. Resistance was broken by shootings, beatings, mass arrest, house burnings and collective fines. The Contai district, for example, was subjected to a reign of terror with 12,000 arrests, 956 houses burned down and hundreds of incidents of rape by police and troops. Niblett, the "hero" of Madhuban, was subsequently removed as a magistrate for objecting to the conduct of troops and police in his area. "To my dismay," he noted, "reprisals were the order of the day." He complained of police in another district carrying out "a pogrom"—"they set fire to villages for several miles" and then crossed into his district to burn more villages. On another occasion 19 men were arrested when they were found "near the railway" by a military patrol. Without any other evidence than suspicion, to his horror, they were sentenced to 30 stripes with the whip and seven years imprisonment. The whipping was immediately carried out in the market place. Officials "were given instructions to set fire to houses of all with Congress leanings". He was transferred after describing government policy as "official arson".[56]

By the time the revolt was finally crushed over 90,000 people had been arrested, many of them to be held until after the war. Arthur Greenwood, the deputy leader of the Labour Party, told the House of Commons that "Quit India" prisoners could hardly be said to be in prison at all because of the "luxurious conditions" they were held in. After the war one of the leaders of the CSP , Rammanohar Lohia, told Harold Laski that on his capture, he had been "ill-treated in one way or another for over four months; I was kept awake day after day, night after night, the largest single stretch running into ten days... If beating and bastinadoing [beating the soles of the feet] to death or near about it and forcing the human mouth to the uses of a sewer were alone to be considered atrocities, these and worse took place." There were prisoners "who died through beating and ill treatment".[57] The official figure for the number of rebels killed by troops and police during the suppression of the revolt was 1,060, but this figure is part of the attempt to minimise the outbreak. Nehru gave a figure of 10,000 killed but other estimates go as high as 25,000.[58] The real figure will never be known.

By the end of September 1942 the popular uprising in the countryside had been crushed. Those militants and activists, often CSP members, still at large established an underground resistance that continued organising against the British and tried to initiate a guerrilla war. In Bombay, CSP militants, led by Lohia, operated a secret radio station broadcasting revolutionary propaganda that survived for 88 days before capture by the police.[59] The underground produced revolutionary newspapers and bulletins (Quit India, War of Independence, Revolt and others) that kept up a propaganda barrage.[60] In early September a Central Directorate was established to organise and coordinate the movement. The cause was given a tremendous boost in October when the CSP leader, Jayaprakesh Narayan, escaped from prison. He became the most forceful advocate of armed resistance. Bands of resistance fighters, the Azad Dastas, were operating in many areas, harassing the British authorities and the police, and Narayan hoped to pull them together into an underground army. They saw themselves as the equivalent of the guerrillas in "occupied Europe...continuously harassing the Hitler regime". Their objective in "occupied India" was "the complete paralysis and demoralisation of British rule".[61]

Narayan issued a series of revolutionary letters making clear the political stance of the resistance. On 1 September 1943 his second letter was issued from "Somewhere in India". He wrote:

The war can be truly ended by the common people of the world. But their voice is stifled. Russia, which could have become the champion of the common man, has herself suppressed him at

THE BLOOD NEVER DRIED

home and disowned him abroad by truckling to the imperialists and supercapitalists of Anglo-America... Neither allied nor axis victory is our aim, nor do we pin our hopes on either. We work for the defeat both of imperialism and fascism by the common people of the world and by our struggle we show the way to the ending of wars and the liberation of the black, white and yellow.[62]

The revolutionary underground never developed beyond small bands engaged in sporadic activity. It was never a serious threat to British rule. Narayan himself was recaptured by the British on 18 September 1943. He was not released until April 1946.

The Quit India revolt, for obvious reasons, hardly figures in British histories of the Second World War. The repression of the movement is a stark contradiction of the principles for which Britain was supposedly fighting. Although it went down to defeat, nevertheless the revolt seriously shook the empire. There were serious doubts as to whether British rule would survive another such challenge.

"The final judgement on British Rule in India"

India still had to face the greatest disaster to befall the country in the 20th century: the Bengal Famine of 1943-44. This was the product of food shortages brought about by the war. Imports of food grains from Burma were cut off by the Japanese occupation and the system of distribution for domestic supplies broke down. For the peasantry, a large number of whom lived at or below subsistence level at the best of times, the consequences were catastrophic. In Bengal the price of rice rose from 7.5 rupees (Rs) a maund in November 1942 to Rs 29.7 in May 1943 and by October that year to as much as Rs 80 in some places. The poor could not afford to feed themselves and began to starve. Tens of thousands trekked to Calcutta, only to die on the city streets. The British administration in the words of one historian responded with "a callous disregard of its duties in handling the famine".[63] Not only were no steps taken to provide against famine, but India continued exporting food grains to Iran at the rate of 3,000 tons a month throughout 1942. The result was a terrible death toll from starvation and disease in 1943-44 that totalled more than 3.5 million men, women and children. This was, as Nehru put it, "the final judgement on British rule in India".[64]

When Lord Wavell succeeded Linlithgow as viceroy, he was

appalled at how little had been done to provide famine relief. Part of the problem was Churchill, "who seemed to regard famine relief as 'appeasement' of the Congress".[65] On one occasion when presented with details of the crisis in Bengal, Churchill commented "on Indians breeding like rabbits". As far as he was concerned "the starvation of anyhow underfed Bengalis is less serious than sturdy Greeks", a sentiment with which Amery concurred.[66] Wavell himself informed London that the famine "was one of the greatest disasters that has befallen any people under British rule". It was, he warned, doing "incalculable" damage "to our reputation". The government was unmoved. Later, when he was attending a cabinet meeting in London (April 1945), Wavell had brought home to him "the very different attitude towards feeding a starving population when the starvation is in Europe" rather than India. When Holland needs food, "ships will of course be available, quite a different answer to the one we get whenever we ask for ships to bring food to India".[67] The previous September, Lord Mountbatten, the British commander in chief in South East Asia, had made available 10 percent of his shipping allocation to carry food to India. Churchill had responded by cutting his allocation by 10 percent.[68]

Churchill's attitude was quite explicitly racist. He told Amery, "I hate Indians. They are a beastly people with a beastly religion." On another occasion, he insisted that they were "the beastliest people in the world next to the Germans". Amery was bemused by his "curious hatred of India" and concluded that he was "really not quite normal on the subject". Indeed, Amery was not sure "whether on this subject of India he is really quite sane". Provoked beyond endurance by Churchill's bigotry, Amery, on one occasion, said, "I didn't see much difference between his outlook and Hitler's".[69] Amery, it is worth reminding the reader, was not a liberal or progressive, but a hard-nosed right wing imperialist. And it was not just to Amery that Churchill made his feelings clear. In February 1945 he told his private secretary, John Colville, that "the Hindus were a foul race...and he wished Bert Harris could send some of his surplus bombers to destroy them".[70] Somewhat predictably, Churchill's part in the failure of famine relief in Bengal, one of the great crimes of the war, is not something that his innumerable biographers have been concerned to explore. This is really quite disgraceful.[71] Let us leave the last word on Churchill with N B Bonarjee, the district magistrate who had loyally helped

THE BLOOD NEVER DRIED

suppress the Quit India revolt. In his memoirs he writes bitterly of how in the Victory broadcast of 13 May 1945 Churchill had thanked Australia, Canada and New Zealand for their contribution to the war effort, but could not bring himself to mention India "although she provided more in men and material than the rest put together".[72]

The end of British rule

According to Clement Attlee, India's independence was "the fulfilment of Britain's mission in India". It was the final step in a long journey whereby the British had led India towards freedom. Indeed, Attlee cast himself in the role of India's "liberator". One recent discussion has actually described independence as "Labour's parting gift to India". This is so much nonsense. The Labour government successfully constructed what one historian has called an "invented tradition" to disguise the fact that independence had to be given o n terms that would have been considered totally unacceptable up until 1947. And, of course, it has been used ever since to endow the 1945-51 Labour government with a completely unjustified reputation for being, at least, progressive as regards imperial policy, if not actually anti-imperialist.[73] As Anita Inder Singh has pointed out, the Labour government's anti-imperialist reputation is, in fact, rather "puzzling", not least because after 1947 "Britain still possessed the rest of her empire and had every intention of holding on to it".[74] This was, after all, the government that was, in 1949, to remove Seretse Khama from his chieftainship in Bechuanaland "for marrying a white woman". Fenner Brockway considered it "beyond belief that a Labour government could act in such a way".[75] Unfortunately not. One of its most senior ministers, Herbert Morrison, the man thought most likely to succeed Attlee as party leader, considered the British Empire to be "the jolly old empire" and described talk of self-government for many colonies as "ignorant dangerous nonsense...it would be like giving a child of ten a latch-key, a bank account and a shotgun".[76] And of course when Hugh Dalton, another senior figure in the Labour Party, a former chancellor of the exchequer, was offered the Colonial Office in 1950, he confessed to "a horrid vision of pullulating, poverty stricken, diseased nigger communities...querulous and ungrateful".[77] There were, of course, some Labour MPs and many rank and file party members who were anti-imperialist, but this was never the motivation of the 1945-1951 Labour government.

What was the Indian policy of the Labour government that took power at the end of July 1945? They intended to concede self-government, but were nevertheless determined to keep India within Britain's informal empire. Independence would be given to a fragmented India, where Congress influence would be minimised by the Muslim League and the princely states, and over which Britain would still be able to exert considerable influence. It was inconceivable that Britain would not retain military bases in an independent India and that India's own considerable military strength would not continue to be at the disposal of the empire. On 17 January 1946 the Labour cabinet decided that it had a "moral responsibility" not to hand India over "without being satisfied that the succession governments were fully aware of the military and economic problems which a self-governing India would have to face". Moreover, if British concerns were not met, "logically we should continue governing India even if it involved rebellion which would have to be suppressed by British troops". As Inder Singh puts it, "Labour's commitment to the maintenance of British power was understandably greater than its so-called commitment to Indian independence." In the Labour scheme of things, a self-governing India would still be required to contribute to "the effort to preserve Pax Britannica".[78] Martin Wainwright makes a similar point, insisting that though "Labour leaders promised to grant India independence...this desire in no way contradicted their intention that Britain should use the military resources of the subcontinent in order to maintain its influence east of Suez". Moreover, India's airfields "were now essential positions from which...the Western allies could launch atomic and, possibly, bacteriological air raids on the Soviet Union".[79] This was not to be.

The Labour government's intentions were to be overthrown by a combination of its own weakness, both military and economic, and by the extent of popular unrest in India that threatened revolution and/or civil war. The harsh reality confronting the government was that while ministers could quite cheerfully talk of an Indian rebellion being "suppressed by British troops" there were not the forces available for the task. Moreover, it was becoming increasingly clear that the Indian armed forces could no longer be relied upon. At the same time, India itself was in the grip of increasing revolutionary unrest combined with increasing communal violence. Attlee found that the situation had escaped beyond his government's control and decided

THE BLOOD NEVER DRIED

on a policy of "scuttle". This was to be successfully disguised as Labour "bestowing the gift of independence on India", a travesty in which all sections of the party, left, right and centre, were complicit.

After his brief involvement with the Nazis, Subhas Chandra Bose had transferred his allegiance to Japan. He had now successfully raised a 20,000-strong force, the Indian National Army (INA), from among Indian prisoners of war. The intention was that the INA would participate in a Japanese invasion of India. Instead Japan surrendered and Bose died in a plane crash. Now the British proposed to put a number of INA men on trial. This precipitated what has been described as "the almost revolution". On 21 November there were student demonstrations protesting against the trials in Calcutta. Police opened fire, killing two protesters, provoking a general strike in the city the following day. A British intelligence report described the situation on the 22nd:

> Conditions are worst the city has experienced during the past 20 years...the police had to open fire on six occasions. Barricades have been erected in many of the streets and are still in position. The burning of military vehicles continues. All the corporation employees are on strike. Employees of a number of jute mills have come out on strike and the coolies are reported to be sitting on the East India Railway line. Students are playing a prominent part in the demonstrations, which are being supported by large sections of labour.[80]

By the time order was restored on the 23rd, police and troops had killed 33 protesters.

The following year, on 10 February 1946, the trial of Captain Abdul Rashid of the INA ended with him receiving seven years imprisonment. A student strike was called in protest in Calcutta on the 14th and demonstrators were once again attacked by the police. The following day the Calcutta trade unions, with the Communist Party playing a leading role, staged a general strike and some 500,000 people marched through the streets chanting "Down with British imperialism" and "Hindus-Muslims unite". That evening British troops were brought into the city to restore order. Street fighting continued until the 14th with the troops making free use of their firearms. By the time the British were back in control, the official figure for the number of protesters killed was 84, but unofficial estimates were "over 200".[81]

Decisive, however, was the outbreak of mutiny in the Royal Indian Navy on 18 February, "one of the most truly heroic, if also largely forgotten episodes in our freedom struggle", as Sumit Sarkar describes it. The mutiny started on the *Talwar* in protest against bad food and racist officers, but the following day it spread to on-shore establishments and embraced 22 ships in Bombay harbour. The mutineers elected a Naval Central Strike Command and drew up a list of demands, including better food, equal pay with British seamen, the release of INA prisoners and the withdrawal of Indian troops from Indonesia where they were being used to restore Dutch rule. Sarkar writes of:

> Remarkable scenes of fraternisation, with crowds bringing food for ratings…and shopkeepers inviting them to take whatever they needed. The pattern of events in fact unconsciously echoed the course of the mutiny on the Black Sea Fleet during the first Russian Revolution of 1905… By 22 February the strike had spread to naval bases all over the country as well as to some ships at sea, involving at its height 78 ships, 20 shore establishments and 20,000 ratings.

On 22 February there was a Communist Party instigated general strike in Bombay in support of the mutineers. Some 300,000 workers walked out and barricades were erected in working class districts. There followed two days of street fighting that left over 200 protesters and three policemen dead. The mutineers were persuaded to surrender by the Congress and Muslim League leaderships on 23 February. They were as alarmed by the outbreak as the British.[82]

In April 1946 Wavell's security adviser told him that in view of the unreliability of the Indian armed forces "I doubt whether a Congress rebellion could be suppressed".[83] This realisation marks the turning point, the decisive moment when it dawned on the British that the game was up. Congress had the whip hand. Wavell later recorded in his journal how he had explained the realities of the situation to Ernest Bevin, the foreign secretary, and A V Alexander, the First Lord of the Admiralty. Bevin "seemed to accept the picture", although Wavell went on, "both he and Alexander are in reality imperialists and dislike any idea of leaving India".[84] Even as late as 1 January 1947, however,

THE BLOOD NEVER DRIED

Bevin was still trying to persuade Attlee that Britain should stay in India and, if necessary, put down any Congress rebellion. Attlee insisted that there was no "practical alternative" to getting out. Any attempt to impose British terms on the Indian people was thought likely to involve another 15 years occupation of the country. This was just not possible. There were neither the troops nor the money.[85] The decision to withdraw, suitably dressed up as a magnanimous act of statesmanship, was taken by the cabinet on 18 February 1947, with June 1948 as the deadline for the handover. Lord Mountbatten was sent out as viceroy to implement the decision. He presented Nehru with the government's rather obviously named "Plan Balkan" in May 1947, but this was completely unacceptable. The British backed down.

Although Congress was using the threat of revolution to intimidate the British, in fact the leadership were themselves seriously concerned about popular unrest and the growing influence of the Communist Party of India. They wanted a handover as soon as possible in order to head off further explosions of rage such as had occurred in Calcutta and Bombay. They were also confronted with increasing communal violence generated by the Muslim League's demand for Pakistan. While the British had certainly exploited communal tensions and had given the Muslim League considerable support, communal violence was taking on a life of its own.[86] In the circumstances, partition was reluctantly accepted as necessary, and 17 August 1947 was settled on as the date for independence when the British Raj finally came to an end. The British had, in reality, been thrown out. The best assessment of the Labour government's policy was provided by General Hastings Ismay: "India in March 1947 was a ship on fire in mid-ocean with ammunition in the hold. By then it was a question of putting out the fire before it actually reached the ammunition. There was in fact no option before us but to do what we did".[87]

The Suez invasion:
losing the Middle East

T HE DOMINANT position in the Middle East that the British Empire had established at the end of the First World War was to collapse in the 1950s. This is usually associated with the Suez invasion of 1956, but important though this was, the British collapse really consisted of four episodes, distinct but nevertheless related. The first, defeat at the hands of the Zionists in Palestine, we have already discussed in Chapter 7. This was followed by the overthrow of the British position in Iran, then in Egypt, and lastly in Iraq. In each episode, a seriously weakened British Empire found itself confronted by militant nationalist movements determined to drive it out and by the United States that hoped to replace it.

The British under both Labour and Conservative governments were fully aware of their predicament although not about how to deal with it. In May 1954 the then Conservative foreign secretary, Anthony Eden, complained of the American failure to support either the French position in Indo-China (today's Vietnam, Laos and Cambodia) or the British position in Egypt. They wanted to "replace the French and run Indo-China themselves" and they "want to replace us in Egypt too". Indeed, he complained, "they want to run the world".[1] What this chapter will explore is both the British attempt to maintain their dominance over the Middle East, and once this had failed, their coming to terms with the United States' new Middle East imperium.

Iranian oil

British interest in Iran had initially been strategic, a concern to counter Russian influence that might pose a threat to British India. This concern had been joined by the discovery of oil in 1908, which transformed the country into one of the British Empire's major economic assets. Although only part of Britain's informal empire, there was a clear understanding that whatever else might be going on, Iranian governments were expected to allow the British controlled Anglo-Iranian Oil Company (AIOC), today's British Petroleum (BP), to exploit the country's resources without interference. Iran's oil was there for the benefit of the British Empire, not for the benefit of Iran. This resulted in the situation in 1950 where the AIOC earned some £200 million profit from its Iranian operations, but only paid the Iranian government £16 million in royalties, profit share and taxes. The company's profits in that year alone were considerably more than the total paid to Iran (£114 million) since the oil concession had been granted. In fact, the British government, a Labour government, was receiving substantially more in taxes from the AIOC's Iranian operations than the Iranian government itself.[2] And this was a company in which the British government held a 51 percent interest. The injustice was compounded by the fact that Iranian oil cost more in Iran than it did in Britain with the Royal Navy, in particular, receiving substantial discounts. The Iranians could buy oil from the Soviet Union at a cheaper price than they could buy it from the AIOC. At the same time, the company behaved "as a typical colonial power, manipulating the host government by making and unmaking ministers", insisting on its privileges and treating "the natives" with contempt.[3]

There was a growing hostility in Iran, both to the privileges of the AIOC and to the regime that sustained them. The nationalist movement, the National Front led by Mohammad Musaddiq, demanded the nationalisation of the company and constitutional curbs on the power of the Shah. If the British had offered a more generous settlement regarding oil revenues then it is possible that a "friendly" government might have been able to survive in power. The idea of the Iranians successfully defying the might of the British Empire was not taken seriously, however. This was to prove a costly mistake. When the British ambassador, Francis Shepherd, considered that what Iran really needed was "a 20-year occupation by a foreign power", one can see that confrontation was inevitable.[4]

On 7 March 1951 the pro-British prime minister, General Ali Razmara, was assassinated to great popular delight. While the Shah and the British looked around "for a suitable strong man to seize the premiership and take control of the country", the Iranian parliament, the Majlis, voted to pardon the assassin.[5] Confronted with a militant nationalist movement and fearful for his throne, the Shah reluctantly bowed to popular pressure and on 29 April appointed Musaddiq as prime minister. On 1 May 1951 Musaddiq signed a bill nationalising the oil industry.

For the Labour government in London this was a disaster. As the Foreign Office made clear, what was at stake was not "the fate of *a* major asset, but of *the* major asset which we hold in the field of raw materials. Control of that asset is of supreme importance".[6] The Abadan oil refinery, in particular, was the largest in the world, with the physical plant alone estimated to be worth £120 million. The loss of the Iranian oil industry would be a tremendous economic and financial blow, but more than that it would also have dire political consequences, seriously damaging British prestige throughout the Middle East. As Emanuel Shinwell, the minister of defence, put it when advocating a military response:

> We must in no circumstances throw up the sponge not only because of the direct consequences of the loss of Persian oil, but because of the effect which a diplomatic defeat in Persia would have on our prestige and on our whole position throughout the Middle East. If Persia was allowed to get away with it, Egypt and other Middle Eastern countries would be encouraged to think they could try things on; the next thing might be an attempt to nationalise the Suez Canal.[7]

There were not the troops available, however, for a protracted occupation of the oil fields. This was one of the consequences of the loss of British India. Instead the government imposed an economic blockade on Iran and initiated covert activities inside the country to try and bring Musaddiq down. They intended wrecking the Iranian economy so that popular opinion would hopefully turn against Musaddiq and he could be overthrown by a coup of some kind.

This might well seem to be unusual behaviour for a Labour government, especially the great reforming government of 1945-51. In fact,

THE BLOOD NEVER DRIED

Clement Attlee's Labour government was wholeheartedly committed to the preservation of as much of the British Empire as was possible, although it did use a different rhetoric from Churchill and the Conservatives. While India, Burma and Ceylon (Sri Lanka) might have gone, British domination of the Middle East was to be maintained no matter what the cost. As Ernest Bevin, the Labour foreign secretary, put it, the Middle East was an area of "cardinal importance...second only to the United Kingdom itself".[8] His successor as foreign secretary, Herbert Morrison, the man who actually had to deal with the Iran crisis, was a strong advocate of military action against Musaddiq and complained that the government was being "too United Nationsy". Even his Foreign Office advisers were surprised at how "hawkish" this former conscientious objector was when confronted with rebellious natives. Morrison started reading Philip Guedalla's biography of Palmerston as soon as he was appointed and actually confided to one official that "I wish I was Lord Palmerston".[9] He urged that if the oil fields could not be occupied then at least the Abadan oil refinery should be seized. This, he argued, "would demonstrate once and for all to the Persians, British determination not to allow the Anglo-Iranian Oil Company...to be evicted from Persia and might well result in the downfall of the Musaddiq regime". He went on to warn that "failure to exhibit firmness in this matter may prejudice our interests throughout the Middle East".[10]

Preparations for the military occupation of Abadan were put under way. If the appropriately named "Operation Buccaneer" had gone ahead then one suspects the Labour government's quite undeserved reputation for being "progressive" in colonial affairs would have been seriously damaged, if not altogether destroyed.[11] What prevented it was not any great principled objection to an act of imperialist aggression on the part of members of the government, but American hostility. The United States made it absolutely clear that they were opposed to any British military action and the government did not feel strong enough to defy them. The chancellor of the exchequer, Hugh Gaitskell, seems to have been the US embassy's spokesman in the cabinet over this and other issues. Attlee made the position clear: "It was...the general view of the cabinet that, in the light of the United States' attitude...force could not be used to hold the refinery and maintain British employees of the Anglo-Iranian Oil Company in Abadan. We could not afford to break with the United States on an issue of this kind".[12]

With the occupation of Abadan ruled out, the British were forced to evacuate the country in a humiliating and damaging retreat. Soon afterwards Labour lost power and Winston Churchill once again became prime minister. The Conservatives had been extremely critical of the Labour government's failure to overthrow Musaddiq in opposition, but once installed in power they found themselves forced to rely on the United States. The coup d'etat that finally overthrew Musaddiq in August 1953 was organised by the American Central Intelligence Agency (CIA) with Britain's MI6 very much in a supporting role.[13] The Shah's new dictatorship rewarded its American sponsors with a renegotiated division of the oil spoils. Under the new arrangements the Shah's government received 50 percent of the profits from the oil industry which was placed in the hands of an international consortium. The AIOC had a 40 percent share in this consortium, along with US oil companies that also had a 40 percent share. Royal Shell had 14 percent and the French state oil company a 6 percent share. This represented a massive shift in the relative position of British and US oil interests, reducing the British owned share of Middle Eastern oil from 53 percent to 24 percent and increasing the American share from 44 to 58 percent. The brutalities of the Shah's dictatorship were a small price to pay for the security of Western oil.

Egypt and the Canal Zone

Egypt was also part of Britain's informal empire, although the presence of British troops in the country gave British influence a directness, even brutality, not so evident in Iran. On 4 February 1942, for example, the British ambassador, Miles Lampson, had surrounded King Farouk's palace with tanks and, accompanied by armed men, forced the monarch to appoint a prime minister of Britain's choosing. This bullying was, Lampson confessed, "something I could not have enjoyed more". While it achieved short term objectives, however, the resentment this humiliation of the Egyptian head of state caused made the British position untenable in the long term. In March 1946 Lampson, by now Lord Killearn, gave Ernest Bevin some advice on what sort of people the Egyptians were and how best to handle them. "The Egyptians", he wrote, "are essentially a docile and friendly people, but they are like children in many respects. They need a strong but essentially fair and helpful hand to guide them: 'Firmness and justice' is the motto for Egypt just as it used to be for the Chinese".[14] The

THE BLOOD NEVER DRIED

days when British governors, ambassadors and officials could get away with this sort of patronising arrogance had gone, however.

The Labour government that took power at the end of July 1945 was confronted with a growing demand for the removal of British troops from Egypt. Under the terms of the Anglo-Egyptian Treaty of 1936, the British were entitled to station 10,000 troops in their Canal Zone bases. In 1946 there were, in fact, still over 100,000 British troops in the country, half of them in Cairo. Their presence was bitterly resented and there were continual clashes with the local people, clashes that were beginning to assume the character of a low level guerrilla war. On 21 February 1946 British troops in Cairo opened fire on demonstrators, killing more than 20 people. This provoked demonstrations and protests throughout the country. In Alexandria there were serious clashes that left two British soldiers and 17 Egyptians dead. After this, attacks on the British became routine with shootings, grenade attacks and bombings a regular occurrence.[15] The British responded by withdrawing their troops to the Canal Zone but still maintained over 60,000 men in the country as late as mid-1947.

As far as the British were concerned, the military bases in the Canal Zone were of vital importance. The scale of the commitment was enormous. The network of bases occupied 750 square miles between the Nile delta and the west bank of the Canal. It was, according to one historian, "the world's most elaborate military complex" and boasted:

Regional communications networks; ten airfields and a facility for seaplanes; docks; a railroad system (50 engines and 900 coaches); depots (for ammunition, ordnance, railroad trucks, and thousands of cars, trucks, motorcycles, and armoured carriers, along with medical and general stores); assembly plants and factories (for jerrycans and clothing, among other commodities); repair shops for everything from vehicles to surgical equipment; power stations, water filtration plants and distribution outlets for water, coal and oil (including storage tanks, pipelines, and filling stations); to say nothing of barracks, hospitals, and recreational facilities.[16]

This hopefully ensured British domination over the Middle East, but was also regarded as indispensable in the event of war with the Soviet Union. The Labour government hoped to use this Cold War consideration to secure American support for the retention of the

Canal Zone. To this end, the British undertook to extend the runway of the Abu Sueier airfield so that it could take American B-29 strategic bombers. They would be able to attack more targets in the Soviet Union flying from Egypt than from the bases the Labour government had handed over in Britain itself.[17]

The Labour government was attempting to maintain military bases in a country that was in a "pre-revolutionary situation".[18] Attempts at reaching an agreement were fatally compromised as the situation in Egypt escalated out of control. The situation finally came to a head on 8 October 1951 when the Egyptian government unilaterally annulled the 1936 treaty and demanded British evacuation. The British responded with a show of strength, pouring troops into the country in an attempt to intimidate the Egyptians. By early November troop levels were again up to over 60,000 men. They took up positions in the Canal Zone and threatened the reoccupation of the whole country. Attlee and Morrison were absolutely determined to maintain the British position, because, they reasoned, "the consequences of allowing ourselves to be ejected from Egypt…would be so disastrous as to leave us no alternative".[19]

With the election into office of Winston Churchill's government, at the end of October, an even stronger line was taken. Troop levels rose to some 80,000 men and a tough response to Egyptian guerrilla attacks was authorised. In November the British commander, General George Erskine, ordered most of the village of Kfr Abdu levelled because it was being used by snipers to harass the Suez water filtration plant. Some 80 houses were bulldozed and the inhabitants evicted in an operation that one British officer subsequently described with some understatement as a "blunder". One Egyptian newspaper placed a bounty of 1,000 Egyptian pounds on Erskine. Violence escalated with the British shelling Egyptian villages in response to increasing guerrilla attacks. Erskine believed that the Egyptian police were heavily involved in assisting, even participating in, the guerrilla campaign. On 25 January 1952, in an attempt to put a stop to this, a large British force surrounded the police station in Ismailia and demanded its surrender. The police refused and, to the surprise of the British, mounted a fierce resistance. An infantry assault was beaten off and so Centurion tanks were brought in to shell the buildings. The police finally surrendered after more than 40 of their number had been killed. One British officer recalled that his men were "far from

THE BLOOD NEVER DRIED

jubilant...Dead and wounded littered the barracks and rooftops".[20] Erskine's political adviser, J de C Hamilton, crowed that the operation had shown "the jackal peoples of the world...that the lion's tail cannot be twisted indefinitely and that he can still bite". The British press was unanimous in its support, with the *Daily Express* welcoming the attack as "a mighty reaffirmation of imperial destiny".[21]

The reality was somewhat different: as one historian has put it, Erskine had "saved Ismailia and lost the Canal Zone".[22] Any prospect of an agreement allowing British troops to stay in Egypt was gone. The day after the battle in Ismailia, 26 January, " Black Saturday", large crowds attacked the European district in Cairo with the police either standing by or joining in. Over 400 buildings were destroyed, many of them symbols of British domination, including Shepherd's Hotel and the Turf Club, and seventeen British subjects were killed. Eventually order was restored and King Farouk, fearful of British retaliation, retreated from further confrontation. This sealed his fate, completing the alienation of the Egyptian army and leaving the country ungovernable. Moreover, his fear of the British was exaggerated. The events of the 25 and 26 January served as a "reality check" with the British recognising they could not reoccupy the country. The opposition to such a move would be too great. Plans for moving troops into Cairo and Alexandria had been prepared, but the Middle Eastern commander in chief, General Brian Robertson, now concluded that the heroism (my word, not his) of the Egyptian police at Ismailia made the undertaking too dangerous. "Any idea that we can waltz into Cairo and find some moderate elements whom we could set up to restore order is out of the question," he told the government. "Our former expectations", he warned, "that the Egyptian army might offer only token resistance will not be realised".[23] The reoccupation of Egypt would meet with fierce resistance and would require more troops. There were no more to be had. Indeed, the chief of the Imperial General Staff, Field Marshal William Slim, feared that the Egyptian crisis had already swallowed up Britain's strategic reserve and that this "might encourage insurgency in other parts of the world to which they would be unable to respond".[24]

Nasser and the road to war

On 23 July 1952 a secret society organised within the Egyptian army, the Free Officers, staged a coup that overthrew Farouk. They installed a Revolutionary Command Council (RCC) headed by General Mohammad Neguib in power. The dominant figure within the RCC, however, was Colonel Gamal Abdel Nasser, who was soon to supercede Neguib.[25] The coup took place with the full support of the CIA and, according to one account, the Americans promised the conspirators that they would prevent the British from intervening on Farouk's behalf.[26] As far as the Americans were concerned, a modernising dictatorship aligned with the US was the way forward and they supported the Egyptians in negotiations over the Canal Zone. For the British, Egyptian demands remained totally unacceptable. Churchill, the prime minister, in particular, regarded it as outrageous that Britain could no longer dictate terms to an inferior people for whom he had the utmost contempt. On one occasion he told Anthony Eden that he should tell the Egyptians "that if we had any more of their cheek we will set the Jews on them and drive them into the gutter from which they should never have emerged".[27] On another occasion, as Eden attempted to secure an agreement on the bases, Churchill sarcastically remarked that "he never knew before that Munich was situated on the Nile".[28] Privately, Churchill made it clear that he supported the "Suez Group", a collection of right wing Tory MPs who opposed any retreat from empire and favoured the use of military force in Egypt and everywhere else. Eden's private secretary, Evelyn Shuckburgh, complained in his diary of the widespread view in Whitehall that "we should sit on the gippies [Egyptians] and have a 'whiff of grapeshot'".[29]

Without American support, however, the British no longer had the ability to impose their will on the Egyptians. On 27 July 1954 the Churchill government finally concluded an agreement to evacuate British troops from Egypt by 18 June 1956. Thereafter military facilities would be maintained by civilian contractors and the British would be allowed to make use of them only in response to outside attacks on Turkey or any Arab state.[30] This was a humiliating retreat, surrendering control of territory the size of Wales to the despised Egyptians. It was a humiliation that rankled.

Even after the 1954 Settlement the British could not accept the notion of Egyptian independence. When Eden met Nasser in Cairo in February 1955, the Egyptian leader was summoned to the British embassy to be lectured on his responsibilities to the British Empire. The British expected the Egyptians to behave as loyal servants and cooperate with the military alliance, the Baghdad Pact (Britain, Turkey, Iran, Pakistan and Iraq) that they were constructing. As far as Nasser was concerned, this was "colonialism in disguise".[31] Egyptian opposition to the pact was seen as a major challenge to the British position throughout the Middle East. Having driven the British out of Egypt, Nasser was now trying to drive them out of the whole region. The problem was that the Egyptian regime had ambitions both to modernise the country and to establish itself as an independent regional power. Nasser was not prepared to be a British client or, as the Americans were to soon discover, an American client. Instead he hoped to adopt a "neutralist" stance in the Cold War, committed to neither side but playing the Russians and the Americans off against each other to Egypt's advantage. This was not acceptable.

By the mid-1950s hostility to British domination was widespread throughout the Middle East. Rather than recognising this as a response to British policy and behaviour, the government blamed it on Nasser personally. According to Anthony Nutting, a junior minister at the Foreign Office, they needed "a whipping boy to explain away the failure of their policies in the Arab world".[32] King Hussein of Jordan's decision in March 1956 to dismiss John Glubb, the British commander of his Arab Legion, finally convinced Eden (by now prime minister) to get rid of the Egyptian leader. Hussein had recognised that if he was to survive the rising tide of Arab nationalism, he had to distance himself from the British. The British, however, blamed Nasser, the new "Hitler" or "Mussolini" who was out to dominate "our" Middle East. The response was "a toughening of British policy everywhere in the Middle East" and the ascendancy of "the 'whiff of grapeshot' school" in the cabinet.[33] Evelyn Shuckburgh wrote of the prime minister wanting "to strike some blow, somewhere, to counterbalance". "Ministers", he wrote, "led by the PM—mad keen to land British troops somewhere to show that we are still alive and kicking". Bahrain, where the foreign secretary, Selwyn Lloyd, had been stoned on a recent visit, was considered as one possibility. On 3 March, however, Eden took Shuckburgh aside "and said I was seriously to consider reoccupation of Suez as a move to counteract the blow to our prestige which Glubb's dismissal means". Everything, Shuckburgh concluded, was "in a mess" with the Arabs "hating us more and more".[34] Nutting, still advocating a restrained response, was told by an outraged Eden to forget all talk of isolating or neutralising Nasser: "I want him destroyed, can't you understand? I want him murdered, and if you and the Foreign Office don't agree, then you'd better come to the cabinet and explain why." When Nutting tried to argue that they had no alternative government to replace Nasser, Eden replied: "I don't give a damn if there's anarchy and chaos in Egypt".[35]

Nasser's refusal to accept a client role was by now alienating the Americans. The Egyptians had become desperate to modernise their own armed forces. They were alarmed by Israel's increasing military strength, courtesy of arms deals with the French, and their exercise of that strength in punitive border raids. The prospect of Israeli aggression made this a matter of life and death for the regime, and when the Eisenhower government refused to help, Nasser turned to the Soviet bloc. In September 1955 the Egyptians concluded an arms deal with the Czechs. This was regarded as a hostile act by the United States and Nasser went on to compound his crime in May 1956 by recognising Communist China. The Americans responded by withdrawing their financial support for Egypt's major development project, the Aswan Dam, on 19 July 1956. Nasser's response was, a week later, to nationalise the Suez Canal.

Collusion and invasion

The nationalisation of the Suez Canal was another blow to British prestige, but it was also an opportunity. While covert efforts were already under way to overthrow both Nasser and the Syrian government ("Operation Straggle"), there was now a pretext for a full-scale military intervention to take back the Canal.[36] The Conservative Party was united, with the chancellor of the exchequer, Harold Macmillan, leading the "hawks". Indeed one leading Conservative described him as "wanting to tear Nasser's scalp off with his own fingernails".[37] Moreover, at least initially, the Labour opposition supported intervention. Hugh Gaitskell, the Labour leader, made it clear that he would support military action against the new "Hitler", but with the proviso that "they must get America in line". A staunch Zionist, Gaitskell urged an alliance with Israel.[38] Even Aneurin Bevan, the leader of the Labour left, joined in the abuse of Nasser who he compared to "Ali Baba". Egypt, he wrote in the *Tribune* newspaper, had "a right to come into her own, but not into someone else's".[39] The key to the crisis, however, was to be the United States.

In order to try and secure US support for an invasion, the British played the Cold War card, arguing that Nasser was a Soviet ally and that through him the Russians aimed to dominate the Middle East. MI6 supposedly had an agent codenamed "Lucky Break" placed in Nasser's inner circle, who was sending back reports of a Soviet sponsored attempt to take over the Middle East. While the Joint Intelligence Committee (JIC), that coordinated intelligence collection and assessment, discounted these reports, Eden took them seriously and passed them on to the Americans. In the words of the JIC's semiofficial history, "He was already falling into the dangerous practice of selecting the pieces of intelligence that fitted his preconceptions and neglecting the committee's more balanced overall view".[40] Indeed, the historian Scott Lucas has gone so far as to argue that the likelihood is that "Lucky Break" never even "existed outside the creative imaginations of MI6 officers who wanted more aggressive operations against Egypt".[41] President Eisenhower would still not come on board, however. The Americans were not interested in helping to bolster British power in the Middle East and, anyway, did not regard military intervention as the most effective way to deal with Nasser. It would alienate Arab opinion. For the British, the situation was beginning to slip out of their hands with the likelihood of the Americans sponsoring a deal over the Canal that would complete their humiliation.

The solution to Eden's predicament was provided by the French. Guy Mollet's Socialist government was determined to strike a blow against Nasser because of his support for the liberation struggle in Algeria. The French were already in an informal alliance with Israel, having armed the country and agreed to help it become a nuclear power. They now proposed extending this alliance to include the British. At this time relations between the Eden government and Israel were poor, with the British concerned that the Israelis were planning an attack on Jordan to seize the West Bank. Despite considerable reservations Eden entered into secret discussions with the French and Israelis that eventually resulted in the Sèvres Protocol of 24 October 1956.[42] Under the terms of this illegal conspiracy, Israel would attack Egypt, whereupon Britain and France, posing as peacemakers, would demand that both sides withdraw from the Suez Canal area. Israel would agree, but the Egyptians could not possibly accept this infringement of their sovereignty, especially as they were the victims of aggression. In response to the Egyptian refusal, an Anglo-French force would invade, ostensibly to separate the two sides, but in reality to overthrow Nasser. The Israelis insisted that the British and French should act quickly because they counted on the British destroying the Egyptian air force. The British were absolutely insistent that the collusion remained secret, something the Israelis, who were quite open about their expansionist aims, regarded as typical "British hypocrisy".[43]

There were a number of problems with the Sèvres plan. First, it would fool no one. It was even more transparent than George Bush and Tony Blair's later "weapons of mass destruction" ruse. When Selwyn Lloyd told a cabinet colleague, R A B Butler, of the plot, Butler "was impressed by the audacity of the thinking behind this plan", but nevertheless was "concerned about the public reaction".[44] Second, even if the operation was successful, there was the practicality of occupying Egypt. The British had pulled back from this very prospect in 1952-1954 and the French were heavily embroiled in Algeria and yet they now proposed what could well be an open-ended military commitment. Humphrey Trevelyan, the British ambassador in Cairo, warned that invasion would be greeted with "guerrilla warfare and it would be difficult for us to disengage without long and widespread operations… No government set up by the occupying forces would last".[45] The British ambassador in Paris, Gladwyn Jebb, later acknowledged "the sheer impossibility of occupying Egypt for very long", and doubted "whether we could succeed in establishing a stooge government in Cairo capable of carrying on after the withdrawal of our troops". In retrospect, he concluded that "the Suez venture on any rational calculation did not make very much sense".[46]

The Suez invasion was not, however, based on any "rational calculation". Nasser, for example, could not believe that the British would commit "the one unforgivable sin" of joining with Israel in an attack on an Arab country. It would irreparably damage "their prestige and interests in the Middle East".[47] Why then did Eden take the gamble? It was an act of desperation by a government that believed the British position in the Middle East was lost unless some dramatic stroke could rescue it. The Americans could not be relied on, British influence was in decline, but perhaps a military demonstration could turn the situation round. The British state no longer had either the financial or the military strength for such demonstrations, but the Conservatives refused to face up to this. In the event, the Suez invasion was to prove a testimony to British weakness. There was, of course, a third problem with the Sèvres plan. The United States were

THE BLOOD NEVER DRIED

to be kept in the dark in the belief that they would oppose any attack on Egypt if they knew in advance, but would have to support it if it was an accomplished fact. After all, the British government had supported the Americans over the CIA-inspired coup that overthrew President Arbenz in Guatemala in June 1954, even to the extent of covering up the sinking of a British freighter by CIA aircraft.[48] Surely the Americans would reciprocate. As far as the Americans were concerned, however, this was one way traffic. One of those who assured Eden that the Americans would go along with the invasion once it was under way was Harold Macmillan. As he later acknowledged, this was "a profound miscalculation".[49]

The Israelis launched their surprise attack on Egyptian positions in Sinai on 29 October. French collusion was hardly disguised with French aircraft supporting the attack from Israeli airfields from day one. The British, however, were desperate to maintain the pretence. The Anglo-French ultimatum was presented to both sides the following day. Nutting, who resigned from the government in protest, later wrote:

> If proof were needed of collusion between Britain and the aggressor, it was written plainly enough in the timing of the ultimatum, which demanded that both belligerents withdraw to a distance of ten miles from the Canal at a moment when the Egyptian army was still engaging the Israelis at distances between 75 miles and 125 miles to the east of the Canal. This meant, at the moment of its issue, the powers who were pretending to put a stop to the fighting by separating the belligerents, were ordering one of them—and the victim of aggression at that—to withdraw up to 135 miles, while the other, who happened to be the aggressor, was told to advance on all fronts between 65 and 115 miles.[50]

The Egyptians rejected the ultimatum and the British bombers began their attacks. The actual invasion began on 5 November with paratroop landings followed by a seaborne assault on Port Said. The following day the British and the French agreed to a ceasefire.

The decisive factor in defeating the Israeli-Franco-British attack on Egypt was the hostile stance taken by the United States. Eisenhower reacted to the invasion with fury. The Americans were not prepared to tolerate independent action on this scale on the part of the British. Not only did they not want any revival of British power and influence in the Middle East, but they were afraid that Britain's old-fashioned imperialism would play into the hands of the Russians. Accordingly, the United States took the lead in condemning the invasion and backed this up with financial and oil sanctions. This forced the British to accept a ceasefire without any of their political or military objectives having been gained. When British troops finally withdrew on 22 December 1956 Nasser was still in power, a popular hero throughout the Arab world. American hostility was also the decisive factor in the Labour opposition's decision to oppose the invasion. Although Gaitskell grounded his opposition on the UN charter, there can be no serious doubt that if the United States had supported the attack on Egypt, so would he. Many Labour MPs and most rank and file party members would have opposed it regardless, but they certainly did not have as much influence with the party leadership at this time or subsequently as the American embassy.

Conservative hardliners have always claimed that, were it not for the Americans, the Suez invasion would have been a great success. Julian Amery, for example, insisted that if operations had continued for only another 48 hours, "we would in my judgement have toppled Nasser and seen the emergence of a new Egyptian regime". Nasser would have fled, "probably to the Soviet Union".[51] A much better case can be made that Eisenhower actually saved the British government from a quagmire. The Egyptians had prepared for guerrilla war, distributing arms to the people, including all the weapons the British had stored in the Canal Zone bases. Nasser ordered the assassination of collaborators. And he put on a display of personal courage and determination that the likes of Amery refused to believe any Egyptian capable of. Moreover, the British and the French had already met determined resistance in Port Said that was put down with considerable violence. Taking the city cost the lives of 11 British and French soldiers and between 650 and 1,000 Egyptians, mainly civilians. The ceasefire agreed on 6 November did not stop guerrilla attacks on the occupation forces which continued up until the moment of the final evacuation. If the British had been successful in installing a "stooge government" in Cairo, they would have faced protracted resistance across the country. The chief of the Imperial General Staff estimated that " to hold Egypt would take eight divisions and five hundred military government officers".[52] A bloody protracted guerrilla war would have led to attacks on the British throughout the

THE BLOOD NEVER DRIED

Middle East. One consequence of this would almost certainly have been the continuation of conscription into the 1960s. Success in 1956 would have been an even bigger disaster than failure.

One last point worth making is that those responsible for the collusion never admitted to it, even after it was common knowledge. Eden, Macmillan and Lloyd all denied that there had been any conspiracy. This is, of course, perfectly understandable when one considers that they had conspired to make an unprovoked attack on Egypt under the guise of peace keeping, no less. This is really quite breathtaking. Nevertheless, Lord Kilmuir insisted, "The wild accusations of collusion between the British, French and Israeli governments which were hurled by the Labour Party had absolutely no foundation in fact".[53] Kilmuir, it is worth remembering was a former attorney general, home secretary and lord chancellor, an absolute pillar of the establishment, a man of unimpeachable integrity. And yet here we have absolute proof that he lied through his teeth until the day he died.

Aftermath

How did the British government respond to the absolutely ruthless way that Eisenhower crushed their imperial pretensions? The contrast with France is interesting. The French responded with a Gaullist strategy of refusing to accept subordination to the United States and attempting instead to build up Western Europe as a rival to the American imperium. The British were to consider such a response themselves, with Selwyn Lloyd putting forward the Gaullist alternative. He was never to forgive the Americans for Suez and even in his posthumously published memoirs insisted that they had "let us down on every occasion, when even silence from them would have helped". This had been evident even before 1956 (he blamed the loss of Iran on them) and he characterised the US State Department's "anti-British" attitude as "a mixture of anti-colonialism and hard-headed oil tycoonery".[54] In early January 1957 Lloyd presented his "Grand Design" to the cabinet. He proposed a:

> closer military and political association between Britain and Western Europe. He went so far as to suggest that Britain could "pool our resources with our European allies so that Western Europe as a whole might become a third nuclear power comparable with the United States and the Soviet Union".[55]

What Lloyd was urging was a revolutionary shift in grand strategy whereby the British state committed itself to building up Western Europe as a means for protecting British interests throughout the world, as, in fact, a rival imperium to both the Soviet Union and the United States. This had some support within the Conservative Party at the time, and still has today, but Macmillan decided instead on the alternative course of voluntary subordination to the United States that was dignified as a "Special Relationship".

In Macmillan's memoirs he revealingly entitles the chapter on the Suez invasion "The Anglo-American Schism". This is not how he saw it at the time, when "Destroying Nasser" would have been a more appropriate title, but it was certainly how he came to regard the crisis subsequently. As far as Macmillan was concerned such a "schism" should never be allowed to happen again. The interests of British capitalism were best served by embracing an alliance with the United States on whatever terms were available. Whereas previous governments had hoped for an alliance of equals, Macmillan accepted that this was not realistic. Maintaining an unequal alliance, with the British very much in the subordinate position, became the primary objective of British foreign policy. This has been the strategy of successive British governments both Conservative and Labour ever since, with the notable exception of Edward Heath's Conservative government (1970-1974), the nearest we have come to a British Gaullism. While this strategy has often involved British leaders in an undignified relationship with American presidents, Macmillan with Kennedy, Wilson with Johnson, and most especially Blair with the appalling George W Bush, in fact, it was every bit as hard-headed as France's Gaullist strategy. What the Macmillan government decided was that Britain's interests, unlike those of the French, were global and could only be effectively protected by a state with a global reach. Once the British state had been able to perform this role itself, but since the Second World War it had become increasingly clear that this was no longer the case. The Suez fiasco was the most dramatic demonstration of this. Instead the British looked to the United States, an imperial state with a considerable reach, to protect its interests. Obviously there were difficulties with this because British interests always took second place to American interests, so that the alliance was often tense and uneasy, but these difficulties were always secondary. As far as successive British governments were concerned, Western Europe did not have the ability to

THE BLOOD NEVER DRIED

protect British interests worldwide so that some British variant of Gaullism was never in the interests of British capitalism.

The Iraqi endgame

While the Suez invasion was certainly important in weakening the British position in the Middle East, it was not the decisive factor in its final destruction. Indeed, after the invasion Macmillan did his best to restore the British position, but always with American support. He remained every bit as committed to the destruction of Nasser as before, but recognised that nothing could be achieved without the United States.[56] Britain still maintained Iraq as a client state and was determined to oppose Egyptian influence everywhere it could. On 14 July 1958, however, a military coup swept away the Hashemite monarchy and dealt the British position in the Middle East a final fatal blow.[57] Certainly the Suez affair played a part in this, compromising any Arab government that remained friendly with Britain, but nevertheless the coup took the British completely by surprise. Macmillan himself described it as "devastating…destroying at a blow a whole system of security which successive British governments had built up".[58]

At the time it was regarded as an Egyptian-sponsored coup, as part of a general offensive to overthrow pro-Western governments throughout the Middle East. To counter this, on 15 July US marines landed in Lebanon to support the Chamoun government and on 17 July British paratroopers began arriving in Jordan to support King Hussein. The British also hoped for intervention in Iraq. Macmillan tried to persuade Eisenhower to agree to an Anglo-American invasion, but the Americans were not prepared to go that far. Despite this, the British continued trying to interest the Americans in a joint occupation of the country as late as August 1959. British plans were advanced enough for it to be proposed that the Americans should occupy Baghdad, while the British occupied Basra.[59] Britain acting alone was not even considered. As it was, the new Iraqi regime quickly distanced itself from the Egyptians. Its provenance was nationalist rather than Nasserist and the British followed the American lead and came to terms with it. This proved only a short-lived "friendship" and in 1963 the CIA supported a coup carried out by the Baath party, a coup whose ultimate beneficiary was, of course, Saddam Hussein.

Crushing the
Mau Mau in Kenya

THE BRITISH campaign to crush the Mau Mau rebellion in the
1950s has become a byword for colonial brutality. Although not
so well known as the French campaign in Algeria or the American
campaign in Vietnam, nevertheless, in terms of the intensity and violence of the repression, the war in Kenya easily stands comparison
and in some respects was worse. The British were just better at covering it up. Why, though, was "decolonisation" in Kenya such a
bloody affair compared to Britain's other African colonies? The
answer is provided by the presence of white settlers, an armed community of white racists that was prepared to resist even the most
minimal concessions to the black population, let alone majority rule
and independence. While the British government was, however reluctantly, to hand over power to black governments—in Ghana in 1957,
Nigeria in 1960, Tanganyika in 1961 and Uganda in 1962—with minimal violence, in Kenya the settlers offered fierce resistance that was to
cost thousands of lives. The British attempt to sustain settler rule in
Kenya led to an unprecedented attempt to crush and cow the African
population. The violence of this attempt was a product of the manner
in which the colony had originally been established. According to
Elspeth Huxley, the best-known settler apologist, "no country in the
empire has ever been opened up and settled with so little bloodshed
and with the maintenance of such friendly relations with the native
population".[1] The realities of conquest starkly contradict this.

Pacification

The British had established their East African Protectorate in 1895 primarily for strategic reasons, but subsequently decided to open up the territory for white settlement. To persuade the African population to accept this required their large-scale slaughter by a succession of punitive expeditions. An expedition mounted against the Kikuyu in 1904 killed over 1,500 people, but the official report was doctored on the orders of the commissioner, Charles Eliot, who had the figure reduced to 400. An expedition against the Nandi in 1905 killed 636 people and seized 10,000 cattle and 18,000 goats and sheep. The following year the Nandi were once again attacked, this time with 1,117 killed and 16,000 cattle and 36,000 goats and sheep seized. In 1906 the award of a timber concession to a British partnership meant that the Embu, who thought the land was theirs, had "to be dealt with". A punitive expedition duly killed over 400 and seized 3,000 cattle, and 4,000 goats and sheep. As a Colonial Office official piously observed, "Unless we are going to abrogate our civilizing mission in Africa such expedition with their attendant slaughter are necessary".[2]

An expedition against the Kisii in 1905 inevitably involved large-scale loss of African life. A British officer, W Robert Foran, described the decisive encounter:

> The machine gun was kept in action so long during this sharp engagement that it became almost red-hot to the touch. Before the Kisii warriors were repulsed, they left several hundred dead and wounded spearmen outside the square of bayonets. This was not so much a battle as a massacre.

The Kisii had to be punished again in 1908, but this time offered no resistance, being, according to Foran, "under the impression that the tribal surrender had been accepted". Nevertheless, the expedition put in "some strenuous work—burning villages, devastating standing crops, capturing livestock and hunting down bolting natives". On this occasion the reports reaching London caused some concern. One official estimated, extremely conservatively it must be said, that casualties were being inflicted on the Africans by more punitive expeditions in the ratio of 40 to one. The colonial under-secretary, Winston Churchill, complained: "I do not like the tone of these reports... It looks like butchery... Surely it cannot be necessary to go on killing these defenceless people on such an enormous scale".[3] The Colonial Office was actually warned at the time that the settlers, "through acts of oppression and cruelty", were trying to provoke trouble "and then to seize the opportunity for general spoliation of African possessions". In April 1908, in the middle of an international scandal over conditions in the Belgian Congo, a report on forced labour in Kenya arrived in London that had noted in the margin, "It must on no account be published." An official who read the report observed, "One might almost say that there is no atrocity in the Congo—except mutilation—which cannot be matched in our Protectorate".[4]

As far as the men on the spot were concerned, massacre was absolutely necessary. As one practitioner, Richard Meinertzhagen, insisted, "When stationed with 100 soldiers amid an African population of some 300,000, in cases of emergency where local government was threatened, we had to act and act quickly".[5] The whites were so few in number that if the African population was to be broken to their will, any resistance had to be bloodily and decisively crushed. Even a severe critic of the settlers such as Norman Leys could still write in 1924 that "slaughter" was "the kindest way of dealing with native risings".[6]

Once broken, the Africans were kept cowed by a regime of flogging. Elspeth Huxley, in her best-selling account of an idyllic childhood in the colony, *The Flame Trees of Thika*, could justify flogging for showing lack of respect on the grounds that:

> Respect was the only protection available to Europeans who lived singly, or in scattered families, among thousands of Africans accustomed to constant warfare and armed with spears and poisoned arrows... The least rent or puncture might, if not immediately checked and repaired, split the whole garment asunder and expose its wearer in all his human vulnerability.[7]

Of course, when she wrote of respect, she really meant fear. It was recognised, though, that "repeated beatings" could well be counterproductive, and Lord Cranforth warned against this in his 1912 volume, *A Colony in the Making*. What was essential was that when a beating was called for it should be "thorough". While recognising that this was not a popular view in Britain, he nevertheless insisted that "for certain crimes, such as lying, petty stealing and more especially cruelty

THE BLOOD NEVER DRIED

to children or animals, the whip is the best and kindest preventative and cure". His wife, Lady Cranforth, contributed a chapter on the supervision of African domestic servants: "One could not, for instance, learn by experience in England when it is the right time to have a servant beaten for rubbing silver plate on the gravel path to clean it, and that after several previous warnings".[8] A regime that was prepared to flog Africans for lying or petty theft or disrespect would commit the most fearful atrocities when confronted with a full-scale rebellion.

The Mau Mau revolt

The revolt was largely the work of the Kikuyu tribe for whom the white settlement had been a complete disaster. They were penned in by the settlers. By 1948 one and a quarter million Kikuyu were restricted to landholding in 2,000 square miles of tribal reserve, while the 30,000 white settlers held 12,000 square miles, including most of the best farmland. In the reserves there was considerable poverty, with almost half of the population landless. Only a small class of collaborators prospered. For the great mass of the people the situation was deteriorating. Outside the reserves some 120,000 Kikuyu lived as squatters on the white farms, receiving a small patch of land in return for their labour, in effect a form of serfdom. This group found their way of life and standard of living under concerted attack in the 1940s, as the farmers tried to transform them into landless labourers. According to one account, the squatters' real income had fallen by 30 to 40 percent in the years before the revolt.[9] These people were to provide the backbone of the revolutionary movement in the countryside. Many Kikuyu were forced off the land altogether and driven to seek work in the towns. The African population of Nairobi more than doubled between 1938 and 1952, increasing from 40,000 to 95,000 with the Kikuyu dominating the Eastlands district. Living conditions were appalling and getting worse. Nairobi was to become the centre of the revolt: in the graphic phrase of one historian, it was "the Mau Mau's beating heart".[10]

What drove the Kikuyu down the road to rebellion was the failure of the Labour government elected with an overwhelming majority in 1945 to offer any hope of improvement or advance. When the colonial secretary, James Griffiths, a former miners' union official, visited Kenya in 1951, the moderate Kenya Africa Union (KAU) repeatedly requested that the African population be given 12 elected representatives on the

Legislative Council. Instead Griffiths offered to increase African representation from four to five nominees. This left the 30,000 settlers with 14 elected representatives, the 100,000 Asians with six, the 24,000 Arabs with one and the five million Africans with five nominees. Even the settlers were astonished at how reactionary the Labour government proved to be. This shattering of hopes for peaceful change fatally compromised the influence of the moderates and strengthened the hand of the revolutionaries.

The revolutionary movement originated in the reserves and on the white farms, a product of Kikuyu land grievances. It was initiated by the banned Kikuyu Central Association (KCA) that in the late 1940s launched an "oathing" campaign to enrol the Kikuyu in a movement of resistance to the British. This movement was originally conceived as a protest movement, but it became increasingly radicalised. It is a testimony to the success of British propaganda that it is known as "the Mau Mau", the bastardised name given to it by the British and their collaborators. To the rebels themselves it was known at the time as "Muingi" or "The Movement" or as "Muigwithania" or "The Unifier" or as the KCA.[11] Whatever the name, it was without any doubt one of the most important revolutionary movements in the history of modern Africa and one of the most important revolutionary movements to confront the British Empire.

The movement was radicalised by a militant leadership that emerged from the trade union movement in Nairobi. Here the Transport and Allied Workers Union led by Fred Kubai, and the Clerks and Commercial Workers Union led by Bildad Kaggia were at the heart of the resistance. Most accounts of the Mau Mau movement either ignore or play down the role of the trade unions in the struggle, but the fact is that without their participation a sustained revolt would not have been possible.

The trade unions came together on 1 May 1949 to form the East African Trades Union Congress (EATUC) with Kubai elected president and an Asian socialist, Makhan Singh, elected general secretary. The organisation was seen as a serious threat by the authorities, a perception wholeheartedly endorsed by the Labour government in London. When on 1 May 1950 the EATUC issued a call for independence and majority rule, the first African organisation to do so, both Fred Kubai and Makhan Singh were arrested. The response was a general strike that saw 100,000 workers walk out throughout the colony.

THE BLOOD NEVER DRIED

The British mounted a massive show of force and after nine days the strike was broken. Makhan Singh was to be interned without trial for the next 11 years, while Fred Kubai was only released early in 1951.[12]

The defeat of the general strike and the banning of the EATUC saw the leaders and militants of the trade unions throw themselves into the revolutionary movement. They established themselves as a new radical leadership committed to overthrowing colonial rule by mass action, strikes, demonstrations and armed struggle. In June 1951 they took control of the Nairobi branch of the KAU, using it as a front for the revolutionary activity. A Central Committee was set up in the city, enrolling the people and organising its own armed squads to protect the oath administrators and to deal with informers and collaborators. Its influence extended beyond the city into the reserves.

By now the colonial government was becoming alarmed. On 6 October 1952 Evelyn Baring arrived to take over as governor of the colony. The very next day a loyalist, Chief Waruhiu, was shot dead in broad daylight. Baring informed London that "we are facing a planned revolutionary movement".[13] On 20 October he declared a state of emergency which was accompanied by mass arrests. Among those rounded up were moderate opponents of the Mau Mau such as Jomo Kenyatta, who actually found himself charged with being its leader.

War

The Mau Mau revolt did not extend to the whole of Kenya. It was largely confined to the Kikuyu, Embu and Meru, and geographically restricted to the Central Province, an area of some 14,000 square miles. Nevertheless, the revolutionary cause had the support of the overwhelming majority of the Kikuyu, with General George Erskine estimating that over 90 percent were behind the movement.[14] This popular support gave the movement the initiative in the first phase of the rebellion, as the Land and Freedom Armies formed in the forests and the network of supporters expanded to sustain them. Even in this phase casualties were heavy, but they were replaced by enthusiastic recruits determined to strike back against the settlers and their African collaborators. Only the rebels' chronic shortage of firearms prevented them from inflicting crippling losses on the police and the settler community. Instead the movement's wrath fell on the collaborators, Kikuyu who had benefited from colonial rule and who took the side of the settlers. In the course of this conflict more than 2,000 loyalists were to die at the hands of the Mau Mau. The most notorious incident was the Lari massacre of March 1953 in which over 70 loyalists, including women and children, were killed.[15] This civil war dimension to the conflict was not something peculiar to the Mau Mau revolt. It is a feature, to one degree or another, of all wars of national liberation, including the American War of Independence.

Kenyatta was brought to trial in December 1952 before Justice Thacker and finally sentenced on 8 April 1953. There was no real evidence against him because, far from being the instigator of Mau Mau, he was its opponent. Indeed, the revolutionary movement's leaders were seriously considering having him assassinated as a collaborator before his arrest. As far as the authorities were concerned, no distinction was possible between moderate and revolutionary nationalism, and the settlers were determined to destroy both. Thacker sentenced Kenyatta to seven years hard labour to be followed by restricted residence in the remote north of the country for life. For his services to British justice, Thacker received a secret payment of £20,000. Far from dealing Mau Mau a blow, however, Kenyatta's travesty of a trial only served to rally people to the rebel cause.[16]

As late as January 1954 a parliamentary delegation from London visiting the colony could warn that Mau Mau influence over the Kikuyu "except in certain localities has not declined; it has on the contrary increased." They believed that "the situation has deteriorated" and that "the danger of infection outside the Kikuyu area is now greater, not less than it was at the beginning of the State of Emergency". As for Nairobi, "the situation is both grave and acute" with "Mau Mau orders…carried out in the heart of the city". "Mau Mau courts", they reported, sat "in judgement and their sentences are carried out by gangsters".[17] Particularly worrying was the intelligence that the revolutionary movement in Nairobi was recruiting members of the Kamba tribe. This was a very dangerous development because the Kamba were the backbone of Africa army units and of the African police. The rebels were also beginning to recruit from the Masai, and troops and police were despatched to the Narok district to prevent the "contagion" taking hold. One settler leader feared that they were in danger of losing "the battle for the mind of the African everywhere".[18]

The tide was about to turn, however. General Erskine took command in Kenya in January 1953 and he had by now come to recognise the crucial strategic role that Nairobi played in the struggle. The Mau

THE BLOOD NEVER DRIED

Mau were so embedded in the African districts of the city that only the most drastic action would break their hold. On 24 April 1954 Operation Anvil was launched. Some 25,000 troops and police cordoned off the city and proceeded to screen its African population. An incredible 27,000 men and women were interned without trial, mostly Kikuyu (indeed nearly half the city's Kikuyu population were interned), and over 20,000 others, once again mostly Kikuyu, were expelled from the city back to the reserves. There can be little doubt that this blanket use of internment was only possible because the victims were black, so that the violation of their civil liberties caused little concern back in Britain. The revolutionary movement was struck a massive blow, one that hit the trade unions particularly hard. Any African in possession of a union card was automatically interned.[19] According to one senior British army officer, Operation Anvil was "the turning point of the campaign".[20]

The success of the operation gave the British the initiative. The loss of Nairobi cut the Land and Freedom Armies off from their most important source of supplies. Erskine followed this success with similar operations in other areas that were once again accompanied by wholesale internment. By the end of 1954 there were 77,000 people interned without trial including thousands of women, and children as young as 12. This was accompanied, once again, by the mass deportation of the Kikuyu back to the reserves, forcibly uprooting the squatter population and expelling them (at least those not interned) from the White Highlands.

To complete the isolation of the Land and Freedom Armies, the British borrowed from their Malayan experience, and in June 1954 introduced a policy of forced villagisation. Over a million Kikuyu had their homes and possessions destroyed and were herded into over 800 guarded villages. Men, women and children were often left to sleep in the open until they had built their own new homes. Poverty, starvation and disease were rife in the new villages where the Kikuyu were concentrated, deprived of all civil liberties and subjected to a brutal and arbitrary police regime.[21] The settlement programme was the second crushing blow that the British inflicted on the Mau Mau. It left the surviving rebel fighters isolated in the forests, remorselessly hunted down by the British "counter-gangs", mixed squads of soldiers, police and renegade Mau Mau. These counter-gangs often behaved as death squads. By September 1956 it was estimated that there were only some 500 rebels still at large. The following month Dedan Kimathi, the commander of the Land and Freedom Armies, was captured by a counter-gang. He was subsequently hanged. The British had successfully defeated the revolt, although the emergency was to continue until January 1960.[22]

Repression

The defeat of the Mau Mau involved a degree of savagery that is quite unprecedented in British 20th century colonial wars. One really has to go back to the suppression of the Great Indian Rebellion of the 1850s to find a comparable episode. The reality was that in Kenya the flogging, torture, mutilation, rape and summary execution of suspects and prisoners were everyday occurrences. The extent of the violence was successfully covered up at the time but when news of particular incidents did leak out, it was overwhelmed by the government-sponsored propaganda campaign that portrayed the Mau Mau as primitive savages, barely human, who had to be put down.

In his account of the Mau Mau, the historian Robert Edgerton provides a graphic portrait of police methods during the emergency:

> If a question was not answered to the interrogator's satisfaction, the subject was beaten and kicked. If that did not lead to the desired confession, and it rarely did, more force was applied. Electric shock was widely used, and so was fire. Women were choked and held under water; gun barrels, beer bottles, and even knives were thrust into their vaginas. Men had beer bottles thrust up their rectums, were dragged behind Land Rovers, whipped, burned and bayoneted... Some police officers did not bother with more time-consuming forms of torture; they simply shot any suspect who refused to answer, then told the next suspect, who had been forced to watch the cold-blooded execution, to dig his own grave. When the grave was finished, the man was asked if he would now be willing to talk.

As far as the settlers were concerned there was open season on the Kikuyu. Anyone thought suspicious could be flogged, tortured and, if necessary, killed, with virtual impunity. When Field Marshall John Harding visited the colony early in 1953, he acknowledged that the settlers had taken the law "into their own hands" but this had been "fortunately hushed up".[23]

THE BLOOD NEVER DRIED

As part of her research into the British conduct during the emergency, Caroline Elkins interviewed a number of former settlers who had been members of the Kenyan Police Reserve. They described the torture they had carried out with as much concern as they talked about the weather. One man told her how he had dropped by a Special Branch interrogation centre to check up on a suspect and had:

> Stayed for a few hours to help the boys out, softening him up. This got a little out of hand. By the time I cut his balls off he had no ears and his eyeball, the right one, I think was hanging out of its socket...he died before we got much out of him.[24]

One should not mince one's words about this. Elements within the security forces in Kenya, particularly the police, used the methods of the Gestapo at their worst. This is no exaggeration or hyperbole, but a plain statement of fact. Except for a few isolated instances, where unwelcome publicity made action unavoidable, they were never held to account. On the few occasions when they were, their punishments were derisory. Unofficial repression was accompanied by the most ferocious official repression. As well as the tens of thousands interned without trial (the best estimate is that over 160,000 people were interned during the course of the emergency), even more were imprisoned for emergency offences. Between 1952 and 1958 over 34,000 women were to be imprisoned for Mau Mau offences, and the number of men imprisoned was probably ten times that figure. According to one historian, "at least one in four Kikuyu adult males was imprisoned or detained by the British colonial administration".[25] At the same time the government presided over what can only be described as a judicial massacre. Between the declaration of the emergency and November 1954, 756 rebels were hanged. By the end of 1954 the number was over 900 and by the end of the emergency had reached 1,090. Of those, 346 were hanged for murder, 472 for possessing arms or ammunition, 210 for consorting with rebels and an incredible 62 for administering illegal oaths.[26] A mobile gallows was specially built so that prisoners could be hanged in their home districts to provide an example. At one point, they were being hanged at the rate of 50 a month. The massacre even caused some concern in London where the prime minister, Winston Churchill, urged "that care should be taken to avoid the simultaneous execution of any large number of people". He was worried about the effect that "anything resembling mass executions" would have on public opinion. Churchill intervened to stop Evelyn Baring adding the possession of incendiary materials to the list of capital offences because they would soon be hanging men for the possession of a box of matches.[27] Despite this slaughter, there is no doubt that Frank Kitson, one of the originators of the counter-gang strategy, was speaking for many when he complained that the army and the police "had firmly fastened one of their hands behind their back with the cord of legal difficulties".[28]

In his outstanding account of the hangings during the emergency, *Histories of the Hanged*, David Anderson puts names to some of the victims. He records the fate of Wakianda Gachunga, hanged for the possession of two rounds of ammunition, and of Karanja Hinga, hanged for the possession of 13 rounds. He tells of the police informer who sold firearms and then promptly betrayed the purchasers to the hangman. He was found dead with his tongue cut out. He tells of the 13 internees at Embakali detention camp who overpowered their guards and escaped. The eight men subsequently recaptured were all hanged for being in possession of the guards' weapons. And he tells the story of Karithii Muthomo, arrested on his way to carry out an assassination in Nairobi in January 1954. He had been betrayed by Hussein Mohamed, a Special Branch informer, who was subsequently shot dead in broad daylight. When Muthomo was sentenced to hang, he told the judge, "I am dying for my land and I am not afraid to die for that".[29] The one-sided nature of the conflict is demonstrated quite dramatically by the casualties suffered by the two sides. The official British figure for rebels killed in action was 11,503, but the real number was much higher. Some estimates go as high as 50,000, and this is much closer to the truth. The casualties suffered by the security forces were considerably lower: only 12 European soldiers and 51 European police were killed, three Asians and 524 African soldiers and police. This disparity is a product of the overwhelming superiority in firepower that the British possessed and their readiness to use it. As for settler casualties, only 32 were killed in the course of the emergency, less than died in traffic accidents in Nairobi in the same period. What was successfully portrayed by the British government as a pogrom against the white settlers was in fact a pogrom against the Kikuyu.

How was it that British governments headed by such respectable figures as Winston Churchill, Anthony Eden and Harold Macmillan were able to preside over the Kenya scandal without British public opinion calling them to account. What happened in Kenya was far worse than anything revealed at Abu Ghraib or Guantanamo Bay but excited considerably less controversy. Certainly, racism was an important factor. The savagery of the repression in Kenya was possible because the victims were black and this undoubtedly constrained public concerns. Moreover, the government was very successful at portraying the Mau Mau as a reversion to a savage barbarism that had to be stamped out by whatever means were necessary. And, of course, the government consistently and systematically covered up and denied what was going on. The colonial secretary, Alan Lennox-Boyd, a fascist sympathiser in the 1930s, was to freely admit after his retirement that he had been actively engaged in "cover-up operations" for the security forces. He remarked on the shock of his successor, Iain Macleod, when he briefed him on what was really going on.[30] A number of Labour MPs—Fenner Brockway, Barbara Castle, John Stonehouse and others—did campaign to expose the atrocities that were being committed in Kenya. They received little help from the Labour front bench, which obviously hoped to become the government in the near future and consequently would have had to continue the cover-up itself.

Only with the Hola camp massacre of 3 March 1959 did the cover-up machinery finally break down. On this occasion detainees who were refusing to do forced labour were attacked by guards. Many of them were injured and 11 were beaten to death. What is interesting is that this was far from the first time that men were beaten to death in the camps. At Manyani camp in 1955 six men had been killed by the guards and their cause of death registered as typhoid. This was the normal way of proceeding. By 1959, with Iain Macleod as colonial secretary, the political situation had changed. He was looking to an agreement with the moderate African nationalists, something bitterly opposed by both the colonial administration and the white settlers. The exposure of the Hola camp atrocity would fatally compromise this opposition, so Macleod, instead of collaborating in the cover-up as Lennox-Boyd had done as a matter of routine, allowed what had really happened to become a cause of public scandal. This indicated a decisive shift in British government policy.

Independence

Even though the Mau Mau had been defeated by the British, the movement did win a posthumous victory over the white settlers. The settlers dreamed of a permanent white supremacist regime in Kenya that would be strong enough to sustain itself with or without the support of the British state. They looked to the example provided by Southern Rhodesia and South Africa. Mau Mau, however, had shown that the settlers did not have the strength to survive on their own. Without the British government coming to their assistance in the 1950s, Mau Mau would have won. Consequently, the white settler community found itself completely dependent on the British at a time when the British government was beginning to separate its interests from those of the settlers. The British recognised that Mau Mau had only been defeated because of its lack of modern weapons. It was also clear that the maintenance of settler rule would sooner rather than later provoke another rebellion. Next time the rebels would be armed by the Communist bloc. The white settler regime was clearly no longer viable. Moreover, as Colin Leys has shown, while the white settlers dominated Kenya politically, they did not dominate it economically. The settlers owned some 20 percent of the foreign assets in Kenya in 1958, the remainder being owned by British and foreign companies. While African rule would be fatal for the settlers, British and foreign business interests were confident that they could reach an accommodation with moderate nationalists.[31] Indeed, settler intransigence increasingly came to be seen as a threat to British strategic and economic interests in Kenya. The settlers found themselves cut adrift, in their terms "betrayed" by the British government as it set about reaching an agreement with the African moderates, including the soon to be rehabilitated Jomo Kenyatta. As late as 1959 Evelyn Baring was assuring the settlers that Kenya would never get full independence. On 12 December 1963 independence was granted and a Kenyatta government was installed in power.

Kenyatta had always been an opponent of Mau Mau, even during his captivity. There was never any acknowledgement on his part that it was only the bravery and sacrifice of the revolutionary movement that eventually brought him to power. Kenyatta promised reconciliation in the new Kenya, but it was a reconciliation between moderate nationalists, collaborators and those settlers prepared to accept the black population gaining the vote. The Mau Mau were excluded.

THE BLOOD NEVER DRIED

Indeed, in 1965 Kenyatta was to tell Baring that "if I had been in your shoes at the time I would have done exactly the same".[32] From being a prisoner of the British, by the end of 1964 Kenyatta had the Special Air Service (SAS) training his bodyguard. The security of his regime was regarded as being in the British national interest. Not until the late 1970s was "the baton", in this respect, taken up by the United States.[33]

The other rebellion : Southern Rhodesia

An interesting comparison can be made between the way the British state went to assist the white settler regime in Kenya against black rebellion and the way that it did not go to the assistance of the black population in Southern Rhodesia when the white settlers rebelled. In Southern Rhodesia the black population was effectively abandoned by Harold Wilson's Labour government and left to free itself from settler rule. As the historian Peter Clarke observed, "its handling of Rhodesia" showed that "it made little difference that a Labour government was now in office".[34]

What was to become Southern Rhodesia had been conquered in 1893 by Cecil Rhodes' British South African Company. This private enterprise exercise in imperial expansion was not unprecedented. For the government, it certainly proved convenient. As the Liberal chancellor of the exchequer, William Harcourt, remarked, Rhodes might be " a great jingo, but he is a cheap jingo".[35] The conquest of the Ndebele was accompanied with little British loss and much slaughter. At Shangani on 24 October 1893 a Ndebele attack was routed by machine gun and artillery fire and a few days later at Imbembesi another attack was beaten off. As Frederick Courtney Selous observed, the Ndebele "were in each case driven off with heavy loss by the fire of the Maxim guns". The conquest, he enthused, "will ever be remembered as one of the most brilliant episodes in the history of British colonisation in Southern Africa".[36] Rhodes, a thief and a murderer, who was really only a gangster who stole countries rather than knocked over banks, was made a privy councillor, and his lieutenant, Starr Jameson, became a Companion of the Bath.

Once the territory had been conquered, the black population were ruthlessly despoiled as white settlers began to move in. According to Frank Sykes, the British South Africa Company "proceeded to administer the land upon the basis of a white dominant race and a helot nation of conquered blacks". Black women, he makes clear, were regarded as part of the spoils.[37] When Rhodes and Jameson tried to seize the Transvaal in 1895, stripping Matabeleland of troops, the Ndebele seized the opportunity to revolt. Taken by surprise, some 140 settlers (127 men, ten women and three children) were killed. The British response was ferocious. According on one historian the settlers' deaths raised "a spirit of fury among the whites unparalleled since the Indian Mutiny". Rhodes ordered no quarter and insisted on personally counting the African dead. "Wipe them all out...everything black", urged one British officer.[38] Another officer, Robert Baden-Powell, the future founder of the Boy Scouts, acknowledged "the extraordinary bloodthirsty rage of our men". Indeed, he confessed that he "felt it myself later on". But he still insisted:

> Don't infer from these remarks that I am a regular nigger-hater for I am not. I have met lots of good friends among them... But however good they may be, they must, as a people, be ruled by a hand of iron in a velvet glove... In the present instance they have been rash enough to pull off the glove for themselves and were now beginning to find out what the hand was made of.[39]

The Ndebele and Shona revolts of 1896-1897, known as the first *Chimurenga*, were put down with considerable brutality and bloodshed. Settler rule was successfully imposed on the country.[40]

The British government's abandonment of the white settlers in Kenya provided their "kith and kin" in Southern Rhodesia with a good indication of their likely fate. Unlike Kenya, however, the Rhodesian settlers felt that they were numerous, wealthy and powerful enough to sustain themselves in power without British assistance. There were some 250,000 white settlers in Southern Rhodesia and, moreover, they were confident of support from neighbouring South Africa. Ian Smith's Rhodesian Front government decided to declare independence from Britain rather than make any of the concessions to the black majority that the British were pressing for. White supremacy was to be maintained at any cost and the aspirations of the black population were to be crushed with whatever amount of force was necessary.

UDI (Unilateral Declaration of Independence) was declared on 11 November 1965. The white settlers had rebelled and Wilson made it clear that under no circumstances would he even contemplate the use of force. There can be no doubt that if the whites in Rhodesia had been threatened by a black revolt, British troops would have been sent to help maintain "law and order" without any problem. A black population threatened by a white revolt was a different thing altogether.

The Wilson government was seriously constrained at the time. It was politically weak with a parliamentary majority of only four and was confronted by open sympathy for the Rhodesian settlers on the part of much of the British establishment. A good instance of this is provided by Wilson's attempt to secure details of Rhodesian sterling holdings in London from Lord Cromer (yet another member of the Baring family!), the governor of the Bank of England. Cromer refused to divulge this information to the elected government and Wilson was too politically weak to replace him. By the time legislation was passed compelling Cromer to release the information, the Rhodesians had, to his great satisfaction, run their balances " down to practically zero".[41] Even more remarkably, the Chiefs of Staff seem to have made it clear to the government that the armed forces could not be used against the settlers. When Wilson ruled out military intervention, according to one historian, he averted a "potential Curragh", a reference to the threat by army officers to resign rather than disarm Ulster in 1914.[42] There is no evidence, however, regardless of the army's attitude, that the Labour government would have been prepared to intervene militarily in Rhodesia. Instead of force, Wilson attempted to force Smith to negotiate by means of economic sanctions. These were to prove futile, with even British Petroleum, the state-owned oil company, overtly breaking sanctions with the secret connivance of both Labour and Conservative governments, the so-called "Oilgate" scandal.[43] In the end, the black majority in Rhodesia were left to overthrow settler rule themselves in a protracted guerrilla war, the second *Chimurenga*, that only finally came to an end in 1979.[44]

Malaya and the Far East

W INSTON CHURCHILL described the surrender of Singapore to the Japanese army on 15 February 1942 as "the worst disaster and largest capitulation in British history".[1] A supposedly impregnable fortress had surrendered to an attacking force that was inferior in numbers. This was more than a defeat: it was a humiliation. Churchill's doctor, Lord Moran, recorded the tremendous impact the surrender had on him:

> How came 100,000 men (half of them of our race) to hold up their hands to inferior numbers of Japanese? Though his mind had been gradually prepared for its fall, the surrender of the fortress stunned him. He felt it was a disgrace. It left a scar on his mind. One evening, months later, when he was sitting in his bathroom enveloped in a towel, he stopped drying himself and gloomily surveyed the floor: "I cannot get over Singapore," he said sadly.

For Churchill, the surrender was more than a "reverse": it was, he feared, "a portent" of the loss of the empire.[2] Certainly it dealt a shattering blow to the mystique of racial superiority with which the British had surrounded their rule in the Far East.

The Japanese military offensive of 1942 overran Malaya and Singapore, Burma, the Dutch East Indies (today's Indonesia), the American-controlled Philippines, and consolidated their grip on French Indo-China. The catastrophe was such that the European empires never really recovered. Indeed, the reoccupation of their colonies by the British, the French and the Dutch in 1945-46 was only accomplished on the back of American military might, which was absolutely decisive in the defeat of Japan. Britain had fared best of the European colonial powers, partly because the country had escaped occupation by the Nazis and still had powerful armed forces under its own control. It was also because, as we have seen with regard to India and Burma, the British were prepared to retreat and withdraw when confronted with the threat of large-scale rebellion. With the surrender of Japan on 2 September 1945, however, British forces under the command of Lord Mountbatten found themselves responsible for restoring colonial rule, not just in Britain's own colony of Malaya, but also in the southern half of French Indo-China and the Dutch East Indies. Let us look first at how Attlee's Labour government performed its two little known acts of colonial generosity towards the French and the Dutch.

The First Vietnam War

The Japanese surrender created a vacuum in Indo-China that the Communist-led Viet Minh resistance, led by Ho Chi Minh, with American encouragement, moved to fill. The United States was initially unsympathetic to the restoration of French rule, and the American OSS (the forerunner of the CIA) had encouraged the Viet Minh to establish a provisional revolutionary government as early as April 1945. With the Japanese collapse, Viet Minh forces took control of much of the north of the country, and on 2 September Ho Chi Minh proclaimed the Democratic Republic of Vietnam in Hanoi. He read out a Vietnamese Declaration of Independence, borrowing from the American Declaration of 1776, to over 100,000 people. OSS officers were photographed, alongside the Viet Minh military commander Vo Nguyen Giap, saluting the flag of the new republic. The American expectation was that the French would have to come to terms with what they hoped would be a Communist-dominated client government.[3]

Further south, however, the Viet Minh hold was much weaker, and on 6 September British troops, commanded by General Douglas Gracey, began arriving in Saigon, with every intention of restoring the French. From the very beginning Gracey refused to even acknowledge the existence of the Viet Minh, introducing what amounted to martial law, disarming the nationalists and arming released French prisoners of war. On 23 September, with his full support, the French seized power in Saigon, taking over its city hall and arresting large numbers of Vietnamese. As one senior French officer told Mountbatten, "Your General Gracey has saved French Indochina".[4]

The Viet Minh responded to the French takeover by calling a general strike, and fighting broke out. According to George Rosie, in his standard account of the British intervention:

> The days immediately after the coup saw much sporadic fighting in which the British-Indian troops fought off desperate nationalist attacks all over the city. In the early stages the Vietnamese casualties were fairly heavy. In one clash with 80 Indian Infantry Brigade on 26 September in the south of the city, 60 Vietnamese were killed. Mortars, 25 pounders and heavy machine-guns were freely used by the British in the street fighting, and non-combatant Vietnamese must certainly have suffered in the process.[5]

The British found themselves under considerable pressure and Gracey was forced to open negotiations with the Viet Minh on 2 October. This was just a ploy while reinforcements were poured in, bringing his strength to over 22,000 men. On 9 October, he gave the Viet Minh an ultimatum: surrender the city or face destruction.

The Viet Minh launched an attack against British positions throughout the city, but were beaten back. On 12 October they attempted to seize the key airfield at Tan Son Nhut. They reached "the doors of the radio station and were within 300 yards of the control tower when they were stopped; the fight for the airfield turned into a grim struggle as its loss would have cut Saigon off from the rest of the world".[6] The Viet Minh attacks were driven off by the reinforced British. After this failure the Viet Minh resorted to guerrilla tactics and the "bitter street battles…gave way to the brutal business of ambushes, small-scale guerrilla attacks, terrorism and repressive counter-measures, all carried out in the midst of a sullen and resentful population. No matter how many nationalists the British killed or captured, more appeared the next day".[7]

Edmund Taylor, as OSS officer, arrived in Saigon towards the end of October to find "a war of extermination marked by appalling atrocities on both sides" under way. He described how:

In retaliation for the murderous Annamese [the majority ethnic group in Vietnam] guerrilla tactics, the British had deliberately burned down great sections of the native quarter in Saigon. This further inflamed the anti-British sentiments of the Annamese whose fanatical if clumsy attacks became such a menace to the inadequate British occupation forces that for a long time they had to cease disarming the Japanese and to use their late enemies as auxiliaries in fighting their newer ones.

According to Taylor, the atmosphere in Saigon "was that of a town newly occupied by Franco's forces in the Spanish Civil War".[8]

By the end of December 1945 the British began their withdrawal, handing Saigon and the South over to the French. Most had left by March 1946 with only some specialist soldiers remaining behind. The last British troops to die in Vietnam were six soldiers killed in an ambush in June 1946. They had fought a short but bloody campaign, the tenor of which is captured by the operation instructions issued to officers: "Always use the maximum force available to ensure wiping out any hostiles we may meet. If one uses too much no harm is done".[9] The disproportion between casualties suffered and inflicted shows that this advice was taken literally. By the middle of January 1946 the British had suffered 40 men killed while they claimed to have killed some 600 Viet Minh. The actual numbers were considerably higher. This British success was to prepare the way for both the French and the American Vietnam Wars.

A forgotten intervention: Indonesia 1945-46
In the Dutch East Indies nationalists, led by Sukarno, had proclaimed the Republic of Indonesia as early as 17 August 1945. With the Japanese collapse, the nationalists proceeded to take control of much of the main island of Java. A republican government was established, supported by a large, if poorly armed and trained, militia. It was determined to resist any attempt to re-establish Dutch rule. When the first British troops began to arrive, conflict was inevitable.

The British intention was to occupy the coastal cities of Jakarta, Semarang and Surabaya, and the hill towns behind them—Bandung, Ambarawa, Magelang and Malang. The nationalist forces would be disarmed and dispersed and the Dutch would be put back in control. To this end, Jakarta was occupied and Dutch prisoners of war were armed. Within days sporadic clashes had broken out as the Dutch "turned on the insurgent Indonesians like savages, ruthlessly machine-gunning the Kampongs, or native compounds, and inviting atrocity for atrocity by all their acts".[10] To one British officer it seemed as if "the Dutch wanted to provoke war and thereby force us to fight on their behalf".[11] The first British fatalities occurred on 11 October when two British officers were killed. The British response provoked heavy fighting that was ended only with the arrival of reinforcements and the rearming of the Japanese. Jakarta was successfully brought under control, although sniping and sporadic attacks continued.

Elsewhere the British placed even more reliance on the Japanese. In Bandung the Japanese arrested nationalist leaders and disarmed nationalist forces before handing the city over to the British. In Semarang, however, they met with fierce resistance. Only after six days of heavy fighting and the use of both tanks and artillery was the city taken, with some 2,000 Indonesians killed. When the British arrived on 20 October, they found a silent, deserted and devastated city. The British were full of praise for the Japanese troops' "incredible gallantry" and their commander, Major Kido, was actually recommended for the Distinguished Service Order (DSO). This was a step too far, as the Labour government was coming under attack in parliament for using Japanese troops. Both Attlee and Bevin defended their use, although they lied about the extent of the practice.[12] Then on 25 October British troops began disembarking in Surabaya.

In Surabaya the British were confronted by a large well-armed nationalist militia that possessed tanks, artillery and anti-aircraft guns seized from the Japanese. The British commander, Brigadier Mallaby, assured the nationalists that he had no intention of disarming them or restoring the Dutch. This agreement was promptly repudiated by Mallaby's superiors, who had no idea of the situation he faced. On 28 October Mallaby's 4,000 troops came under attack from over 20,000 Indonesians with a hostile population solidly behind them. A number of British positions were overrun with heavy losses and Sukarno was flown into the city to negotiate a ceasefire. This broke down almost immediately. British troops were besieged in a bank in Internatio Square and Mallaby himself went to investigate. As he arrived, the troops opened fire and in the confusion Mallaby was killed, almost certainly shot by an Indonesian youth.[13] The ceasefire was successfully reinstated, but only after the British agreed to withdraw their forces back into the port area of the city. After a week of fighting, Mallaby's brigade had lost over 200 men killed, including its commander.

The British proceeded to pour reinforcements into Surabaya. On 9 November, General E C Mansergh demanded the immediate surrender of the city and at 6am the next morning ordered an all-out attack. Against ferocious opposition, British and Indian troops fought their way into the city. They were assisted by a tremendous artillery and naval bombardment that devastated large areas and killed many civilians. Two cruisers and three destroyers shelled the city. Mosquito and Thunderbolt warplanes bombed and strafed targets. One RAF history enthusiastically describes an air raid on a nationalist strongpoint on the first day of the attack: 18 1,500 lb bombs were dropped and only eight missed the target![14] This was a densely populated city. The Indonesians defended themselves as best they could against the onslaught. According to David Wehl, fighting was particularly severe in the centre of the city where "streets had to be occupied one by one, doorway by doorway. Bodies of men, horses, cats and dogs, lay in the gutter, broken glass, furniture, tangled telephone lines, cluttered the roads, and the noise of battle echoed among the empty office buildings".[15]

After three days of continuous bombardment and intense street fighting, most of the city was in British hands. For another three weeks, however, the Indonesians fought on before finally admitting defeat and withdrawing their forces from the city. Even after this, sporadic fighting continued. When the 2nd Battalion of the Buffs arrived in the city early in January 1946, they found it "encircled by a large force of uniformed and reasonably well-organised and well-equipped Indonesians". Surabaya was to all intents and purposes "invested", effectively under siege, and clashes with the Indonesians were a daily occurrence.[16] The battle for Surabaya had cost the nationalists at least 10,000 casualties and the British in the region of 600. So stubborn had been Indonesian resistance that the British refused to believe they had organised it themselves and saw instead the hand of renegade Japanese and even of German advisers.[17] Unknown in Britain, the battle became for the Indonesians "a symbol and rallying-cry for revolution".[18] It unleashed a nationalist uprising that spread throughout Java and threatened to engulf the British. The battle of Surabaya is still celebrated in Indonesia every year on "Heroes Day".

After heavy fighting, British forces were driven out of Magelang on

21 November and, the following month, out of Ambarawa, effectively abandoning central Java to the nationalists. Meanwhile serious fighting had broken out in Bandung where the British forcibly evicted some 100,000 people from the northern half of the city. When, on 24 March 1946, the British demanded the evacuation of the rest of the city, the nationalists withdrew, setting fire to whole districts as they went. According to John Smail, "Bandung [was] a sea of flames...and the picture is fixed in the memories of those who were in the city on 24 March ".[19] Between a third and half of the city was razed rather than surrender it to the British. The fighting spread to the island of Sumatra where there were serious clashes in Medan early in December. Although the conflict never reached the same level of intensity as in Java, the British still lost 55 soldiers killed and 243 wounded. One particular incident deserves notice, however. On 13 December, Japanese troops sacked the Sumatran town of Tebing Tinggi and massacred over 2,000 people. This was while it was under British command.[20] The scale and intensity of the fighting brought home most forcibly to the British that restoring Dutch rule was not practicable. At the end of December 1945 Mountbatten informed the Chiefs of Staff in London that to achieve a military solution in Indonesia would require another three divisions in a "full-scale war", which would be followed by a guerrilla war "situation analogous to Ireland after the last war, but on a much larger scale".[21] Instead the British held on to their coastal bridgeheads, but abandoned the rest of the country to the nationalists. As late as September 1946 there were still 45,000 British troops in the country, but withdrawal was already under way as the Dutch built up their forces. The last British troops were evacuated by the end of November 1946. By and large, the Dutch forces were armed and equipped by the British, by a Labour government, without whose assistance their offensives of the summer of 1947 and the winter of 1948-49 would not have been possible.

Britain's Indonesian intervention had proven extremely costly. Over a 14-month period some 620 British and Indian troops had been killed and 1,447 wounded. Another 327 were missing, most of them dead, but some Indian troops had defected to the nationalists. The 23rd Indian Division suffered heavier casualties in these months than in four years fighting the Japanese in Burma. Over 1,000 Japanese troops were also killed, fighting alongside the British, more than had been killed capturing Indonesia from the Dutch in the first place.

Indonesian casualties have been estimated at some 20,000 killed.[22] One would, naively perhaps, have expected this episode to have left the Attlee government's reputation in imperial affairs in tatters, but far from it. The whole episode is simply written out of the historical record. The battle of Surabaya, so important in Indonesia, is almost completely unknown in Britain.[23]

Reoccupying Malaya

In Malaya the British had cooperated with the Malayan Communist Party (MCP) and with the Communist-led resistance movement during the Japanese occupation. By the time the Japanese surrendered, the Malayan People's Anti-Japanese Army had some 4,000 armed members, but a considerably larger support network, the Malayan People's Anti-Japanese Union.[24] Rather than oppose the return of the British, the Malayan Communists, unlike the Vietnamese Communists and the Indonesian nationalists, decided to cooperate with the colonial power in the hope of securing a legitimate place in the post-war order. The election of a Labour government in London undoubtedly created serious illusions with regard to future developments in the colonies. Instead of fighting the British, a Communist guerrilla unit actually took part in the victory parade in London, and Chin Peng, soon to be the most wanted man in Malaya, was actually awarded the Order of the British Empire (OBE). The Communists proceeded to disband their guerrilla army and instead concentrated their efforts on building up a strong, militant trade union movement and on establishing a left wing nationalist movement, uniting Chinese, Malays, and Indians.

In retrospect, the decision to cooperate with the British seems a serious mistake. The Communists could certainly have launched an insurrection in 1945 and the British would have found themselves seriously over-stretched in trying to deal with it. The fighting in Indo-China and Indonesia was a great drain on resources. A number of factors militated against it, however. First, Communist support was largely confined to the Chinese minority of the population (about 38 percent), and, indeed, there were serious clashes between the Malayan People's Anti-Japanese Army and Malays in 1945-46. Second, the British would certainly have made use of Japanese troops to bolster their position. And third, although unknown at the time, the general secretary of the MCP, Lai Tek, was a police agent who had worked for both the British and the Japanese. He argued most forcefully for a peaceful road. Nevertheless, the prospects for success in 1945 were considerably greater than they were to be in 1948 when the guerrilla insurgency was actually launched.

Communist efforts at building a militant trade union movement were particularly successful. The appalling economic and social situation after the war saw thousands of workers turn to the MCP. These efforts were met with determined hostility by the British authorities. Despite this, the Communists established the Pan-Malayan Federation of Trade Unions (PMFTU), a considerable achievement. Alongside its trade union work, the MCP set about constructing a progressive alliance of Malay, Chinese and Indian organisations committed to democracy, social reform and independence. The British responded in July 1946 by putting forward proposals for a federation of Malaya that safeguarded the position of the Malay sultans, most of whom had collaborated with the Japanese, and severely restricted the citizenship rights of non-Malays. The MCP was instrumental in establishing a broad-based opposition to this, organising protest meetings and demonstrations, culminating in a one-day general strike on 20 October 1947. The British ignored these protests and on 1 February 1948 inaugurated the Federation of Malaya. The road to peaceful change, as far as the MCP and its supporters were concerned, had been closed and the Labour government had decided on a return to pre-war colonialism.[25]

The federation scheme seriously weakened the position of those in the MCP advocating the peaceful road. This was compounded in March 1947, when Lai Tek disappeared with the party's funds, just before his exposure as a police agent. He was replaced as general secretary by Chin Peng.[26] The new leadership found itself confronted by a British offensive against the trade union movement. With the full support of the authorities, the employers launched a concerted attack on trade union organisation, cutting wages, victimising activists and carrying out mass sackings and evictions. Police and troops were deployed as strikebreakers, beating and on occasion opening fire on striking workers. The employers, according to one account, "demanded 'death, banishment and particularly flogging'".[27] By the beginning of 1948 the employers "had recovered to a considerable extent the position they had lost in the immediate post-war years".[28]

With the road of constitutional advance closed and with the trade

THE BLOOD NEVER DRIED

unions under attack, the MCP leadership took the decision to prepare for armed struggle. No actual timetable was laid down but steps were put under way to reactivate elements of the MPAJA and establish jungle camps and an underground network. Events outstripped the MCP's preparations, however. Some of its activists responded to the increasingly violent attempt to batter the trade unions into submission with terrorist attacks, shooting strikebreakers, and estate and mine managers. On 12 June 1948 the British banned the PMFTU and then, on 19 June, declared a state of emergency. The MCP was taken completely by surprise.

One important question that has to be considered is why it was that the Labour government set out to smash the left in Malaya. It is clear that there was no place for any kind of left in Malaya, Communist or otherwise, according to the government's thinking. The simple reason for this was that the Labour government was determined to increase its exploitation of Malaya, and the left and the trade unions were an obstacle to this. Malaya was too important for any alternative to be seriously contemplated. In 1947, for example, Malayan rubber was the British Empire's biggest dollar earner, bringing in $200 million, compared with the $180 million earned by British manufacturing industry. By 1950 Malayan tin and rubber were earning $350 million out of the sterling area's total dollar earnings of $2,385 million. It was under Attlee's government that British colonies were to be most ruthlessly and successfully exploited. Between 1946 and 1951 the colonial sterling balances held in London increased from £760 million to £920 million, a massive transfer of funds that gives the lie to the pious rhetoric of the time regarding colonial development.[29] While the Labour government might well have withdrawn from India and Burma, in the words of one historian, this was "only to reveal an expanded appetite for African and South East Asian exploitation".[30]

The emergency

The British launched a wave of repression against the left. By the end of August 1948 well over 4,000 men and women had been detained, a substantial proportion of them Malays. The British were absolutely determined to eradicate the Malay left, while all the time warning of the danger of a Chinese takeover, deliberately exacerbating and exploiting ethnic divisions. The blows also fell particularly heavily on the trade unions, with hundreds of militants arrested. In May 1949 the general secretary of the banned PMFTU, S A Ganapathy, was hanged for possessing a revolver. There was some concern in Malaya as to whether a Labour government would allow the execution of a trade union leader, especially in the light of a pleas for clemency from the Indian prime minister, Nehru, but as one British official observed, "there was no comeback from Attlee".[31] Union membership plummeted from 154,000 in April to 75,000 in September.

As we have seen, the MCP was taken by surprise by the declaration of the emergency. Although it was in the process of embarking on a strategy of guerrilla warfare, preparations were still at an early stage. The MCP faced the problem of organising its forces for revolutionary war with the full weight of the colonial state bearing down on it. Not until 26 June was it able to stage the first guerrilla attacks in response to the wave of repression. For their part, the British expected to be able to crush the MCP in a matter of months. Instead the Communists managed to find sanctuary in the jungle where they set about organising their guerrilla forces, the Malayan National Liberation Army (MNLA), and re-establishing their underground support network, the Min Yuen. The MNLA rallied some 5,000 men and women, most of them unaccustomed to the jungle, poorly trained and armed with only light weapons. This force was too weak to establish liberated zones as was originally planned, but it did begin a campaign of assassinations, ambushes and attacks. By the end of 1948 the MNLA had killed 149 troops and police, and wounded another 211. They had also killed over 300 civilians, mostly Chinese collaborators. Their own losses were 374 killed and another 319 surrendered or captured. By the end of 1949 incidents were averaging 400 a month and the insurgency was beginning to have an impact.

With the declaration of the emergency, the government imposed a police regime on Malaya. Between 1948 and 1957, when Malaya became independent, nearly 34,000 people were interned without trial. Thousands more Chinese suspected of rebel sympathies were deported from the colony (over 10,000 in 1949). And the government introduced a battery of legal measures, including the death penalty for a wide range of offences, including possession of firearms. In the course of the emergency 226 Communists were hanged, a figure only exceeded in the post-1945 period by the judicial slaughter carried out in Kenya.[32] All of this was introduced "with the full consent of the Labour government".[33]

THE BLOOD NEVER DRIED

By the end of 1949, however, the MNLA had managed to seize the initiative. The guerrillas carried out hit and run attacks, striking and disappearing into the jungle. The British responded with large-scale cordons and search operations, combing the jungle with hundreds of troops and police, hunting an elusive enemy that had already slipped away. Unable to find the guerrillas, the British became increasingly brutal towards the Chinese civilian population. Suspects were routinely beaten and on occasions killed (the worst known incident was the massacre of 24 Chinese civilians at Batang Kali in December 1949), and their homes, sometimes whole villages, were destroyed.[34] Far from intimidating the Chinese population, their methods only increased support for the MNLA. British methods attracted little criticism back home. When on 28 April 1952, the British Communist Party's *Daily Worker* carried the photograph of a smiling Royal Marine holding up the severed head of a dead guerrilla, the government expected an outcry. No other British newspaper made use of the photograph or took up the story.[35]

What broke the cycle of repression and resistance was the strategy developed by the new director of operations, General Harold Briggs, when he took over the conduct of the war in April 1950. The so-called "Briggs Plan" conceptualised the war against the Communists as a "competition in government", a competition for control of the population. Instead of trying to hunt down the guerrillas, the British determined to establish effective control over the Chinese rural population, the squatters, miners and plantation workers, in order to isolate them.[36] To this end, in June 1950 a massive resettlement programme was launched. It was carried out with considerable determination and ruthlessness. By the beginning of 1952 over 400,000 Chinese had been resettled in "new villages", surrounded by barbed wire, heavily policed and effectively deprived of all civil rights. Parallel with this, mine workers and plantation workers were compulsorily regrouped in defended compounds, once again behind barbed wire.

Resettlement and regroupment broke the back of the Communist insurgency. By successfully isolating the guerrillas from the Chinese rural population, these measures made their defeat inevitable. This did not seem the case at the time, however. In 1950 the MNLA killed 393 soldiers and police and in 1951 the figure was 504. They achieved their most spectacular success on 6 October 1951 when the high commissioner, Henry Gurney, was killed in an ambush. The situation seemed desperate, but the tide had already turned. When General Gerald Templer took over as high commissioner and director of operations in February 1952, he inherited a situation where the initiative had already passed into the hands of the British. With the guerrillas increasingly on the defensive, Templer was to develop the tactics and methods for hunting them down.[37] Templer admitted to the use of "killer squads", though as he told the colonial secretary, Oliver Lyttelton, "I won't call them that, with a view to the questions you might have to answer".[38] Later, as the MNLA retreated deeper into the jungle, the British sprayed suspected guerrilla gardens from the air with trichlorophenoxyacetic acid (24ST), preparing the way "for future American involvement in herbicidal warfare in South East Asia".[39]

As early as September 1952 Templer was cautiously informing London that, "in a small way, we have to some extent got the initiative at last...the situation is improving a bit".[40] The following year was to be the "breakthrough year" with the MNLA forced on the defensive, engaged in a struggle to survive rather than contending for victory. This military success was underpinned by movement towards political independence. The British sponsored the development of the Alliance Party, bringing together a moderate Malay and Chinese leadership committed to private enterprise and Western interests. In the first federal elections in July 1955 the Alliance won over 80 percent of the vote and secured 51 out of 52 seats. The Alliance leader, Tunku Abdul Rahman, began pressuring the British for an early declaration of independence. When independence was finally granted on 31 August 1957, Malaya remained firmly within the British sphere of influence and the campaign against the weakening Communists continued.

The extent to which the MNLA had been forced on the defensive is shown by the fact that in 1956 and 1957 they only killed 58 police and soldiers while having nearly 600 of their own number killed and another 300-odd surrendered. The following year the guerrillas killed ten police and soldiers but had over 150 killed themselves, but, more important, over 500 surrendered. The MNLA had ceased to be an effective fighting force and the MCP took the decision to "fold up the banner and silence the drums".[41] The emergency finally ended on 31 July 1960.

This British victory has subsequently been celebrated as proof that the British, unlike the French or the Americans, had discovered the

THE BLOOD NEVER DRIED

way to defeat Communist insurgency. Indeed, it was offered up as an experience that the United States could learn from, with Robert Thompson leading a British advisory mission to South Vietnam from 1961 to 1965 and hundreds of South Vietnamese police and soldiers being trained at the Jungle Warfare School in Malaya.[42] In fact, a good case can be made that there were few strategic lessons to be learned because the reasons for British success were so specific. The MCP failed to win any real support among the Malay population that was successfully enlisted on the British side. The British were able to bring overwhelming force to bear against the MNLA, force that was applied with increasing sophistication. And the MCP received no aid from outside Malaya. There was no Ho Chi Minh trail bringing the modern weapons and trained reinforcements. In retrospect, the MNLA was doomed to defeat. What was remarkable was the protracted nature of the resistance they put up against overwhelming odds in the most difficult circumstances.[43]

Confrontation

The British hoped to build up their new client regime in Malaya as a counterweight to Sukarno's neutralist Indonesia. Sukarno not only refused to subordinate Indonesia to the United States in the Cold War, but also took a strong anti-imperialist stance in international affairs and tolerated, indeed collaborated with, a mass Communist Party that the Americans and the British wanted suppressed. He was inevitably the victim of systematic denigration and ridicule in the British media, much of it government inspired. The British proposed the establishment of a Federation of Malaysia, bringing together Malaya, Singapore, Britain's two colonies on the island of Borneo, Sarawak and North Borneo, and the British protectorate on the island, the Sultanate of Brunei. As David Easter makes clear in his account of these events, "Malaysia was largely conceived in response to Britain's defence needs" and was seen as a way for Britain to "maintain herself as a global power".[44] As far as the Indonesians were concerned this was a very real threat to their national interests. Their expectation was that the Borneo colonies would revert to Indonesia and, moreover, they had good reason for regarding both Britain and the United States as enemies. Both governments gave covert support to separatist movements in Indonesia, and in 1958 the CIA had given considerable assistance, including air support, to separatist rebels on the islands of

Sumatra and Kalimantan. The British had cooperated in this attempt to break up the country and overthrow Sukarno.[45] Although the rebellion had been crushed, the Indonesians saw the establishment of Malaysia as compounding the threat with separatist movements being encouraged to break away and join the federation. This was very much the policy of the Malaysian government that looked forward to the break-up of Indonesia and the acquisition of Sumatra.

Sukarno launched what was known as "the Confrontation" with Malaysia in April 1963, initiating a conflict that was to continue until August 1966 when the Indonesians finally admitted defeat. This small-scale frontier war, fought largely in Borneo, cost the British some 80 soldiers killed, while Indonesian fatalities were officially put at 590, but were almost certainly substantially higher. It was according to Denis Healey, the Labour minister of defence, "one of the most efficient uses of military force in the history of the world".[46] Inevitably, the British contrasted their success with American failure in Vietnam. In reality, however, the Confrontation was only a "small war", a war of border skirmishes, although it did, on occasion, threaten to become something more serious. Even so, it still put a serious strain on British resources. At the height of the conflict Britain had 59,000 military personnel stationed in Malaysia. The naval presence was built up to some 80 vessels, including submarines and aircraft carriers, and for a time V-bombers visited Singapore, "an event which raised the prospect of the ultimate deterrent against any Indonesian escalation of the conflict".[47]

While British military prowess in Borneo, particularly the role of the SAS, has been widely celebrated in recent years, much less attention has been given to the covert war that Britain waged, once again providing support for separatist elements.[48] This covert activity was to be transformed into support for the military takeover in Indonesia that took place in October 1965. While Sukarno was left in place as a figurehead president, the army under General Suharto effectively took power and launched a general massacre of the left. Even while the Confrontation was still under way, the British collaborated with the generals in a massacre that cost the lives of over 500,000 men, women and children, many of them slaughtered with the utmost brutality. As the British ambassador in Jakarta, Andrew Gilchrist, told Michael Stewart, the Labour government foreign secretary, "I have never concealed from you my belief that a little shooting in

THE BLOOD NEVER DRIED

Indonesia would be an essential preliminary to effective change".[49] The British, cooperating once again with the United States, played their part in inciting and encouraging the killing. To be blunt, Harold Wilson's Labour government was complicit in what has been described as "one of the worst mass killings of the 20th century". The destruction of Indonesian Communism was one of the great Western triumphs of the Cold War, and in London policymakers enthusiastically "celebrated the destruction of the PKI [Indonesian Communist Party]".[50] For some reason neither Harold Wilson nor Denis Healey celebrate this triumph in their memoirs.

With the army installed in power, Indonesia moved into the American sphere of influence with Suharto becoming the West's favourite dictator. The Confrontation was speedily ended and cordial relations were established between London and Jakarta—so cordial, in fact, that when the New Labour government published its annual report on human rights in 1998, it featured a photo of foreign secretary Robin Cook shaking hands with the mass murderer Suharto.[51]

Britain and the American Empire

O N 15 December 1950 South Korean police carried out a public mass execution of Communist suspects, men, women, *and* children, in the area of Seoul under British occupation. The massacre, one of many, outraged the British troops who witnessed it. One journalist quoted a soldier to the effect that "it was just mass murder". Another soldier wrote to the Labour foreign secretary Ernest Bevin personally, "wondering which side was right in Korea". So strong was the troops' response to the killings that the British commander banned any further public executions and authorised the use of force to prevent them.[1] The episode caused serious concern in London where it was seen as contributing to the Korean War's growing unpopularity. The government, however, as one historian has pointed out, "was less concerned with the killings than with the publicity that surrounded them". The mass executions could continue, but only "behind prison walls". The government "was satisfied with a cosmetic measure" which hopefully would "contain public disillusion" with both the war and "the Atlantic alliance".[2] This was not the only bad news from Korea. A story by the journalist James Cameron, detailing the murderous brutality of the South Korean police, was suppressed by Edward Hulton, the proprietor of the *Picture Post*. The magazine's editor, Tom Hopkinson, was sacked for objecting. Cameron's story was subsequently carried by the *Daily Worker*. The government responded by publicly toying "with the idea of prosecuting the *Daily*

Worker and introducing a draconian press law prohibiting journalism which brought 'aid and comfort to the enemy'." Intimidation was the real objective, however. Another story by the journalist René Cutforth, this time for the BBC, described the American use of napalm in Korea. It too was suppressed.[3] Nothing could be allowed to interfere with the American alliance.

There are obvious parallels between the despatch of British troops to Korea in 1950 and the despatch of British troops to Iraq in 2003. While Tony Blair's New Labour government might well have abandoned any vestiges of social democracy and embraced neo-liberalism domestically, in foreign and defence policy there is a remarkable degree of continuity with Attlee's government of 1945-51. Attlee was every bit as determined as Blair to prioritise the American alliance, even to the extent of participation in a brutal war, a war far more murderous than that waged against Iraq. The only British "national interest" at stake in Korea in 1950 was the need to safeguard the American alliance. The lives of over a thousand British soldiers were sacrificed to this end. What this chapter will explore is this element of continuity in British foreign policy since the end of the Second World War, the pressures it has come under, and the very different contexts in which it has been sustained. Whereas in 1950 Attlee and Bevin saw the alliance as one between two imperial powers, by 2003 Tony Blair and Gordon Brown saw Britain as a junior partner in what was very much an American Empire.

Labour and the American alliance

The Labour government elected into office in July 1945 was determined that Britain should maintain its position as a great imperialist power, one of the three superpowers, along with the United States and the Soviet Union, that had emerged from the wreckage of the Second World War. That conflict had left Britain exhausted, virtually bankrupt, militarily overextended (there were British troops in over 40 countries in 1945), and dependent on the United States. In these circumstances, sustaining the British Empire required a revolution in strategy and a historic reshaping of the British warfare state.[4]

Let us consider the Labour government's revolution in strategy first. In the post-war years the United States remained a rival of the British Empire, hoping to hasten its liquidation, so that the newly liberated colonies could be incorporated into America's own informal global empire. This conflict was particularly evident, as we have already seen, in the Middle East. Despite this, the Labour government was absolutely committed to continuing Churchill's wartime alliance with the United States into peacetime. As partners in Churchill's coalition government during the war, Labour had, of course, been a party to that alliance. Now, they considered its continuation essential, both to meet the much more dangerous threat posed by the Soviet Union and to help withstand nationalist agitation and unrest in the colonies. It was hoped that once the Americans had recognised the scale of the Soviet menace, they would help sustain the British Empire. As far as the Attlee government was concerned, this post-war alliance was between two superpowers, albeit of unequal strength. Indeed, it was determined to make every effort to restore British power in the post-war period. As events were to show, however, the British need for the Americans was to prove far greater than the Americans' need for them.

This unequal alliance was to involve the Labour government in historically unprecedented developments that were to decisively shape the post-war era. These developments have been successfully naturalised, so much so that they are completely taken for granted today. It is time to revisit them. Labour's part in the creation of the modern welfare state, most notably the National Health Service, is well known. More important for the British ruling class, however, was the contemporaneous creation of what can be usefully described as Britain's modern warfare state. It was Attlee's government that took the decision in January 1947 to develop the British atomic bomb. This decision was taken in secret, without parliament, let alone the British people, being consulted. Interestingly, possession of the atomic bomb was not aimed at the Soviet Union, but was rather considered vital if Britain was to maintain some sort of equality with and independence from the United States. As Ernest Bevin put it:

> I don't want any other foreign secretary of this country to be talked at by a Secretary of State in the United States as I have just had in my discussions with Mr Byrnes. We have got to this thing over here whatever it costs…we've got to have the bloody Union Jack flying on top of it.

Attlee later made much the same point: "If we had decided not to have it, we would have put ourselves entirely in the hands of the

THE BLOOD NEVER DRIED

Americans. That would have been a risk a British government should not take".[5] Later that same year the government took the unprecedented decision to continue conscription into peacetime. Initially, conscripts would only serve for one year, but in 1950 this was increased to two.[6]

Even more dramatic was the decision in July-August 1949 to allow the Americans to establish bases for B-29 bombers in Britain. This initiated the permanent establishment of foreign, that is American, military bases on British soil. As Bevin acknowledged, "Permanent peacetime bases involved quite new principles." Indeed, it was without any historical precedent and yet it was accomplished without any serious public debate and is completely taken for granted today, supported unquestioningly by New Labour, the Conservative Party and the Liberals. Britain, as chancellor of the exchequer Stafford Cripps observed in October 1947, "must be regarded as the main base for the deployment of American power".[7] By 1950 the Americans were basing bombers carrying nuclear weapons in Britain. And in April 1949 Bevin was instrumental in establishing the North Atlantic Treaty Organisation (NATO). This involved the permanent stationing of British forces on the Continent, another unprecedented development. NATO was to become one of the most important international organisations through which the United States controlled its allies and exercised its power.

A "blood price" had to be paid for the American alliance. It came due when the simmering conflict in Korea finally flared up into a full-scale war when the Communist North invaded the South in June 1950. Initially, the British Chiefs of Staff were opposed to sending troops to Korea. It was a sideshow in the great confrontation with the Soviet Union as far as they were concerned and British forces were already overstretched. Moreover, there were serious fears that involvement in the war would damage relations with Communist China. The Labour government did not share the ferocity of American enmity towards China and, indeed, in the face of considerable US opposition, had recognised Mao Zedong's regime in January 1950. Hong Kong was too important, and too vulnerable, to risk Chinese hostility. Nevertheless, once the United States, under the banner of the United Nations, had committed itself to rolling back the North Koreans, Attlee concluded that Britain had no alternative but to despatch troops and ships. The British ambassador in Washington, Oliver Franks, made it clear that "refusal to provide troops would harm Anglo-American relations". The cabinet decided that "British land forces should be sent in order to consolidate Anglo-American friendship and to placate American public opinion".[8] British troops were to fight and die in an American war. First naval forces and then troops were dispatched. Eventually a Commonwealth Division was formed, made up of British, Canadian, Australian and New Zealand troops.

The North Koreans were quickly routed, and the American forces under General Douglas MacArthur, crossed the 38th Parallel and invaded the North, with the full support of the Labour government. They intended unifying the country under their client, Syngman Rhee. Once again the Chiefs of Staff initially opposed this, forcefully warning of the dangers of Chinese intervention. They subsequently dropped their opposition, one suspects, under pressure from Bevin. The North Korean capital, Pyongyang, fell to the Americans on 20 October 1950. A week later the Chinese launched their first offensive. By the end of November the Americans and their allies were in headlong retreat.

The Chinese intervention and the likely American response caused panic in London where the government was terrified that the war was about to escalate out of control. These fears intensified when on 30 November, at a press conference, President Truman stated that the use of nuclear weapons in Korea was under "active consideration".[9] Certainly this was what General MacArthur and his supporters were advocating, together with the bombing of Manchuria and action against the Chinese mainland. Truman's remarks provoked what one journalist described at the time as "a rebellion of free Europe against the kind of leadership America was giving the West on the Korean issue".[10] On 4 December, Attlee flew to Washington to put the concerns of America"s European allies to the president. They feared that any nuclear escalation would precipitate a third world war with the Soviet Union. Now that the Russians had their own nuclear weapons, Europe and especially Britain (where US air bases were an obvious target), faced certain devastation.[11] The Korean conflict had to be contained. In the event, it is unlikely that Attlee's representations had any decisive effect. American preponderance in Korea was so overwhelming that they would take the decision whether or not to escalate. The British were certainly not conceded any veto over the use of nuclear weapons, only the right to be kept in the loop by the Americans. If the

THE BLOOD NEVER DRIED

decision were taken, they would be the first to know. The stabilisation of the battlefront in 1951 eventually removed the danger.

Attlee confronted yet another crisis in January 1951 when the United States tabled a motion at the UN, condemning Chinese intervention in Korea. This provoked a cabinet rebellion on the 25th when the remarkable decision was taken to vote against. The revolt was short-lived. The decision was reversed the next day after the chancellor of the exchequer, Hugh Gaitskell, a fervent pro-American, threatened to resign. The reversal was the work of what one junior minister, Kenneth Younger, described sarcastically as the "don't be rude to the Americans school". He complained that "'America right or wrong' is a very powerful sentiment in the cabinet". The left proved to be so many paper tigers with even Aneurin Bevan conceding that "if the clash came, we could do nothing but support the Americans".[12] Britain voted for the resolution even though there was general agreement in the government that it was counter-productive, if not dangerous.

British participation in the Korean War made the Labour government and its Conservative successor party to a terrible conflict that left Korea effectively laid waste. While often described as a "limited war", it was in fact waged with little restraint as far as the Korean people were concerned. Even General MacArthur, certainly no sentimentalist, confessed, "I have never seen such devastation." According to one of his air force commanders, US bombing left "nothing standing worthy of the name".[13] Whole cities and small hamlets were bombed out of existence in one of the worst crimes of the post-1945 era. According to one military historian, the war cost the lives of between 500,000 and 1 million South Korean civilians and of 1.5 million North Korean soldiers and civilians.[14] British governments stood shoulder to shoulder with their American ally throughout the slaughter, desperately trying to cover up what was going on.[15]

The Labour government's overriding determination to maintain the American alliance, no matter what the cost, was to eventually bring it down. Under American pressure, in 1950, the government introduced a massive rearmament programme. Labour committed itself to doubling defence expenditure to £3,400 million spread over the next three years. This was despite the fact that Britain was already spending a higher proportion of GDP on defence than the United States. The following year, in January 1951, this commitment was increased to £4,700 million (the Americans wanted £6,000 million). What this involved was the government throwing away the fruits of economic recovery achieved by the sacrifices of ordinary people in order to appease the Americans. Attlee, as one historian has observed, put Labour's electoral fortunes at serious risk for the sake of the American alliance. The massive increase in military spending was motivated less by fear of the Russians than by the need to keep in with the United States: "Britain spent what she had to do to make the alliance secure".[16] The economic consequences were disastrous. Whereas in 1950 there was a £244 million balance of trade surplus, by 1951 this had been converted into a £521 million deficit. The chancellor, Hugh Gaitskell, proposed cuts in welfare to help pay for rearmament (the introduction of charges in the NHS) and increased taxes.[17] The introduction of NHS charges split the government, with Bevan, Harold Wilson and others resigning in protest. In the general election of October 1951 the Conservatives under Winston Churchill were elected into power. They quickly scaled down the rearmament programme.[18]

From Suez to Vietnam

As we have already seen in Chapter 9, little more than a decade after the Second World War the British position in the Middle East had been reduced from one of hegemony to dependence on the United States. The Eden government's futile attempt at reasserting British power in 1956, invading Egypt in alliance with France and Israel, was brutally cut short by American economic and political pressure. It is worth emphasising that Britain's greatest post-war humiliation was inflicted not by the Soviet Union or by France or by Germany, but by the United States. And yet the British ruling class remained whole-heartedly committed to restoring and maintaining its alliance with the Americans, no matter what. Whereas the French response to the Suez humiliation was to look to Europe as a counter-balance to American power, the British embraced dependency. In 1966 President de Gaulle was actually to close down US bases in France and order the removal of all US forces from French soil. At the same time, the British were seeking a junior partnership in America's global empire. Even when Britain finally joined the European Economic Community (forerunner to the EU) in January 1973, it soon became clear, once the Heath government had fallen, that the American alliance still came first. In fact, Britain was a deliberate obstacle to

THE BLOOD NEVER DRIED

Europe becoming a counter-balance to the United States. That remains the situation today.

The different trajectories of the French and British states reflected the different interests of French and British capitalism. British interests were and are global. Whereas the British state had once been powerful enough to protect those interests, now only the United States had the necessary military might. From this point of view, the American alliance can be seen as a fundamental ruling class interest. This is not to say that there were not sections of the capitalist class who looked primarily to Europe. Indeed, the conflict between the protagonists of America and Europe was one of the factors that tore the Thatcher and Major governments apart in the 1990s. At the moment, however, this conflict seems to have been decisively resolved in favour of the American alliance, a resolution symbolised both by the failure to join the euro and British participation in the invasion and occupation of Iraq under Blair.

The government that determined Britain's particular trajectory was the Macmillan government. In the aftermath of Suez, Macmillan set about restoring relations with the United States. This determination had an important military dimension. As far as the Chiefs of Staff were concerned, Suez had shown that the Americans could not be relied on to defend British interests. The answer was to abandon any interests that conflicted with those of the United States. As G Wyn Rees has pointed out:

> The chiefs emerged from the Suez debacle with a determination not to seek greater independence, as might have been expected, but rather to seek closer cooperation with their Atlantic partner in order to avoid such a split ever recurring. They realised how dependent future overseas operations would be upon American support and resolved to tie Britain more closely to the United States... As Sir William Dickson, chairman of the Chiefs of Staff Committee, declared: "We and the Americans are the only two powers with global interests..."[19]

There was no alternative. Indeed, an alliance with France had already proven incapable of defending British interests in Egypt. A partnership with the Americans on whatever terms was the only option.

Dependence was even more marked as far as nuclear strategy was concerned. "While the quest for a British deterrent had all along been driven by the wish to avoid dependence upon the United States", as Ian Clark points out, under Macmillan, "the final creation of a special nuclear axis with America" became the objective.[20] As we have already seen, Attlee's government had initiated development of a British atom bomb in 1947. By the time this was delivered in 1952 it was already obsolete. Both the United States and the Soviet Union developed the hydrogen bomb. Not until the summer of 1957 did Britain explode its own hydrogen bomb, a consolation for the Suez debacle as far as British Conservatives were concerned. As Randolph Churchill MP boasted:

> Britain can knock down 12 cities in the region of Stalingrad and Moscow from bases in Britain and another dozen in the Crimea from bases in Cyprus. We did not have that power at the time of Suez. We are a major power again.[21]

Such optimism was misplaced. By now the problem was that Britain's delivery system, the V-bomber force, was obsolescent, as was its proposed replacement, the Blue Streak missile, still only in development at the time.

As far as the British government was concerned, it was absolutely essential that Britain should be armed with nuclear weapons. It was a guarantee of great power status. In 1960 Blue Streak was cancelled and Macmillan negotiated the purchase of a missile the Americans had in development, the Skybolt, which could be delivered by the V-bomber force. In return, the Americans were given the Holy Loch submarine base for their Polaris submarines. When Skybolt was cancelled late in 1962, Macmillan was forced to go cap in hand to beg President Kennedy for Polaris. He emphasised British support during the Cuban crisis (Macmillan had described Castro to Kennedy as "your Nasser")[22] and warned that refusal to give him Polaris might well lead to the fall of his government and its replacement by Labour. In April 1963 the Americans agreed. Interestingly enough, even at this point there were ministers who disagreed with becoming dependent on the United States. Julian Amery and Peter Thorneycroft both argued that Britain should develop nuclear weapons with the French. Instead the Polaris deal was concluded with "far-reaching consequences". As David Reynolds has argued, "It locked Britain into a

THE BLOOD NEVER DRIED

transatlantic nuclear dependence that has endured to the present day".[23] Britain's celebrated *independent* nuclear "deterrent" was, in fact, very much a *dependent* nuclear capacity, an emblem of British subordination to the United States.

This brings us to the question of Vietnam. The Americans had first proposed military intervention in 1954, when the French were facing defeat at the hands of the Vietnamese. They had backed away from the idea when the Churchill government refused to support them. Churchill had made the point to the head of the US Joint Chiefs of Staff that it was hardly likely that British troops who had not fought to keep India in the British Empire would be prepared to fight to keep Indochina in the French Empire.[24] Later, when the United States was supporting the Diem regime in South Vietnam, the Macmillan government was positively enthusiastic about assisting in counter-insurgency operations against the Vietcong. As we saw in the last chapter, in 1961 the government had sent an advisory mission to Saigon to advise the South Vietnamese (in the face of US opposition).[25] Given this initiative, there seems little doubt that if the Conservatives had been returned to office in 1964 at least a token British force would have been sent to Vietnam to fight alongside the Americans as the war intensified.

In October 1964 Harold Wilson became Labour prime minister. He was confronted with the escalation of the Vietnam conflict in 1965 and its transformation into a full-scale war. Throughout the fighting the Labour government made clear that it fully supported the United States in its bloody colonial war, but when the Americans pressed for British troops to be despatched to Vietnam, Wilson refused. One justification for this refusal was that Britain was already heavily involved in the confrontation with Indonesia. Indeed, it was hinted that if British forces were sent to Vietnam then some American commitment to Malaysia would be expected. The most important factor in Wilson's calculations, however, was the danger of splitting the Labour Party in parliament together with the strength of anti-war feeling in the country at large. Labour was confronted by a mass anti-war movement, the Vietnam Solidarity Campaign (VSC), that opposed Wilson's support for the Americans in the most militant terms. In October 1968 the VSC was able to stage a march of 100,000 people in London in support of the Vietcong and in opposition to the Labour government.[26] Michael Foot, one of the leaders of the Labour left, warned Wilson that, if

British troops set foot in Vietnam, "they would tear to pieces even the secure majority which they now have in the House".[27] If Hugh Gaitskell had still been Labour leader (he had died in 1963) there is little doubt that he would have sent troops regardless of the any damage it did to the Labour Party. One can feel absolutely confident that Tony Blair too would have had no hesitation in this regard either.

But while Wilson was concerned to keep the Labour Party together, he still gave full support to America's war. The Labour government defended the war as a war against communist aggression and only faltered in this respect on one occasion. In June 1966 the Americans stepped up their bombing of North Vietnam and Wilson publicly disassociated himself from the decision. This display of independence was not all it seemed: the terms of the disassociation had actually been cleared with the Americans beforehand![28] What is absolutely clear, however, is that in a brutal imperialist war in which the United States once again laid waste much of another Asian country, the British government remained steadfast in their support. According to Jonathan Neale, in their bombing of Vietnam (North and South), Laos and Cambodia, the Americans:

> dropped over 8 million tons of explosives. This was roughly three times the weight of bombs dropped by all sides in World War Two, and the explosive force was equal to 640 of the atom bombs used on Hiroshima… There are no precise counts of the number of dead Vietcong and civilians. The best estimate is between 1.5 and 2 million, though the Vietnamese estimates are higher. Hundreds of thousands more people died in both Laos and Cambodia. That puts the total dead at roughly 3 million, most of them from the air war.[29]

There was hardly a war crime that the United States did not commit in Vietnam (the torture and killing of prisoners, the massacre of civilians, indiscriminate shelling and bombing, chemical warfare, even medical experiments on prisoners), but the Labour government continued to champion America's cause. Inevitably, however, there was some US resentment at the refusal to send troops. Dean Rusk, the American secretary of state, complained to a journalist in 1968 that "all we needed was one regiment. The Black Watch would have done. Just one regiment…"[30] Such a commitment would, of course, have made no difference to the final outcome: American defeat.

THE BLOOD NEVER DRIED

Before moving on, let us consider one other revealing episode in the Wilson government's relations with the United States: the question of British Guiana.[31] The Kennedy administration had earlier made it clear to Harold Macmillan that they regarded Britain's South American colony as being within their sphere of influence and that the democratically elected left wing government of Cheddi Jagan and his People's Progressive Party was unacceptable. The Americans wanted Jagan removed before British Guiana became independent. Dean Rusk, the US Secretary of State told the British Foreign Secretary, Lord Home, that the United States "would not put up with an independent British Guiana under Jagan" and warned of "strains on Anglo-American relations". The British did not regard Jagan as any sort of threat, and, moreover, considered him infinitely preferable to his main opponent, Forbes Burnham. Nevertheless, they were bullied into giving the CIA a free hand to destabilise an elected government in a British colony. Macmillan actually met CIA director John McCone to discuss the situation.

Once given the go-ahead, the CIA poured money and agents into the colony, financing Jagan's opponents, deliberately fostering racial conflict and communal violence that cost hundreds of lives, and corrupting much of the trade union movement. The Americans hoped that the disorder and violence they had orchestrated would provide the British with a pretext to remove Jagan, but the British were extremely reluctant to take such a step. The CIA bombarded the British with false intelligence of Russian and Cuban interference in the colony. In February 1962 the British were informed that a Cuban freighter was smuggling 50 tons of weapons into the country. A search of the ship revealed printing presses. In 1963 the CIA organised a general strike, accompanied by considerable violence, including bombings and shootings, against the Jagan government. Corrupt company unions were financed to the tune of a $1 million to bring him down. Under intense pressure, the British finally gave way and agreed to a constitutional coup to remove the PPP from power. They decided to impose a system of proportional representation on the colony, so that Jagan's opponents, under American auspices, could unite to keep him from power. The Labour opposition in London was extremely critical of these proceedings, with Harold Wilson dismissing the new electoral arrangements as a "fiddled constitution".

Jagan hoped somewhat naively that when Labour came to power in

October 1964 Wilson would reverse Conservative policy. This would have meant defying the United States and so Wilson went ahead and put the Conservative plan into effect. In the December 1964 general election in British Guiana the PPP increased its share of the vote. But a combination of proportional representation, massive American financial subsidies and electoral fraud brought the US client, Forbes Burnham, to power. The Labour government gave independence to British Guiana, or Guyana as it became, in May 1966. Forbes Burnham subsequently maintained himself in power by corruption, electoral fraud on a massive scale, gangster violence and the encouragement of race hatred. Among his victims was the Marxist historian and activist Walter Rodney, murdered by Burnham's thugs in June 1980.[32]

A British Gaullism

The Wilson government lost the 1970 general election and was replaced by the Conservatives under Edward Heath. Heath's government was the closest Britain has ever come to a "Gaullist" turn, taking Britain into the European Economic Community and very deliberately distancing himself from the United States. According to Heath's biographer, John Campbell:

> The most radical aspect of Heath's foreign policy—differentiating his government sharply from every previous post-war administration, Conservative and Labour, and from all of his successors…as well—was his determination not to have a special relationship with the United States. On the contrary, he was determined to assert Britain's European identity…he was specifically determined to show Pompidou (the French president) that Britain was not an American Trojan Horse.

Instead of Heath hurrying across the Atlantic to offer fealty to President Nixon, "Nixon had to come and see him". As Campbell observes, the Americans were used to "Wilson fawning on Johnson" and "Macmillan's avuncular relationship with Kennedy", and consequently "could not understand a British prime minister deliberately wanting to keep relations cool".

Even while he looked to Europe, Heath remained a strong Cold Warrior and anti-Communist. He continued British support for the American war in Vietnam, publicly supporting President Nixon's murderous bombing offensive against the North in December 1972. Where the government did take an independent stand, however, was over the "Yom Kippur" war between Israel, and Syria and Egypt in 1973. Britain, together with France and West Germany, refused to allow the United States to use their facilities or air space to fly arms and munitions to Israel. This was an unprecedented step for any British government to take. Moreover, Heath made it clear that he blamed the conflict on American support for Israeli intransigence. Harold Wilson, the Labour leader, was a staunch Zionist and would have inevitably supported the United States, had he still been in power. Heath, on the other hand, as Campbell points out, believed that "membership of a united Europe offered to Britain a means of recovering in partnership the leadership role in the world which she could no longer hope to play alone". In Heath's own words, "There are some people who always want to nestle on the shoulder of an American president. That's no future for Britain".[33]

The Heath government was eventually brought down by the scale and intensity of the class struggle in Britain in the early 1970s. The miners' strike of 1974 proved the final blow that returned Harold Wilson to power. Once Heath was gone, replaced as Conservative leader by Margaret Thatcher, both Labour and the Conservatives once again embraced the American alliance as the cornerstone of British foreign policy. What this reversion demonstrates is that Heath's "Gaullism" had too narrow a social base to ever succeed in reshaping British policy. While it had some support among the ruling class, the American alliance still seemed the best guarantee of British capitalism's global interests. Under Margaret Thatcher, who became prime minister in 1979, the American alliance was to be prosecuted with renewed fervour. What is interesting is that while the "Gaullist" elements within the Conservative Party were eventually able to bring Thatcher down, they were not strong enough to actually change the party's direction. Indeed, under the Blair government, both New Labour and the Conservative opposition seem to have decisively rejected the European option in favour of the American alliance. It is important to remember that what Heath and those of like mind in both the Conservative and Labour parties were looking for in Europe was an imperial counter-balance to American power. Their belief was that British capitalism's global interests would be best served by an equal partnership with France and Germany rather than by an unequal and subordinate one with the United States. As far as the British ruling class as a whole is concerned, however, American military power is so overwhelming that only the United States can effectively protect and advance British capitalism's global interests.

New Labour

When he was appointed ambassador to Washington in 1997, Christopher Meyer had British policy explained to him by Blair's chief of staff, Jonathon Powell: "We want you to get up the arse of the White House and stay there".[34] This was, of course, much more accurate anatomically than Blair's claim that Britain stood shoulder to shoulder with the Americans, but for obvious reasons the latter description was preferable for public consumption. There was nothing new in this policy. Indeed, while New Labour can quite correctly be seen as making a decisive break with the Labour Party's social democratic politics domestically, there is remarkable continuity in foreign and defence policy. Just as Attlee sent troops to Korea to appease the Americans, so Blair sent troops to Afghanistan and Iraq. Harold Wilson's government stands out as an aberration in this respect, but only because of the strength of the left at the time. Under Wilson, anti-war sentiment outside the Labour Party could still find expression within it, something that Blair and his supporters have made effectively impossible today. Where Blair has been unfortunate is that he has had to subordinate himself to one of the most right wing, reactionary and openly imperialist administrations in US history, led moreover by a president of the sorry calibre of George W Bush. A man of profound ignorance, lacking in both character and application, although certainly possessed of some cunning, which the Blairites desperately try to pass off as intelligence, Bush is certainly the worst post-war president, and arguably one of the worst ever.[35] And yet this is the man Blair has to defer to, accept praise from and attempt to influence. The effort has cost him both his credibility and his reputation. It has cost many, many other people their lives.

More important than personalities, however, is the fact that Britain's determination to ally itself with the United States involves an alliance with a superpower whose world economic domination is a thing of the past. The United States is increasingly reliant on military might to substitute for economic muscle, something that is not sustainable in the long term. And, moreover, even in terms of military

THE BLOOD NEVER DRIED

power, the American Empire's reach is not equalled by its hold. This has, of course, been amply demonstrated by the ease with which the Americans overthrew Saddam Hussein in 2003 and by their subsequent failure to effectively occupy and pacify Iraq. Britain will increasingly come to share in America's difficulties.

First, though, let us examine the New Labour phenomenon. The enormity of New Labour's break with its reformist and social democratic past is perhaps best demonstrated by its open embrace of the interests of big business and the rich. Under Tony Blair and Gordon Brown, New Labour proclaimed itself unequivocally the party of business. To this end, it kept in place Thatcher's anti trade union legislation, consistently opposed any extension of workers' rights proposed by the European Union, curbed civil liberties at every opportunity, carried out further privatisations and introduced public-private partnerships as a covert way of transferring state assets to business. New Labour has actually begun the privatisation of both the NHS and the state education system. Whereas once even the right wing of the Labour Party was committed to increasing social equality, the New Labour government has quite happily presided over increased social inequality. Moreover, under Blair there has been a revival of the sale of honours, knighthoods and peerages, on a scale not seen since the days of Lloyd George. The only electoral promise that New Labour has regarded as absolutely sacrosanct is the promise not to increase taxes on the rich. So we have the remarkable situation under the New Labour government where the very poorest pay a higher proportion of their income in taxes than the wealthy. New Labour's embrace of big business and the rich is perhaps best symbolised by its relationship with the News International boss, Rupert Murdoch. This reactionary union buster was assiduously courted by Blair in opposition and continues to be one of the most powerful influences on the government. In many ways Murdoch can be seen as the patron saint of New Labour. Whereas the Labour Party was originally founded to challenge this state of affairs, under Blair, New Labour has enthusiastically embraced it.

How has this come about? It is not the result of a Blairite coup at the top of the Labour Party or of the lack of backbone of a particularly contemptible generation of Labour MPs. These are symptoms, not the cause. Rather the transformation is a response to and consequence of the decisive shift in the balance of class forces accomplished under Thatcher. Put crudely, but nevertheless accurately, big business and the rich are more powerful in Britain today than at any time since the end of the 19th century.[36] One consequence of this has been a breakdown of the border between the public and the private. The state, its assets and revenues have become a source of pillage for private business on an unprecedented scale. This has fundamentally corrupted the British political system. We live in the age of what can be meaningfully described as "the New Corruption", just as "the Old Corruption" defined politics at the end of the 18th century. Doing favours for the rich and for big business is what politics is all about today.[37]

The ideology informing New Labour can best be described as "globalisation". This involved a belief that developments in the world economy had made the policies traditionally associated with the Labour Party irrelevant. Market forces were now too powerful for any nation-state to be able to stand against them. Indeed, they had actually become benevolent, so that the only way forward was to embrace them. The heroes of New Labour were not trade union militants or socialist activists but international bankers and multinational businessmen. These were the people who could make a difference.[38] This ideology pervaded the whole government and the bulk of the Parliamentary Labour Party. Even one of Blair's critics, Clare Short, when in charge of the Department for International Development, awarded contracts to the free market fundamentalist Adam Smith Institute to advise aid recipients on privatisation.[39] New Labour's domestic policies obviously derived from this ideology of globalisation, but it also informed its commitment to the American alliance. Blair, an admirer of the British Empire (like every previous Labour prime minister, it has to be said), was convinced that the world had entered into a new period of benevolent informal empire or "postmodern imperialism", as one of his advisers called it. Instead of the British Empire acting as a force for good in the world that burden had now fallen to the United States. The American state would police the world market for everyone's benefit. Blair seriously bought into the Bush administration's fantasies of world domination. He was a convert to the "Project for the New American Century". The American state, with its historically unprecedented military superiority, was to be the world's policeman and Britain would be its faithful police dog. He literally could not understand why France and Germany refused to subordinate themselves to the United States. This was the future. Once again there was no alternative.[40]

One last point worth considering here concerns New Labour's reputation for dishonesty. While all governments lie, this has been identified by critics, both on the left and the right, as having been carried to new heights by the Blair government.[41] At least in part, the responsibility for this lies with Alistair Campbell, Blair's press spokesman and right hand man, arguably the de facto deputy prime minister for most of Blair's period in office. Nevertheless, the phenomenon can best be seen as deriving from the fact that New Labour is itself a lie. A party whose electoral support still rests on the working class but that has in practice transformed itself into the party of big business is living a lie. It cannot ever afford to tell the truth. This had infected every aspect of New Labour's conduct of affairs and created just the sort of environment where someone like Campbell could thrive.[42]

Invading Iraq

Once in power Blair prosecuted the American alliance with considerable energy and enthusiasm, identifying himself as closely as possible with President Clinton. The Blairites saw themselves as the British version of Clinton's New Democrats, both pulling their respective parties sharply to the right. In November 1997 Blair told the Lord Mayor's Banquet in London that when Britain and the United States "work together on the international scene there is little we cannot achieve. Our aim should be to deepen our relationship with the USA at all levels." What he really meant, of course, was that there was little the United States could not achieve and that Britain would be part of it no matter what. An opportunity soon presented itself in August 1998. In retaliation for Al Qaida attacks on the US embassies in Kenya and Tanzania, Clinton ordered attacks on targets in Afghanistan and Sudan. In Khartoum cruise missiles destroyed the al-Shifa pharmaceutical factory, a target with no terrorist or military connections, but that produced most of the country's antibiotics. As John Kampfner, the chronicler of Blair's wars, observes, "Blair was virtually alone in defending the action." He quotes an anonymous member of Blair's inner circle: "Everyone knew that what Clinton was doing was wrong—bombing that plant—but we also knew that supporting him was right".[43] America right or wrong was to be the watchword.

Indeed, far from Blair being reluctant to support the United States, he actually thought Clinton was too reluctant to use military force, that the Americans were not aggressive enough internationally.

So from day one New Labour was committed to supporting American policy, any American policy, with regard to Saddam Hussein's regime in Iraq, regardless of the consequences. In December 1998, when Clinton launched punitive air raids, Operation Desert Fox, against Iraq, British aircraft took part in the attacks that hit 250 targets. The government supported UN sanctions, sanctions that by 1996 were estimated to have killed some half a million Iraqi children. On one occasion a shipment of vaccines to protect children against diphtheria and yellow fever was blocked. Kim Howells, a New Labour minister, told parliament that the vaccines were blocked "because they are capable of being used in weapons of mass destruction".[44] One would have to be a satirist of the calibre of Jonathan Swift to plumb the depths of this moral universe.

Blair's government was also an enthusiastic participant in the war the United States and Britain fought under the banner of NATO in Yugoslavia and Kosovo, in March 1999, when air attacks were launched that lasted for 11 weeks. The justification for this was that the Milosevic regime in Yugoslavia was committed to a massive programme of ethnic cleansing and the bombing was to prevent this crime being perpetrated. Blair was central to providing the ideological ammunition for this claim. In a speech in Chicago he invoked "humanitarian intervention" as a new "doctrine of the international community". The argument that this was a war being fought for no economic or strategic gain, but for human rights alone, was almost universally accepted in the media.

Yet it was based on lies. The scale of atrocities in Kosovo prior to NATO's intervention was dramatically exaggerated. Geoff Hoon, a minister in the Foreign Office, claimed that 10,000 ethnic Albanians had been killed. There was even talk from some in US administration of 100,000 being "missing". But when a British government memo after the NATO bombing gave a figure for 10,000 people killed in Kosovo during 1999, Robin Cook, the foreign secretary, admitted that only 2,000 occurred before the bombing started. This referred to casualties on both sides of the brutal war between Yugoslav forces and the Kosovo Liberation Army. As Mark Curtis has said, "The mass deaths alleged to be taking place before the bombing seem to have been a

THE BLOOD NEVER DRIED

NATO fabrication." Worse still, the bombing itself *precipitated* mass ethnic cleansing, the very action it was supposedly preventing, with 850,000 now pushed out of Kosovo, dwarfing the pre-war numbers.

There were two main reasons for the bombing of Kosovo. First was the desire by the US administration under Clinton to deepen the process of reasserting US military power, this time in the European Union's own backyard. Secondly, it was part of the process of expanding NATO eastwards into the vacuum left by the retreating Russian state following the collapse of the Soviet Union at the start of the decade. Blair's apparent rhetorical successes over Kosovo would soon be utilised by another US president in the run-up to a much more serious assertion of US military might. This time he would meet with rather less success.[45]

With the election of George W Bush to the presidency, Iraq moved dramatically up the agenda. The new administration took office committed to the overthrow of Saddam Hussein by whatever means necessary and whenever the opportunity presented itself. This was intended to re-establish the American hegemony over the Middle East that had been profoundly challenged by the Iranian Revolution of 1979. Initially, though, the Bush administration was too weak to even consider launching foreign adventures. Bush was deeply unpopular and on the defensive domestically, having stolen the presidency by means of a coup carried out by the Supreme Court. The Al Qaida attacks on 11 September 2001 were to change all that.

The 11 September attacks were a terrible outrage that cost thousands of innocent people their lives. This is indisputable. The way that the outrage was seized on by both Bush and Blair in order to justify their later aggressions has no justification, however. The 11 September attacks were not the worst atrocity since the Second World War. American bombing in Korea and Vietnam killed hundreds of thousands of innocent people, outrages that completely dwarf 11 September. Moreover by any objective criteria the most dangerous terrorist organisation in the post-war world has not been Al Qaida, but the American CIA. The CIA has assassinated and tortured people across the world, sponsored covert wars that have cost hundreds of thousands of lives and overthrown democratically elected governments. Indeed, a CIA-sponsored coup actually took place on an earlier 11 September in 1973 in Chile, overthrowing the elected president, Salvadore Allende, and installing the brutal Pinochet dictatorship.

And, of course, many of the perpetrators of the Twin Towers attack had actually been America's allies when they had been fighting the Russians in Afghanistan.[46] The CIA, needless to say, is welcome in Britain, where it maintains a substantial secret establishment completely outside any parliamentary scrutiny. One of its representatives routinely attends meetings of the Joint Intelligence Committee.[47] Moreover, today the New Labour government effectively condones the CIA use of torture, including, incredibly enough, the torture of British prisoners (Moazzam Begg, Ruhal Ahmed, Asif Iqbal, Shafiq Rasul and others)[48] held at the Guantanamo concentration camp. What was distinctive about 11 September 2001, one has to conclude, was not the enormity of the outrage, but rather who it was done to.

The importance of the 11 September attacks was not that they revealed a massive terrorist threat to the very existence of the West, but that they provided an opportunity for Bush to go on the offensive, both domestically and internationally. There certainly was a terrorist threat to American imperialism, but it was not as dangerous as was claimed and, according to security specialists, what it required was an intelligence-led response. Instead Bush proclaimed a "War on Terror" that was to serve as a convenient vehicle for American imperial ambitions. American aggression anywhere in the world could now be dressed up as part of the War on Terror and presented to the American people as self-defence. This was done with quite breathtaking cynicism. The Blair government wholeheartedly bought into this fiction.[49] For the Bush administration, however, the opportunity to attack Iraq had finally presented itself. Iraq, which had had no involvement with the 11 September attacks whatsoever, was to be invaded and occupied as part of the War on Terror. Ironically, not only did this mean neglecting the hunt for the actual perpetrators of the 11 September attacks, but it also gave their cause a tremendous boost. Iraq, since the invasion, has become a cockpit for terrorist activity and a potent symbol, rallying support and sympathy for Al Qaida. The suicide bombings in London on 7 July 2005, for example, were a response to the invasion of Iraq and would never have taken place but for Blair's participation in America's war.[50]

This is not the place to go into detail with regard to the road to war.[51] Instead a number of salient points will be made. First, as should have become clear in the course of this book, all colonial wars are based on lies. The strong can only ever justify their wars of aggression against the weak by lying about the threat they pose or the offence they have offered, whether it was attacking China in 1842 and 1857, Burma in 1852 or Egypt in 1882. The Suez invasion of 1956 provides a particularly dramatic example of official mendacity. *What would have been surprising, indeed astonishing, is if the Bush and Blair governments had not lied!* The Bush administration took the decision to invade Iraq early in 2002 and Blair committed himself to support the attack in April of that year. Once he had committed himself, all of Blair's subsequent actions were intended to convince public opinion that Saddam Hussein was an imminent threat, that he was the aggressor, and that this would be a war for democracy. Blair's urging that Bush should seek UN sanction for the war was primarily for domestic purposes, to shore up support, because, as he well knew, the Americans would invade regardless, and British troops would be fighting alongside them. The now notorious dossiers of September 2002, *Iraq's Weapons of Mass Destruction*, and February 2003, *Iraq: Its Infrastructure for Concealment, Deception and Intimidation*, were cynical attempts to manipulate public opinion and intimidate Labour MPs. The fact was that, if Iraq had actually possessed the weapons of mass destruction they were accused of having, there would have been no invasion. The invasion was actually premised on the assumption that Iraq was virtually defenceless, that the country had never recovered from its defeat in the 1991 Gulf War and had been crippled by sanctions thereafter. This was, as we have already said, a war to re-establish American hegemony over the Middle East. Blair was determined that Britain should share in the spoils. He was not trying to restrain the Bush administration, as some Labour MPs deluded themselves, but was actually urging them to use their military might to re-establish a domination over the Middle East from which he believed British capitalism would benefit. To this end the British people were told a pack of lies.

One unforeseen problem that confronted the New Labour government was the rise of a mass anti-war movement, the Stop the War Coalition. This was the most powerful anti-war movement in British history. It was able to stage massive demonstrations, including the great 15 February 2003 demonstration, involving some 2 million people. This was the largest demonstration in British history, a demonstration against a Labour government, about to launch an illegal war of aggression.[52] New Labour's ability to go to war regardless of this mobilisation is a good indication of how successfully the

Blairites have severed the party's popular roots. Despite this, when the House of Commons voted on whether to go to war, 139 Labour MPs voted against and 20 abstained. Robin Cook,[53] the former foreign secretary, two junior ministers and six parliamentary aides resigned from the government. Only one Labour MP, however, George Galloway, was to be expelled from the party for the ferocity of his opposition to this illegal war.[54] Given the scale of the government's deception and the consequences that have followed, this is quite astonishing. A majority of Labour MPs, together with an over-whelming majority of Conservative MPs, voted for war. What Blair assumed was that a successful war would be popular after the event, but instead he has found himself presiding over an unfolding disaster that has exposed him as a liar and a hypocrite of historic proportions with the blood of thousands of people on his hands.

It is worth noting one other indication of the atrophy of parliamentary democracy under Blair. On 29 May 2003, after Iraq had been occupied, the BBC *Today* programme broadcast a report by journalist Andrew Gilligan, revealing that Alistair Campbell had "sexed up" the September 2002 dossier. This was the story of the decade. In the event, it was to cost Gilligan his job, led to the resignations of both Greg Dyke, the director-general of the BBC and Gavyn Davies, the chairman of the BBC's Board of Governors, and drove the government scientist David Kelly to suicide. It is as if the exposure of the Watergate scandal had led not to the impeachment of President Nixon and the jailing of his henchmen, but instead to the sacking of the journalists, Bob Woodward and Carl Bernstein, who broke the story, the resignation of the editor and senior executives at the *Washington Post*, and the suicide of "Deep Throat". The main difference between the two episodes is that Watergate concerned a burglary, whereas Gilligan's was a rather more important story about an illegal invasion that has cost the lives of over 100,000 people. The architect of the BBC's downfall was Alistair Campbell. While Woodward and Bernstein represented the best of journalism, telling truth to power, Campbell very definitely represented the worst. Interestingly, Greg Dyke himself noticed similarities with Watergate. In his memoirs he wrote of how Campbell had:

> turned Downing street into a place similar to Nixon's White House. You were either for them or against them. And if you

opposed them on anything you became the enemy... I was quite shocked when writing this book by these similarities between the Nixon White House and Blair's Downing Street.[55]

The American political system, however reluctantly and belatedly, called Nixon to account; the British political system has signally failed with regard to Blair.

The invasion of Iraq began on 19 March 2003. Its catastrophic consequences for the Middle East have been well documented.[56] Far from learning from this disaster, however, the New Labour government, with the support of the Conservative opposition, remains absolutely committed to supporting the United States in future adventures. At the time of writing, a US military attack on Iran seems only a matter of time, inevitably with the support of the British government. Only the lies to be told and the pretexts to be invented remain to be decided. New Labour has actually reconfigured the British armed forces, so that their main role, for the foreseeable future, is to participate in America's overseas interventions. British capitalism's allegiance to the American Empire is for the time being sacrosanct. Only mass protest and mass resistance in Britain, in the United States and throughout the American Empire can bring this to an end.

Notes

Introduction:
the blood never dried

1 N Ferguson, *Empire: How Britain Made the Modern World* (London, 2003); *Colossus: The Rise and Fall of the American Empire* (London, 2004). Rudyard Kipling (1865-1936) was a short-story writer, novelist and poet (his best known work today is *The Jungle Book*). Kipling's poem "The White Man's Burden" (1899) glorified the British Empire.

2 N Ferguson, *Empire*, pxiv.

3 For Orwell and the British Empire see my *Orwell's Politics* (Basingstoke, 1999).

4 See M Leven, "'Butchering the brutes all over the place': Total war and massacre in Zulu land, 1879", *History*, 84 (1999), for an overview, and more particularly A Greaves, *Rorke's Drift* (London, 2002), pp140-144.

The Jamaican rebellion and the overthrow of slavery

1 For the Antiguan conspiracy see D B Gaspar, "The Antigua Slave Conspiracy of 1736: A Case Study of the Origins of Collective Resistance", *The William and Mary Quarterly*, 35 (1978), and D B Gaspar, *Bondmen and Rebels: A Study of Master-Slave Relations in Antigua* (Durham NC, 1993).

2 R B Sheridan, *Sugar and Slavery: An Economic History of the British West Indies 1623-1775* (Kingston, 1994), p256.

3 A Bakan, *Ideology and Class Conflict in Jamaica: The Politics of Rebellion* (Montreal, 1990), p22.

4 R Dirks, *The Black Saturnalia: Conflict and its Ritual Expression on British West Indies Plantations* (Gainesville, 1987), p161.

5 H Beckles, "The 200 Years War: Slave resistance in the British West Indies", *Jamaica Historical Review*, 13 (1982).

6 See J Rawley with S Behrendt, *The Transatlantic Slave Trade* (Lincoln, 2005).

7 J Walvin, *Black Ivory: A History of British Slavery* (London, 1992), p57.

8 H S Klein, *The Atlantic Slave Trade* (Cambridge, 1999), pp158, 159, 182.

9 J Walvin, *Questioning Slavery* (London, 1996), pp50-51, 57.

10 As above, pp233, 234, 235. See also L Greene, "Mutiny on the Slave Ships", *Phylon*, 5 (1944); W McGowan, "The Origins of Slave Rebellions in the Middle Passage", in A O Thompson (ed), *In The Shadow of the Plantation: Caribbean History and Legacy* (Kingston, 2002); and R B Sheridan, "Resistance and Rebellion of African Captives in the Transatlantic Slave

Trade before Becoming Seasoned Labourers in the British Caribbean 1690-1807", in V Shepherd (ed), *Working Slavery, Pricing Freedom* (Kingston, 2002).

11 For a discussion of the Zong episode see I Baucom, *Spectres of the Atlantic: Finance, Capital, Slavery and the Philosophy of History* (Durham NC, 2005).

12 R B Sheridan, "Resistance and Rebellion of African Captives in the Transatlantic Slave Trade before Becoming Seasoned Labourers in the British Caribbean 1690-1807", pp24-25.

13 E Goveia, *Slave Society in the British Leeward Islands at the End of the Eighteenth Century* (New Haven, 1965), pp130, 133.

14 B Bush, *Slave Women in Caribbean Society 1650-1835* (Oxford, 1990), p44.

15 P Wright, *Knibb The Notorious: Slaves' Missionary 1803-1845* (London 1973), p60.

16 D Hall, *In Miserable Slavery: Thomas Thistlewood in Jamaica 1750-1786* (London, 1989), p72.

17 B Bush, *Slave Women in Caribbean Society 1650-1835*, p44.

18 R Coupland, *Wilberforce* (Oxford, 1923), p460.

19 See J Andrew, *The Hanging of Arthur Hodge* (New York, 2000). Hodge's defence was that "a negro being property, it was no greater offence in law for his owner to kill him than it would be to kill his dog" (p18).

20 R Dirks, *The Black Saturnalia*, pp161-162.

21 R Blackburn, *The Overthrow of British Slavery 1776-1848* (London, 1988), p20.

22 H Klein, *The Atlantic Slave Trade*, p158.

23 R B Sheridan, "Resistance and Rebellion of African Captives in the Transatlantic Slave Trade before Becoming Seasoned Labourers in the British Caribbean 1690-1807", p254. "Seasoning" was the process where the African slaves were prepared for the new life that faced them on the plantations. It could last for two or three years.

24 As above, pp166-169; B Bush, *Slave Women in Caribbean Society 1650-1835*, p15.

25 E V da Costa, *Crowns of Glory, Tears of Blood: The Demerara Slave Rebellion of 1823* (Oxford, 1994), pp115, 173.

26 O Patterson, "Slavery and Slave Revolts: A Socio-Historical Analysis of the First Maroon War 1655-1740", *Social and Economic Studies*, 19 (1970), p289.

27 For the Jamaican Maroons see in particular M Campbell, *The Maroons of Jamaica 1655-1796* (Trenton, 1990). See also R Price, *Maroon Societies* (New York, 1973).

28 M Craton, *Testing The Chains: Resistance to Slavery in the British West Indies* (Ithaca, 1982), pp127, 136-137; M Mullin, *Africa in America: Slave Acculturation and Resistance in the American South and the Black Caribbean* (Urbana, 1994), p41. See also R Hart, *Slaves Who Abolished Slavery* (Kingston, 2002), pp130-156.

29 O N Bolland, *Colonialism and Resistance in Belize* (Belize, 2003), p29. He quotes Edward Despard, the superintendent of the settlement, to the effect that slaves deported from Jamaica to the Honduras "showed a continuance of their dispositions as to create a rebellion...when it was found necessary to put several of the ringleaders to death by burning, gibbeting and other methods of torture". This was the same Despard who in 1803 was involved in a revolutionary conspiracy against the British government in alliance with the Irish Republicans. He was himself publicly hanged, drawn and beheaded.

30 R Blackburn, *The Overthrow of British Slavery 1776-1848*, p30.

31 D P Geggus, *Slavery, War and Revolution: The British Occupation of*

Saint Domingue, 1793-1798 (Oxford 1982), p89.

32 O Blouet, "Bryan Edwards and the Haitian Revolution", in D P Geggus (ed), *The Impact of the Haitian Revolution in the Atlantic World* (Columbia, 2001), p46.

33 D Geggus, *Slavery, War and Revolution*, pp90-92. The French colony of St Domingue made up a third of the island of Hispaniola with the rest under Spanish rule. The French colony became Haiti and the Spanish colony became today's Dominican Republic.

34 J W Fortescue, *A History of the British Army*, 4 (London, 1915), p427.

35 For the Grenada revolt, see E L Cox, "Fedon's Rebellion 1795-96: Causes and Consequences", in *Journal of Negro History*, 67 (1982). See also B Steele, *Grenada* (Oxford, 2003), pp115-148.

36 J W Fortescue, *A History of the British Army*, 4, pp463-465.

37 For the Second Maroon War, see M Campbell, *The Maroons of Jamaica 1655-1796*, pp209-249. For the Trelawny Maroons in exile see J Grant, *The Maroons in Nova Scotia* (Halifax, 2000).

38 R N Buckley, *Slaves in Redcoats: The British West Indies Regiments 1795-1815* (New Haven, 1979), p55. In April 1802 there was a serious mutiny in the Eighth West Indian Regiment after it was rumoured that they were to be sold off as plantation slaves. This effectively secured Britain's slave soldiers their freedom.

39 R Blackburn, *The Overthrow of British Slavery 1776-1848*, p231. For the St Lucia campaign see D B Gaspar, "La Guerre de Bois: Revolution, War and Slavery in Saint Lucia 1793-1838", in D B Gaspar and D P Geggus (eds), *A Turbulent Time: The French Revolution and the Greater Caribbean* (Bloomington, 1997). See also L Dubois, *A Colony of Citizens: Revolution and Slave Emancipation in the French Caribbean 1787-1804* (Chapel Hill, 2004).

40 The best account of the revolution in St Domingue remains C L R James's *The Black Jacobins* (New York, 1963). See also D P Geggus, *Haitian Revolutionary Studies* (Bloomington, 2002) and L Dubois, *Avengers of the New World* (Cambridge, Ma, 2004).

41 See D P Geggus, "The Enigma of Jamaica in the 1790s", *The William and Mary Quarterly*, 44 (1987).

42 R B Sheridan, "From Jamaican Slavery to Haitian Freedom: The Case of the Black Crew of the Pilot Boat, Deep Nine", *Journal of Negro History*, 67 (1982). The Haitians made the interesting point that if the men had landed in England they would have been free and the same went for landing in Haiti.

43 See, for example, K O Lawrence, "The Tobago Slave Conspiracy of 1801", *Caribbean Quarterly*, 28 (1982), and M Craton, *Testing the Chains*, pp224-238.

44 H Beckles, *Black Rebellion in Barbados: The Struggle Against Slavery 1627-1838* (Bridgetown, 1984), pp25, 46-47, 92.

45 M Craton, *Testing the Chains*, p264. H Beckles, *A History of Barbados* (Cambridge, 1990), p84.

46 M Craton, *Testing the Chains*, p270.

47 E V da Costa, *Crowns of Glory, Tears of Blood*, p216.

48 S G Checkland, "John Gladstone as Trader and Planter", *Economic History Review*, 7 (1954), pp225-226. For John Smith see N Titus, "Reassessing John Smith's Influence on the Demerara Slave Revolt of 1823", in A Thompson (ed), *In The Shadow of the Plantation*, pp223-245.

49 E Williams, *Capitalism and Slavery* (London, 1964), p206.

50 H G C Matthew, *Gladstone 1809-1874* (Oxford, 1986), p31.

51 M Craton, *Testing The Chains*, p295.

52 R Hart, *Slaves Who Abolished Slavery*, pp252, 253.

53 M Turner, *Slaves and Missionaries: The*

THE BLOOD NEVER DRIED

Disintegration of Jamaican Slave Society 1787-1834 (Kingston, 1998), pp148, 154; A Bakan, *Ideology and Class Conflict in Jamaica*, p55.

54 M Mullin, *Africa in America*, p257.

55 Sharpe had sent emissaries to the Maroons in an attempt to secure their neutrality, but they handed them over to the British who shot them. See R Hart, *Slaves Who Abolished Slavery*, pp269-270.

56 A Bakan, *Ideology and Class Conflict in Jamaica*, p65.

57 R Hart, *Slaves Who Abolished Slavery*, pp257, 320.

58 P Sherlock and H Bennett, *The Story of the Jamaican People* (Kingston, 1998), p220.

59 R Hart, *From Occupation to Independence* (London, 1998), p39.

60 J Walvin, "The Rise of British Popular Sentiment for Abolition 1787-1832", in C Bolt and S Drescher (eds), *Anti-Slavery, Religion and Reform: Essays in Memory of Roger Anstey* (Folkestone, 1980), pp157, 159. For a recent account of the abolitionist movement see A Hochschild, *Bury The Chains: The British Struggle To Abolish Slavery* (London, 2005).

61 S Drescher, *From Slavery to Freedom: Comparative Studies in the Rise and Fall of Atlantic Slavery* (Basingstoke, 1999), p74. See also his *Capitalism and Anti-Slavery: British Mobilization in Comparative Perspective* (New York, 1986).

62 P Wright, *Knibb The Notorious*, pp120-121.

63 See R Frucht, "Emancipation and Revolt in the West Indies, St Kitts, 1834", *Science and Society*, 39 (1975); R Shelton, "A Modified Crime: The Apprenticeship System in St Kitts", *Slavery and Abolition*, 16 (1995); and G Heuman, "Riot and Resistance in the Caribbean at the Moment of Freedom", *Slavery and Abolition*, 21 (2000).

64 For apprenticeship and resistance to it in Jamaica see T C Holt, *The Problem of Freedom: Race, Labor and Politics in Jamaica and Britain 1832-1938* (Baltimore, 1992), pp63-66. Flogging continued to be a routine feature of life for "apprentices".

65 A Tyrell, "The Moral Radical Party and the Anglo-Jamaican Campaign for the Abolition of the Negro Apprenticeship System", *English Historical Review*, 99 (1984), pp498.

66 G Heuman, "The Killing Time": The *Morant Bay Rebellion in Jamaica* (London, 1994), p98. For the dismal role of the Maroons, see J Lumsden, "'A brave and loyal people': the Role of the Maroons in the Morant Bay Rebellion in 1865", in V Shepherd (ed), *Working Slavery*.

67 C Hutton, "The Defeat of the Morant Bay Rebellion", *Jamaican Historical Review* (1996), p35.

68 A Erickson, "Empire or Anarchy: The Jamaican Rebellion of 1865", *Journal of Negro History*, 44 (1959), pp115-119.

69 B Semmel, *The Governor Eyre Controversy* (London, 1962), pp88-95.

The Irish Famine

1 For the 1798 and 1803 Rebellions see in particular K Whelan, *The Fellowship of Freedom* (Cork, 1998); R O'Donnell, *Robert Emmet and the 1798 Rebellion* (Dublin, 2003), and *Robert Emmet and the Rising of 1803* (Dublin, 2003); and my own *United Irishman: The Autobiography of James Hope* (London, 2000).

2 W F Monypenny, *The Life of Benjamin Disraeli, Earl of Beaconsfield*, 2 (London, 1912), p86.

3 C O Grada, *Black '47 and Beyond: The Great Irish Famine in History, Economy and Memory* (Princeton N J, 1999), p24.

4 There is inevitably considerable controversy about the government's culpability and there has never been any shortage of historians prepared to endorse the official position. Recently,

for example, Trevelyan has been the subject of a massive biography (600+ pages) defending his record: R Haines, *Charles Trevelyan and the Great Irish Famine* (Dublin, 2004). More useful is James S Donnelly Jr's assessment: "The famished children who Mitchel viewed as he travelled from Dublin across the Midlands to Galway in the winter of 1847 prompted the vitriolic remark: 'I saw Trevelyan's claw in the vitals of those children, his red tape would draw them to death; in his government laboratory he had prepared for them the typhus poison'... The harsh words which Mitchel had for Charles Trevelyan, who effectively headed the Treasury in London, do not seem—to me, at any rate—to have been undeserved, even if the professional historian would choose different language", from J S Donnelly Jr, *The Great Irish Potato Famine* (Stroud, 2001), pp18-20.

5 C Kinealy, *A Death-Dealing Famine* (London, 1997), p70.

6 D Kerr, *A Nation of Beggars* (Oxford, 1994), p37. See also J Prest, *Lord John Russell* (London, 1972), p246. He describes Russell's claim that government intervention "would lead to a greater number of deaths from famine" as "a high water mark of laissez-faire".

7 G O Tuathaigh, *Ireland before the Famine* (Dublin, 1972), pp219-220.

8 P Gray, *Famine, Land and Politics* (Dublin, 1999), p294.

9 As above, pp314-315.

10 C O Murchadha, *Sable Wings Over The Land: Ennis, County Clare And Its Wider Community During the Great Famine* (Ennis, 1998), pp77, 82-83, 93, 95. For another valuable local study see D Marnane, "The Famine in South Tipperary", *Tipperary Historical Journal*, 9 (1996) and 10 (1997).

11 P Gray, *Famine, Land and Politics*, p333.

12 C O Grada, *Black '47 and Beyond*, p78. Christine Kinealy has made the point that the money "advanced by the Treasury during the whole of the famine was less than one-half percent of the annual Gross National Product...or as has been aptly pointed out, merely 10 percent of what had been spent in one year alone during the Napoleonic Wars"—from C Kinealy, *This Great Calamity* (Dublin, 1994), p295.

13 For the evictions see in particular J Donnelly Jr, "Mass Eviction and the Great Famine", in C Poirteir (ed), *The Great Irish Famine* (Dublin, 1995); T P O'Neill, "Famine Evictions" in C King (ed), *Famine, Land and Culture* (Dublin, 2000); and C O Murchadha, "One Vast Abbatoir: County Clare 1848-1849", *The Other Clare*, 21 (1997).

14 R F Foster, *Modern Ireland 1600-1972* (London, 1989), p374. For critiques of Foster see T P O'Neill, "Famine Evictions", and my own "Walking Away from the Abyss: Foster on the Famine", *Socialist History*, 10 (1996).

15 See T C Smout, *A History of the Scottish People 1560-1830* (London, 1998), and T M Devine, *The Scottish Nation 1700-2000* (London, 2000).

16 J Killeen (ed), *The Famine Decade: Contemporary Accounts 1841-1851* (Belfast, 1995), pp232-233.

17 I Murphy, *The Diocese of Killaloe* (Blackrock, 1992), pp216-217.

18 J Donnelly Jr, "Mass Eviction and the Great Famine", p163.

19 J Donnelly Jr, *The Great Irish Potato Famine*, p139.

20 J Prest, *Lord John Russell*, p286.

21 D Kerr, *A Nation of Beggars*, p333.

22 For the press campaign around the Mahon shooting and the attacks on the Catholic church that were part of it, see D Kerr, as above, pp93-107, and L Williams, *Daniel O'Connell, The British Press and the Irish Famine* (Aldershot, 2003), pp249-255. As well as attempting to intimidate the clergy,

THE BLOOD NEVER DRIED

the government gave serious consideration to introducing a scheme of state payment in an attempt to buy their loyalty. As Nassau Senior had succinctly put it, "Troops are more expensive than priests"—from P Gray, *Famine, Land and Politics*, p12. The Catholic hierarchy rejected Russell's various proposals, but although many bishops attacked the government, they never presented a united front with regard to the starvation of so many of their flock.

23 E Ashley, *The Life of Henry John Temple, Viscount Palmerston 1846-1865* (London, 1876), pp44-46.

24 J Ridley, *Lord Palmerston* (London, 1970), pp322-323.

25 G Moran, *Sending Out Ireland's Poor: Assisted Emigration to North America in the Nineteenth Century* (Dublin, 2004), p107.

26 See, for example, J Chambers, *Palmerston: The People's Darling* (London, 2004). See also P O Laighin, "Grosse-Ile: The Holocaust Revisited", in R O'Driscoll and L Reynolds (eds), *The Untold Story: The Irish In Canada* (Toronto, 1988).

27 J Mitchel, *Jail Journal* (Dublin, 1913), pxlvii.

28 P Gray, *Famine*, p292.

29 J Mitchel, *Jail Journal*, pxxxix; J Mitchel, *The History of Ireland*, 2 (Glasgow, 1869), pp214-215. Most historians reject Mitchel's claim that there was enough food in Ireland to sustain the population, although Christine Kinealy has offered a powerful defence of his stance (see C Kinealy, *Death-Dealing Famine*, pp77-83). Regardless of this, the export of food in front of a starving population is still incredible, and even if it was not enough to keep everyone alive, would still have saved many thousands of people. This is not a judgement after the event, but was argued at the time.

30 J Mitchel, *The Last Conquest of Ireland* (Glasgow, no date), p94.

31 J Mitchel, *The History of Ireland*, pp224-227.

32 For the Chartists and the Irish Confederation see J Saville, *1848: The British State and the Chartist Movement* (Cambridge, 1990). See also T Koseki, "Patrick O'Higgins and Irish Chartism", in T Matsuo (ed), *Comparative Aspects of Irish and Japanese Economic and Social History* (Tokyo, 1993).

33 *United Irishman*, 12 February 1848.

34 P S O'Hegarty, *A History of Ireland Under the Union* (London, 1952), p343. In the course of the famine the Irish electorate shrank from some 121,000 voters in 1845 to 45,000 in 1850.

35 *United Irishman*, 4 March 1840.

36 D Gwynn, *Young Ireland and 1848* (Cork, 1949), p159.

37 J R Hill, *The Role of Dublin in the Irish National Movement 1840-1848*, PhD thesis (Leeds, 1973), p275.

38 D Kerr, *A Nation of Beggars*, pp132-138. Clarendon had been pleading to be allowed to introduce internment since November 1847. His complaints were continual: in Ireland "every man was in favour of the criminal: law and order have no friends"—from Sir H Maxwell, *The Life and Letters of George William Frederick, Fourth Earl of Clarendon*, 1 (London, 1913), p285; and that he was governing what was only "a half conquered country"—from C Kinealy, *The Great Calamity*, p216.

39 A M Sullivan, *New Ireland* (Glasgow, 1882), p64.

40 J McCarthy, *A History Of Our Times*, 1 (Glasgow, 1882), p64.

41 G P Gooch, *The Later Correspondence of Lord John Russell 1840-1878*, 1 (London, 1925), p230.

42 H Maxwell, *The Life and Letters of George William Frederick*, p289.

43 R Davis, *Revolutionary Imperialist: William Smith O'Brien 1803-1864* (Dublin, 1998), p243. See also R Sloan,

William Smith O'Brien and the Young Ireland Rebellion of 1848 (Dublin, 2000), and R Davis and S Petrow (eds), *Ireland and Tasmania 1848* (Hobart, 1998).

44 Carthage was a North African sea power and the Roman Empire's great rival.

45 J Mitchel, *Jail Journal*, pp83, 377.

46 There is, astonishingly, no modern scholarly biography of John Mitchel, but see my "John Mitchel and Irish Nationalism", *Literature and History*, vol 6 (1980).

47 For the Fenians see my *Fenianism in Mid-Victorian Britain* (London, 1994).

48 For the history of the Irish Republican Brotherhood see L O Broin, *Revolutionary Underground* (Dublin, 1976).

The Opium Wars

1 D Judd, *Empire* (London, 1996).

2 A Porter (ed), *Oxford History of the British Empire: the Nineteenth Century* (Oxford, 1999).

3 F Wakeman, "The Canton Trade and the Opium War", in J K Fairbanks (ed), *The Cambridge History of China*, 10, 1 (Cambridge, 1992), p172.

4 J K Fairbanks, "The Creation of the Treaty System", in J K Fairbanks, as above, p213.

5 According to John Richards, in India, Burma and Sri Lanka, "The British so managed opium with a limited excise system that they circumscribed domestic use of the drug...for the Indian consumer, opium remained relatively scarce and expensive whether legally or illegally acquired"—"The Opium Industry in British India", *Indian Economics and Social History Review*, 39 (2002), p154. For more on the East India Company see Chapter 4.

6 M Greenberg, *British Trade and the Opening of China 1800-1842* (Cambridge, 1951), p232.

7 J Gray, *Rebellions and Revolutions: China from the 1800s to the 1980s*

(Oxford, 1990), p27.

8 C Trocki, *Opium, Empire and the Global Political Economy* (London, 1999), pp10, 26, 73-74.

9 R Murphey, *The Outsiders* (Ann Arbor, 1977), p85.

10 J Wong, *Deadly Dreams: Opium, Imperialism and the Arrow War* (Cambridge, 1998), pp411-412.

11 H Gelber, *Opium, Soldiers and Evangelicals* (Basingstoke, 2004), pp63, 68.

12 R Blake, *Jardine Matheson* (London, 1999), p106.

13 P J Maythornthwaite, *The Colonial Wars Sourcebook* (London, 1995), p237.

14 Lord Jocelyn, *Six Months With The Chinese Expedition* (London, 1841), pp55-57.

15 J Beeching, *The Chinese Opium Wars* (London, 1975), p116.

16 J Ouchterlony, *The Chinese War* (London, 1844), pp238-239, 241.

17 "A Field Officer", *The Last Year in China* (London, 1843), pp143, 150-151, 152.

18 Lord Jocelyn, *Six Months With The Chinese Expedition*, pp39-41, 142-143.

19 S Guan, "Chartism and the First Opium War", *History Workshop*, 24 (1987), p22.

20 J Beeching, *The Chinese Opium Wars*, p109.

21 J Morley, *The Life of William Ewart Gladstone*, 1 (London, 1904), pp226, 227.

22 P Lowe, *Britain in the Far East* (London, 1981), p16.

23 K Marx and F Engels, *Collected Works*, 12 (London, 1979), p98.

24 For the Taiping see F Michael, *The Taiping Rebellion*, 3 vols (Seattle, 1972), and V Shih, *The Taiping Ideology* (Seattle, 1967). The most recent discussion of Taiping Christianity is in T Reilly, *The Taiping Heavenly Kingdom* (Seattle, 2004). For an excellent biography of Hong Xiuguan see J Spence, *God's Chinese Son* (London, 1996).

25 T Meadows, *The Chinese and Their Rebellions* (London, 1856), pp457-458.

THE BLOOD NEVER DRIED

26 J Edkins, *Religion in China* (London, 1878), p197.

27 A F Lindley, *Ti-Ping Tien-Kwoh: The History of the Ti-Ping Revolution* (London, 1866), pp154-155. See also my "Taiping Revolutionary: Augustus Lindley in China", *Race and Class*, 42 (2001).

28 J Wong, *Deadly Dreams*, pp9-10.

29 For Bowring see G Bartle, *An Old Radical and his Brood* (London, 1994).

30 J K Fairbanks, *Trade and Diplomacy on the China Coast* (Cambridge Ma, 1954).

31 J Wong, *Deadly Dreams*, p23.

32 E Steele, *Palmerston and Liberalism* (Cambridge, 1991), p121.

33 For Elgin see my "Elgin in China", *New Left Review*, May-June 2002.

34 Sir F Stephenson, *At Home And On The Battlefield* (London, 1914), pp219-220, 223. See also K Bruner and others (eds), *Entering China's Service: Robert Hartley's Journals 1854-1863* (Cambridge, Ma, 1986), pp193-201.

35 Rev R J L M'Ghee, *How We Got to Pekin* (London, 1862), pp114-115. The manufacturer of the Armstrong guns, William Armstrong, explained the thinking behind the weapon: "We, as a nation, have few men to spare for war and we have need of all the aid that science can give us to secure us against aggression and enable us to hold in subjection the vast and semi-barbarous population which we have to rule in the East"—from D Dougan, *The Great Gunmaster* (Newcastle, 1970), pp67-68.

36 D Rennie, *The British Arms in North China and Japan* (London, 1864), p208.

37 G J Wolseley, *Narratives of the War with China in 1860* (London, 1862), p227.

38 J T Harris, *China Jim* (London, 1912), pp81-117.

39 D Boulger, *The Life of Gordon* (London, 1896), pp45-46.

40 F Wakeman, *The Fall of Imperial China* (New York, 1975), p162.

41 J L Hevia, *English Lessons: The Pedagogy of Imperialism in Nineteenth Century China* (Durham NC, 2003), p89.

42 A Lindley, *Ti-Ping Tien-Kwoh*, pp277-279.

43 As above, p607-609.

44 A Wilson, *The Ever Victorious Army* (Edinburgh, 1868), p155-156.

45 A Lindley, *Ti-Ping Tien-Kwoh*, p759.

The Great Indian Rebellion, 1857-58

1 M Edwardes, "The Mutiny and its Consequences", introduction to W H Russell, *My Indian Mutiny Diary* (London, 1957), pxv.

2 T Lowe, *Central India During The Rebellion of 1857 and 1858* (London, 1860), pp103, 104, 166. He writes approvingly of his commander, General Hugh Rose, having "strewn the plains of India with corpses" (p304).

3 For the United Irish Rebellion see my *United Irishman*.

4 D Judd, *The Lion and the Tiger* (Oxford, 2004), p47.

5 V G Kiernan, *European Empires From Conquest to Collapse* (London, 1982), p42.

6 J A Hobson, *Richard Cobden: The International Man* (London, 1919), pp90; S Hobhouse, *Joseph Sturge* (London, 1919), pp119-120.

7 See O Pollak, "The Origins of the Second Anglo-Burmese War 1852-53", *Modern Asian Studies*, 12, 3 (1978). For the Anglo-Burmese Wars see G Bruce, *The Burma Wars 1824-1886* (London, 1973).

8 J A Hobson, *Richard Cobden*, pp87, 91-92.

9 T Blackburn, *The British Humiliation of Burma* (Bangkok, 2000), p58.

10 S L Menezes, *Fidelity and Honour: The Indian Army From The Seventeenth to the Twenty-First Century* (New Delhi, 1999), p77.

11 R Mukherjee, *Awadh in Revolt 1857-1858* (London, 2002), p35. See also

S Mohan, *Awadh Under the Nawabs* (New Delhi, 1997), and F A Taban, "The Coming of the Revolt in Awadh: Evidence of Urdu Newspapers", *Social Scientist*, 26 (1998).

12 C A Bayly, *Indian Society and the Making of the British Empire* (Cambridge, 1988), pp79, 116.

13 K Marx and F Engels, *The First Indian War of Independence 1857-1859* (Moscow, 1959) pp24, 26, 27, 30. It is worth quoting Marx on the role of the British capitalist class in the regeneration of India: "All the English bourgeoisie may be forced to do will neither emancipate nor materially mend the social condition of the mass of the people, depending not only on the development of the productive powers, but on their appropriation by the people. But what they will not fail to do is to lay down the material premises for both. Has the bourgeoisie ever done more? Has it ever effected a progress without dragging individuals and peoples through blood and dirt, misery and degradation? The Indians will not reap the fruits of the new elements of society scattered among them by the British bourgeoisie, till in Great Britain itself the new ruling class has been supplanted by the industrial proletariat, or till the Hindus themselves shall have grown strong enough to throw off the English yoke altogether" (pp29-30).

14 As above, pp59, 60, 63.

15 R Mukerjhee, *Spectre of Violence: The 1857 Kanpur Massacre* (New Delhi, 1998), p175.

16 One of the few academic discussions of torture is D Peers, "Torture, the Police, and the Colonial State in the Madras Presidency 1816-55", *Criminal Justice History*, 12 (1991). See also A Rao, "Problems of Torture, States of Terror: Torture in Colonial India", *Interventions*, 3 (2001).

17 T Walrond (ed), *The Life and Diaries of the English Lord Elgin* (London, 1878), pp199-200.

18 W H Russell, *Indian Mutiny*, pp284-285.

19 W Trousdale (ed), *War in Afghanistan: The Personal Diary of Major General Sir Charles Metcalfe Macgregor* (Detroit, 1985), p157.

20 K Marx and F Engels, *The First Indian War of Independence*, p40.

21 S Gopal, *British Policy in India*, (London, 1965), p1.

22 K Marx and F Engels, *The First Indian War of Independence*, pp32-33.

23 Sir G MacMunn, *The Indian Mutiny In Perspective* (London, 1931), px.

24 S L Menezes, *Fidelity and Honour*, p162. He writes that "she was hanged without trial for 'egging on the mutineers'", observing that British writers invariably ignore "the killing by the British themselves of a British woman".

25 For popular involvement in the rebellion see in particular R Mukerjhee, *Arwadh in Revolt*; T Roy, *The Politics of a Popular Uprising: Bundelkand in 1857* (Delhi, 1994); and E Stokes, *The Peasant Armed: The Indian Rebellion of 1857* (Oxford, 1986). These are all invaluable although written from differing perspectives. See also G Bhadra, "Four Rebels of Eighteen-Fifty-Seven", *Subaltern Studies*, iv, and the special Indian Rebellion issue of *Social Scientist*, 26 (1998), in particular P Rag, "1857: Need for Alternative Sources". Urban involvement in the rebellion urgently requires exploration.

26 D Domin, *India in 1857-59: A Study of the Role of the Sikhs in the People's Uprising* (Berlin, 1977), p2.

27 R Mukherjee, *Spectre of Violence*. See also R Muckherjee, "'Satan Let Loose Upon Earth': The Kanpur Massacres in India in the Revolt of 1857", *Past and Present*, 128 (1990); B English, 'The Kanpur Massacres in India in the Revolt of 1857', *Past and Present*, 142

(1994); and Mukherjee's rejoinder, "Reply", *Past and Present*, 142 (1994). For Nana Sahib see P C Gupta, *Nana Sahib and the Rising at Cawnpore* (Oxford, 1963).

28 According to Michael Edwardes it was the hangings and shootings carried out by Colonel James Neill that "led to the massacre of his countrywomen at Cawnpore". See his *Red Year: The Indian Rebellion of 1857* (London, 1973), p84. John Pemble also argues that the women and children "had been murdered in retaliation for British atrocities"— see his *The Raj, The Indian Mutiny and the Kingdom of Oudh 1801-1859* (Hassocks, 1977), p179. And more recently Heather Streets has insisted that Neill's murder of thousands "of sepoys and suspected rebels as well as innocent men, women and children" bears "directly on the events surrounding the Kanpur Massacre". See her *Martial Races: The Military, Race and Masculinity in British Imperial Culture 1857-1914* (Manchester, 2004), p39.

29 K Marx and F Engels, *The First Indian War of Independence 1857-1859*, pp74-75.

30 W H Russell, *My Indian Mutiny Diary*, p29.

31 See S Malik, "The Panjab and the Indian Mutiny: A Reassessment", *Journal of Indian History*, l (1972).

32 E Stokes, *The Peasant Armed*, pp48, 49.

33 C A Bayly, *Empire and Information: Intelligence Gathering and Social Communication in India 1780-1870* (Cambridge, 1996), p317.

34 See I Husain, "The Rebel Administration in Delhi", *Social Scientist*, 26 (1998).

35 B Watson, *The Great Indian Mutiny: Colin Campbell and the Campaign at Lucknow* (Westport, Ct, 1991), p68. See also the discussion in K Roy, *From Hydaspes to Kergil: A History of Warfare in India* (New Delhi, 2002), pp149-181.

36 F Cooper, *The Crisis in the Punjab* (Lahore, 1858), pp38, 98-100, 108.

37 F A V Thurburn, *Reminiscences of the Indian Rebellion of 1857-1858* (London, 1889), p35.

38 M Edwardes, "The Mutiny and its Consequences", p84.

39 R H Haigh and P W Turner, *The Lions of the Punjab* (Sheffield, 1998), p204.

40 W H Russell, *My Indian Mutiny Diary*, p45.

41 J Pemble, *The Raj, The Indian Mutiny and the Kingdom of Oudh*, pp177-178.

42 Sir J Kaye, *History of the Indian Mutiny of 1857-8*, 2 (London, 1889), pp301, 302.

43 C J Griffiths, *A Narrative of the Siege of Delhi* (London, 1910), pp90, 101, 102, 106, 108. See also P Speer, *A History of Delhi Under the Later Moghuls* (London, 1951), pp218-228.

44 Lord Roberts, *Forty-One Years in India*, 1 (London, 1897), pp328-329.

45 C Hibbert, *The Great Mutiny: India 1857* (London, 1980), p341.

46 Viscount Wolseley, *The Story of a Soldier's Life* (London, 1903), p306.

47 G B Malleson, *History of the Indian Mutiny*, 4 (London, 1889), p133.

48 C Hibbert, *The Great Mutiny*, p341.

49 W Forbes-Mitchell, *Reminiscences of the Great Mutiny 1857-59* (London, 1894), p170.

50 W H Russell, *My Indian Mutiny Diary*, pp87, 110, 114, 161.

51 M Maclagan, *"Clemency" Canning* (London, 1962), pp140.

52 H Anson, *With HM 9th Lancers During the Indian Mutiny* (London, 1896) pp177-178, 225-226, 229, 231, 266.

53 S Malik, "Nineteenth Century Approaches to the Indian 'Mutiny'," *Journal of Asian History*, 7 (1973), pp105, 113.

54 W Oddie, "Dickens and the Indian Mutiny", *The Dickensian*, 68 (1972,) pp4-5.

55 N Edsall, *Richard Cobden, Independent Radical* (Cambridge, Ma, 1986), pp312-313; W H Dawson, *Richard*

Cobden and Foreign Policy (London, 1926), p199.

56 J Byrne, "British Opinion and the Indian Revolt", in P C Joshi (ed), Rebellion 1857: A Symposium (New Delhi, 1957), pp302-311.

57 J Saville, Ernest Jones, Chartist (London, 1952), pp66, 219-221. The most recent biography of Jones, Miles Taylor's Ernest Jones, Chartist and the Romance of Politics 1819-1869 (Oxford, 2003), devotes just over a page to his support for the Great Rebellion which, of course, tells you considerably more about Taylor than it does about Jones.

58 S L Menezes, Fidelity and Honour, pp176-177; A Sharar (ed), The Lucknow Omnibus (New Delhi, 2002), pp32-33.

59 L James, Raj: The Making and Unmaking of British India (London, 1997), p257.

60 C A Bayly, Empire and Information, p332.

61 W Forbes-Mitchell, Reminiscences of the Great Mutiny, pp183-192.

The invasion of Egypt, 1882

1   E F Biagini, Liberty, Retrenchment and Reform (Cambridge, 1992), pp405, 409.

2   W E Gladstone, Political Speeches in Scotland (London, 1879), pp36, 49.

3   As above, pp202-203.

4   T Rothstein, Egypt's Ruin (London, 1910), pp34-41.

5   J Marlowe, Anglo-Egyptian Relations 1800-1956 (London, 1965), p91.

6   L H Jenks, The Migration of British Capital to 1875 (London, 1927), p311.

7   J Marlowe, Anglo-Egyptian Relations 1800-1956, p91.

8   T Rothstein, Egypt's Ruin, p39.

9   R A Atkins, British Policy Towards Egypt (Ann Arbor, 1969), p12.

10 T J Spinner, George Joachim Goschen: the Transformation of a Victorian Liberal (London, 1973), p53.

11 M Schwartz, The Politics of British Foreign Policy in the Era of Gladstone and Disraeli (Basingstoke, 1985), p30.

12 R Wilson, Chapters from my Official Life (London, 1916), p182.

13 W S Blunt, Secret History of the English Occupation of Egypt (New York, 1922), p9. For Blunt see M Berdine, The Accidental Tourist, Wilfred Scawen Blunt and the British Invasion of Egypt in 1882 (London, 2005).

14 For "Muslim Modernism" see F Rahman, "Revival and Reform in Islam", in P M Holt, A K S Lambton and B Lewis (eds), The Cambridge History of Islam, 2B (Cambridge, 1977), pp632-656. For al-Afghani see N R Keddie, Sayyid Jamal Ad-Din "Al-Afghani": A Political Biography (Berkeley, 2001).

15 R A Atkins, British Policy Towards Egypt, p200.

16 J I Cole, Colonialism and Revolution in the Middle East (Cairo, 1999), p44.

17 W S Blunt, Secret History of the English Occupation of Egypt, p157.

18 J I Cole, Colonialism and Revolution in the Middle East, p16.

19 Sir E Malet, Egypt 1879-1883 (London, 1909), pp239, 242, 248-250. See also J S Galbraith and A L al-Sayyid Marsot, "The British Occupation of Egypt: Another View", International Journal of Middle Eastern Studies, 9 (1978).

20 J I Cole, Colonialism and Revolution in the Middle East, p255.

21 D Nicholls, The Lost Prime Minister: A Life of Sir Charles Dilke (London, 1995), p97.

22 J Galbraith and A Marsot, "The British Occupation of Egypt", p485.

23 P Knaplund, Gladstone's Foreign Policy (London, 1970), p183.

24 C Royle, The Egyptian Campaigns 1882-1885 (London, 1900), p63.

25 Sir P Scott, Fifty Years in the Royal Navy (London, 1919), pp47, 48.

26 Sir R Harrison, Recollections of Life in the British Army (London, 1908), p261.

27 Sir W F Butler, Autobiography (London, 1911), p219.

28 M E Chamberlain, "Sir Charles Dilke and the British Intervention in Egypt

THE BLOOD NEVER DRIED

1882", *British Journal of International Studies*, 2 (1976), p272.

29 D Nicholls, *The Lost Prime Minister*, p102.

30 R A J Walling, *The Diaries of John Bright* (New York, 1931), p489, 486.

31 J Morley, *The Life of William Ewart Gladstone*, 3 (London, 1904), p85. The best account of Gladstone and Egypt is R T Harrison's *Gladstone's Imperialism in Egypt* (Westport, 1995).

32 W S Blunt, *Secret History of the English Occupation of Egypt*, p181.

33 W F Butler, *Autobiography*, pp235-236, 251.

34 Rev A Male, *Scenes Through the Battle Smoke* (London, 1901), pp453-454, 477.

35 M W Daley (ed), *The Road to Shaykan: Letters of General William Hicks Pasha* (Durham, 1983), p25.

36 D W R Bahlman, *The Diary of Sir Edward Walter Hamilton*, 1 (Oxford, 1972), pp325, 339, 342, 344.

37 H C G Matthew, *The Gladstone Diaries*, 10 (Oxford, 1990), pplxxii-lxxiii.

38 *London Illustrated News*, 23 September 1882. Contemporary critics of the invasion of Egypt condemned it as a bondholders' war, fought to put down a legitimate nationalist movement aspiring to parliamentary government. The invasion's supporters championed it as a war of liberation to free the Egyptian people from military dictatorship and/or as necessary to protect vital British strategic interests, that is the Suez Canal. In 1961 John Gallagher and Ronald Robinson published their *Africa and the Victorians* (London, 1961) arguing that the British motive was indeed primarily strategic. This thesis was effectively answered quite early on by D A Farnie's magisterial *East and West of Suez: The Suez Canal in History* (Oxford, 1969). Recent research has reinforced this rebuttal. While not denying the importance of strategic concerns as a factor in imperial motivation, the Egyptian war was indeed a bondholders' war.

39 D W R Bahlman, *The Diary of Sir Edward Walter Hamilton*, 1, p352.

40 W S Blunt, *Gordon at Khartoum* (London, 1912), pp79-80.

41 T Mitchell, *Colonising Egypt* (Berkeley, 1991), p97.

42 D W R Bahlman (ed), *The Diary of Sir Edward Walter Hamilton*, 2 (Oxford, 1972), p794.

43 *Commonweal*, March 1885. Available at marxists.org/archive/bax/1885/03/gordon.htm

44 N Kelvin, *The Collected Letters of William Morris 1885-1888*, 3 (Princeton 1987), pp388, 410.

45 E M Spiers, *The Victorian Soldier in Africa* (Manchester, 2004), p151.

46 M W Daly, *Empire on the Nile: The Anglo-Egyptian Sudan 1898-1934* (Cambridge, 1986), pp3, 4.

47 J Pollock, *Kitchener* (London, 2002), p150.

The post-war crisis, 1916-26

1 Lloyd George himself revealed what the war was all about: "We have nothing to complain of in this war. We shall get Mesopotamia, Palestine, the German colonies in South Africa and the islands in the Pacific, including one containing mineral deposits of great value… Mesopotamia contains some of the richest oil fields in the world"— from C Wrigley, *Lloyd George and the Challenge of Labour: The Post-War Coalition 1918-1922* (Hemel Hempstead, 1990), pp181-182.

2 K Jeffery (ed), *The Military Correspondence of Field Marshal Sir Henry Wilson 1918-1922* (London, 1985), pp177-178.

3 See K Morgan, *Harry Pollitt* (Manchester, 1993), pp19-20.

4 See my *Rebel City: Larkin, Connolly and the Dublin Labour Movement* (London, 2004), pp135-153.

5 The most recent and best accounts of the Easter Rising are M Foy and

B Barton, *The Easter Rising* (Stroud, 2000), and C Townshend, *The Easter Rising* (London, 2005).

6 V I Lenin, *British Labour and British Imperialism* (London, 1969), p166.

7 R Taylor, *Michael Collins* (London, 1958), pp57-58; H Talbot, *Michael Collins's Own Story* (London, 1923), p41.

8 For Michael Collins see in particular, G Doherty and D Keogh (eds), *Michael Collins and the Making of the Irish State* (Dublin, 1998).

9 M Hopkinson, *The Irish War of Independence* (Dublin, 2002), p41.

10 For the radical potential of the Irish revolutionary movement see C Kostik, *Revolution in Ireland: Popular Militancy 1917-1923* (London, 1996), and my *Rebel City*, pp156-171.

11 For MacSwiney, see F J Costello, *Enduring The Most: The Life and Death of Terence MacSwiney* (Dingle, 1995).

12 M Gilbert (ed), *Winston S Churchill*, companion vol 4, July 1919-March 1921, part 2 (London, 1997), pp1194-1195, 1214.

13 As above, p1237.

14 M Hopkinson, *The Irish War of Independence,* pp90-91.

15 The quality of British intelligence is shown by the report written by the head of the organisation in Ireland, Ormonde Winter. Here he advised that "the Irishman, without any offence being intended, somewhat resembles a dog, and understands firm treatment", and that "the heads of the rebel organisation are recruited from a low and degenerate type, unequipped with intellectual education." See P Hart (ed), *British Intelligence In Ireland 1920-1921* (Cork, 2000), pp65, 94.

16 M Hopkinson, *The Irish War of Independence*, p83.

17 F J Costello, *The Irish Revolution and Its Aftermath 1916-1923* (Dublin, 2003), p107.

18 K Jeffery, *The British Army and the Crisis of Empire 1918-1922* (Manchester, 1984), p90.

19 As above, p93.

20 For the situation in the North see M Farrell, *The Orange State* (London, 1976) and J McDermott, *Northern Divisions: The Old IRA and the Belfast Pogroms* (Belfast, 2001).

21 A Clayton, *The British Empire as a Superpower 1919-1939* (Basingstoke, 1986), p112.

22 J Beinin and Z Lockman, *Workers On The Nile: Nationalism, Communism, Islam and the Egyptian Working Class 1882-1954* (Princeton, 1987), p91.

23 P J Vatikotis, *The History of Egypt* (London, 1980), p255.

24 J Keay, *Sowing The Wind* (London, 2004), p107.

25 K Jeffery (ed), p98-99.

26 J Keay, *Sowing the Wind*, p117.

27 A Clayton, *The British Empire as a Superpower*, p133.

28 S Sarkar, *Modern India 1885-1947* (Basingstoke, 1989), pp171-177.

29 S Sen, *Working Class of India* (Calcutta, 1997), pp114-115.

30 D A Low, "The Government of India and the First Non-Cooperation Movement 1920-1922", in R Kumar (ed), *Essays on Gandhian Politics: The Rowlatt Satyagraha of 1919* (Oxford 1971), p321.

31 G Minault, *The Khilafat Movement* (New York, 1982), p70.

32 J M Brown, *Gandhi: Prisoner of Hope* (New Haven, 1989), p132.

33 H Fein, *Imperial Crime and Punishment: The Massacre at Jalliarwalla Bagh and British Judgement 1919-1920* (Honolulu, 1977), pp20, 21. See also N Collett, *The Butcher of Amritsar: General Reginald Dyer* (London, 2005), and K H Tuteja, "Jalliarwala Bagh: A Critical Juncture in the Indian National Movement", *Social Scientist*, 25 (1997).

34 S Sarkar, *Modern India 1885-1947*, p192.

35 See D Sayer, "British Reactions to the Amritsar Massacre 1919-1920", *Past and Present*, 131 (1991).

36 See B Robson, *Crisis On The Frontier:*

THE BLOOD NEVER DRIED

The Third Afghan War and the Campaign in Waziristan 1919-1920 (Staplehurst, 2002), and A Clayton, The British Empire as a Superpower, pp159-179. For the debate over the use of poison gas see E M Spiers, "Gas and the North-West Frontier", Journal of Strategic Studies, 4 (1980).

37 M Jacobsen (ed), Rawlinson In India (Stroud, 2002), pp12, 16.

38 B Chandra and others, India's Struggle For Independence (New Delhi, 1989), p189.

39 G Minault, The Khilafat Movement 1885-1947, p167.

40 S Sarkar, Modern India, pp205, 206.

41 R Hardgrave, "The Mappilla Rebellion, 1921: Peasant Revolt in Malabar", Modern Asian Studies, 11 (1977), pp88-89.

42 S Sarkar, Modern India 1885-1947, p217.

43 R Hardgrave, "The Mappilla Rebellion, 1921", p89.

44 See the innovative study by S Amin, Event, Metaphor, Memory: Chauri Chaura 1922-1992 (Berkeley, 1995).

45 S Sarkar, Modern India 1885-1947, pp225-226. He also makes the point that when the British sentenced 172 people to death for the Chauri Chaura killings, there were no nationalist protests, "a matter of shame". In the event 19 were hanged and the rest transported for life.

46 R Khalidi, Resurrecting Empire (Boston, 2004), p1.

47 G Simons, Iraq: From Sumer to Post-Saddam (Basingstoke, 2004), p200.

48 See S Eskander, "Britain's Policy in Southern Kurdistan: The Formation and Termination of the First Kurdish Government 1918-1919", British Journal of Middle Eastern Studies, 27 (2000).

49 M Jacobson, "'Only By The Sword': British Counter-Insurgency in Iraq, 1920", Small Wars and Insurgencies, 2 (1991), p323.

50 E B Maunsel, Prince of Wales's Own, The Scinde Horse (London, 1926),

p280. See also H C Wylly, History of the Manchester Regiment, 2 (London, 1925), pp218-221. High Commissioner Wilson himself acknowledged that when the prisoners were released they had "a healthy and well-nourished appearance...only one having died in captivity"—from A Wilson, Mesopotamia 1917-1920: A Clash of Loyalties (London, 1931), pp298-299.

51 M Jacobsen, "'Only By The Sword'", p341.

52 A Wilson, Mesopotamia 1917-1920, p293.

53 C Townshend, "Civilization and 'Frightfulness': Air Control in the Middle East Between the Wars" in C Wrigley (ed), Warfare, Diplomacy and Politics (London, 1986), p148. Churchill, it should be noted, was a strong advocate of the use of "poisoned gas against uncivilised tribes"—G Simons, Iraq, p213.

54 As above, p214. See also J Cox, "A Splendid Training Ground: The Importance to the Royal Air of its role in Iraq 1919-32", Journal of Imperial and Commonwealth History, 13 (1985).

55 For the undeservedly neglected Jangali movement see C Chaqueri, The Soviet Socialist Republic of Iran (Pittsburgh, 1995).

56 H Sabahi, British Policy in Persia 1918-1925 (London, 1990), p39.

57 As above, p75.

58 As above, pp164-165.

59 According to M G Majd, "Iran was completely controlled by Britain" in the decades after 1918 with Reza Khan richly rewarded for his compliance. He writes of "massive financial corruption and embezzlement by Reza Khan...at the time of his abdication in 1941, he had on deposit at Bank Melli more than 760 million rials ($50 million). Vast amounts were deposited in foreign banks." He also had between £20-30 million deposited in London, "an

unbelievable amount in 1941" as well as "vast sums in Swiss and New York banks". Out of the $155 million paid to Iran in oil royalties during his rule, "at least $100 million was stolen by Reza Shah"—see *Great Britain and Reza Khan* (Gainesville, 2001), pp3, 9. Reza Shah was the model for later pro-Western dictators such as Marcos of the Philippines and Suharto of Indonesia.

60 See N Clifford, *Shanghai 1925: Urban Nationalism and the Defence of Foreign Privilege* (Ann Arbor, 1979).

61 R Bickers, *Empire Made Me: An Englishman Adrift in Shanghai* (London, 2003), pp166, 170.

62 R Rigby, *The May 30 Movement* (Canberra, 1980), p63. See also S A Smith, *Like Cattle and Horses: Nationalism and Labor in Shanghai 1895-1927* (Durham NC, 2002), pp168-169.

63 C L Kit-Ching, *From Nothing To Nothing: The Chinese Communist Movement and Hong Kong 1921-1936* (New York, 1999), p58. See S Tsang, *A Modern History of Hong Kong* (New York, 2004), pp92-101 and J Chesneaux, *The Chinese Labor Movement 1919-1927* (Stanford, 1968), pp290-318.

The Palestine revolt

1 A W Kayyali, *Palestine: A Modern History* (London, 1973), p56.

2 See M Verete, "The Balfour Declaration and its Makers", *Middle Eastern Studies*, 6 (1970).

3 For an interesting discussion see A W Kayyali, "Zionism and Imperialism: The Historical Origins", *Journal of Palestine Studies*, 6 (1977).

4 S Tebeth, *Ben Gurion: The Burning Ground 1886-1948* (Boston 1987), pp85-91. Ben Gurion supported Turkey during the First World War because "Russia was the Jews' worst enemy in the world" (p91); G Sheffer, *Moshe Sharett* (Oxford, 1996), p24.

5 R Sharif, *Non-Jewish Zionism: Its Roots in Western History* (London, 1983), p122.

6 See A W Kayyali, "Zionism and Imperialism", pp107-108.

7 I Friedman, *The Question of Palestine 1914-1918* (London, 1973), pp38-39. See also J Kimche, *The Unromantics: the Great Powers and the Balfour Declaration* (London, 1968), pp3, 8 15-16.

8 D Lloyd George, *The Truth About The Peace Treaties*, 2 (London, 1938), pp1117, 1121, 1122, 1139. See also M Levene, "The Balfour Declaration: A Case of Mistaken Identity", *English Historical Review*, 107 (1992).

9 J Reinharz, "The Balfour Declaration and its Maker: A Reassessment", *Journal of Modern History*, 64 (1992), p496.

10 The standard work on the Balfour Declaration remains Leonard Stein, *The Balfour Declaration* (London, 1961). As for Balfour himself, he was an anti-Semite. When he was prime minister, his government had introduced the 1905 Aliens Act to rescue Britain from "the undoubted evils that had fallen upon the country from an immigration that was largely Jewish": M Egremont, *Balfour* (London, 1980), p205. Later he was to defend the declaration, for which he actually bore little personal responsibility, as something of benefit to "western civilisation" because it would remove a presence "too long regarded as alien and even hostile, but which it was equally unable to expel or absorb": J Tomes, *Balfour and Foreign Policy* (London, 1997), p206.

11 Samuel was home secretary at the time of the Easter Rising in Dublin and had gone along with the decision to hang Sir Roger Casement, which his biographer describes with some understatement "as one of the less creditable episodes in Samuel's career"—B Wasserstein, *Herbert Samuel: A Political Life* (Oxford, 1992), p185.

12 Viscount Samuel, *Memoirs* (London, 1945), pp156, 168.

13 S Huneidi, *A Broken Trust: Herbert Samuel, Zionism and the Palestinians* (London, 2001), pp22, 95,107. While acting as an adviser to the Zionist leaders before his appointment as high commissioner, Samuel had gone along with the "removal" of the Palestinians, but only "with some kind of financial inducement" and "with complete agreement and goodwill" (p91).

14 P A Smith, *Palestine and the Palestinians 1876-1983* (London, 1984), p33

15 M Y Muslih, *The Origins of Palestinian Nationalism* (New York, 1938), p71. See also N Mandel, *The Arabs and Zionism before World War 1* (Berkeley, 1980). He writes of Zionist immigrants being "genuinely taken aback to find Palestine inhabited by so many Arabs", p31.

16 A W Kayyali, *Palestine*, p64.

17 S K Farsoun with C Zacharia, *Palestine and the Palestinians* (Boulder Colorado, 1997), p71.

18 Y Porath, *The Emergence of the Palestinian-Arab National Movement 1918-1929* (London, 1974), p243.

19 According to Simha Flapan, the Revisionists had "earned for themselves a reputation as fascists due to the viciousness of their anti-socialist propaganda, their unbridled hatred of kibbutzim, their 'character assassinations', the unconcealed sympathy of some members towards authoritarian regimes (Hitler, for example, was described as the saviour of Germany, Mussolini as the political genius of the century), and their military parades, drills, training and brown shirts…resembled the fascist movements in Europe"—S Flapan, *Zionism and the Palestinians* (London, 1979), pp111-112. During the Second World War, Jabotinsky's successor, Abraham Stern, actually tried to ally the Revisionist movement with the Italians and the Germans. He proposed a Zionist state allied with Germany and urged the recruitment of an army of 40,000 European Jews, under Nazi auspices, to invade Palestine and drive the British out—see C Shindler, *Israel, Likud and the Zionist Dream* (London, 1995), p25. When Yitzhak Shamir, a follower of Stern, became Israeli prime minister in 1983, the peculiar trajectory of the Zionist right meant that Israel was the only country in the world led by a man who had regarded Hitler as an ally during the Second World War.

20 M Kolinsky, *Law, Order and Riots in Mandatory Palestine 1928-1935* (Basingstoke, 1993), p42.

21 Y Porath, *The Palestinian National Movement: From Riots To Rebellion 1929-1939* (London, 1977), pp39, 140. The immigration figures were, of course, for legal entry. There were thousands more people being illegally smuggled into the country.

22 N Barbour, *Nisi Dominus: A Survey of the Palestine Controversy* (London, 1946), p155.

23 W Khalidi, *Palestine Reborn* (London, 1992), p33.

24 G Antonius, *The Arab Awakening* (London, 1938), p411.

25 F R Nicosia, *The Third Reich and the Palestine Question* (London, 1935), pp57, 63, 161. See also K Polkehn, "The Secret Contacts: Zionism and Nazi Germany 1933-1941", *Journal of Palestine Studies*, 5 (1976), and G Deschner, *Heydrich* (London, 1981), pp149-152.

26 L Brenner, *Zionism in the Age of the Dictators* (London, 1983), p149.

27 P A Smith, *Palestine and the Palestinians*, pp52, 53.

28 For the Histadrut see Z Lockman, *Comrades and Enemies: Arab and Jewish Workers in Palestine 1906-1948* (Berkeley, 1996). See also Steven Glazer, "Picketing for Hebrew Labour: A Window on Histadrut

Tactics and Strategy", *Journal of Palestine Studies*, 30, 2001.

29 P A Smith, *Palestine and the Palestinians*, p54.

30 N Barbour, *Nisi Dominus*, p161.

31 P Mattar, *The Mufti of Jerusalem* (New York, 1988), p67.

32 A W Kayyali, *Palestine*, p181.

33 S Flapan, *Zionism and the Palestinians*, p141.

34 R Sayigh, *Palestinians: From Peasants To Revolutionaries* (London, 1979), p43.

35 Stephen Howe, for example, in his standard work, *Anticolonialism in British Politics: The Left and the End of Empire 1918-1964* (Oxford, 1993) does not mention the revolt.

36 P Mattar, *The Mufti of Jerusalem*, pp70, 71.

37 G Antonius, *The Arab Awakening*, p406.

38 Z Lockman, *Comrades*, p243.

39 Y Porath, *Palestinian National Movement: From Riot to Rebellion*, p171.

40 A W Kiyyali, *Palestine*, p196.

41 J Marlowe, *Rebellion in Palestine* (London, 1946), p160.

42 Y Heim, *Abandonment of Illusions: Zionist Political Attitudes Towards Palestinian Arab Nationalism 1936-1939* (Boulder, 1983), p88.

43 S Flapan, *Zionism and the Palestinians*, p263.

44 P Keleman, "Looking the Other Way: The British Labour Party, Zionism and the Palestinians", in C Collette and S Bird (eds), *Jews, Labour and the Left 1918-1948* (Aldershot, 2000), p147. Labour's commitment to Zionism came under serious strain when the Attlee government was in power. The Zionist settlement was seen as compromising the British position throughout the Middle East and this led to armed conflict. Once the British had evacuated Palestine, the Labour Party once again embraced Zionism.

45 Sir A Kirkbride, *A Crackle of Thorns* (London, 1956), pp99, 100.

46 A M Lesch, *Arab Politics in Palestine 1917-1939* (Ithaca, 1979), p124.

47 H Foot, *A Start In Freedom* (London, 1964), pp48-49.

48 E Keith-Roach, *Pasha of Jerusalem* (London, 1994), pp192-193.

49 A W Kayyali, *Palestine*, p215.

50 J Baynes, *The Forgotten Victor* (London, 1989), p52.

51 D Smiley, *Irregular Regular* (Norwich, 1994), pp15-16.

52 A J Sherman, *Mandate Days* (London, 1997), pp108-109.

53 E Keith-Roach, *Pasha of Jerusalem*, p191.

54 N Shepherd, *Ploughing The Sand: British Rule in Palestine* (London, 1999), p212.

55 C Townshend, *Britain's Civil Wars*, (London, 1986), p110.

56 C Bowyer, *RAF Operations 1918-1938*, (London, 1988), p142.

57 T Swedenburg, *Memories of Revolt: The 1936-1939 Rebellion and the Palestinian National Past* (Minneapolis, 1995), p109.

58 J Baynes, *The Forgotten Victor*, pp61-62.

59 H Foot, *A Start in Freedom*, pp51-52.

60 B Morris, *Righteous Victims: A History of the Zionist-Arab Conflict 1881-1999* (London, 1999), p47.

61 For Zionist relations with the Soviet Union see A Krammer, *The Forgotten Friendship: Israel and the Soviet Bloc 1947-1953* (Urbana, 1974).

Quit India

1 For Reginald Reynolds see his *My Life and Career* (London, 1956).

2 S R Bakshi, *Gandhi and the Mass Movement* (New Delhi, 1988), pp133-134.

3 S N Qanungo, "The Struggle for Purna Swaraj", in R Kumar, *A Centenary History of the Indian National Congress 1919-1935*, ii (Delhi, 1986), p212.

4 L Fischer, *Gandhi and the Mass Movement* (New York, 1950), pp298-299.

5   S R Bakshi, *Gandhi and the Mass Movement*, p142.

6   D G Tendulkar, *Abdul Ghaffar Khan* (Bombay, 1967), pp68-70.

7   S N Qanungo, "The Struggle for Purna Swaraj", pp239-240.

8   S Gopal, *The Viceroyalty of Lord Irwin 1926-1931* (Oxford, 1957), p73.

9   S Sen, *Working Class of India* (Calcutta, 1997), p284.

10 D Arnold, *Gandhi* (Harlow, 2001), p148.

11 S Wolpert, *Nehru: A Tryst With Destiny* (Oxford, 1996), p118. He was released at the end of January 1931 as part of moves towards the so-called Gandhi-Irwin Pact.

12 S Sarkar, *Modern India 1885-1947* (Basingstoke, 1983), p271.

13 For the Meerut trial see P Ghosh, *Meerut Conspiracy Case and the Left-Wing in India* (Calcutta, 1978).

14 One looks in vain in recent histories of the Labour Party for any account of the colonial repression in India during this period. There is no mention in Andrew Thorpe's *A History of the British Labour Party* (Basingstoke, 1997); in Duncan Tanner and others, *Labour's First Century* (Cambridge, 2000); or in Matthew Worley's *Labour Inside The Gate* (London 2005). Similarly with biographies of MacDonald: see D Marquand, *Ramsay MacDonald* (London, 1977), and A Morgan, *J Ramsay MacDonald* (Manchester, 1987).

15 S Wolpert, *Nehru*, p97.

16 J Nehru, *An Autobiography* (London, 1936), p176.

17 P S Gupta, "British Labour and the Indian Left", in his *Power, Politics and the People*, (London, 2002), p389.

18 J Nehru, *An Autobiography*, p174.

19 The popular outrage felt at Lajpat Rai's death prompted an underground revolutionary group, the Hindustan Socialist Republican Army, to shoot the police officer responsible, Superintendent J A Scott. Raj Guru and Bhagat Singh shot the wrong man, Assistant Superintendent J P Saunders, on 18 September 1928. The assassination was tremendously popular and widely regarded even within the ranks of the Congress as vindicating the nation's honour. See S R Bakshi, *Revolutionaries and the British Raj* (New Delhi, 1988).

20 B Porter, *Critics of Empire* (London, 1968), p185-186.

21 J R MacDonald, *Labour and the Empire* (London, 1907), pp108-109. MacDonald's sentiments were often positively Blairite, reflecting a shared taste for empty, pious rhetoric.

22 H H Tiltman, *James Ramsay MacDonald* (London, 1929), p247.

23 R Lyman, *The First Labour Government 1924* (London, 1957), p106.

24 P Ward, *Red Flag and Union Jack* (Woodbridge, 1998), p185.

25 A Roberts, *The Holy Fox* (Basingstoke, 1991), p39. In 1934 Irwin was to become Lord Halifax by which title he is best known as one of the architects of appeasement.

26 S Sarkar, *Modern India 1885-1947*, p322.

27 C Markovits, *Indian Business and Nationalist Politics* (Cambridge, 1985), pp77-78.

28 C Ponting, *Churchill* (London, 1994), p342.

29 MacDonald had actually suggested Thomas for the post, but the king had not been impressed with the idea and they had finally agreed on Lord Willingdon—H Tinker, *Viceroy: Curzon to Mountbatten* (Oxford, 1997), p127.

30 S Sarkar, *Modern India 1885-1947*, p321.

31 Under the 1935 act nearly 7 million adults had the vote (13.4 percent), and of the 250 seats in the Legislative Assembly, only 48 were elected by the general franchise; the rest were allocated to 17 different groups. This arrangement was

weighted very heavily against Congress. One of the 17 groups was the British who were allocated 25 seats (0.0004 percent of the population elected 10 percent of the seats). See M Bose, *Raj, Secrets, Revolution: A Life of Subhas Chandra Bose* (London, 2004), pp149-150.

32 R Chandravarkar, *Imperial Power and Popular Politics: Class, Resistance and the State* (Cambridge, 1998), p225.

33 S Sarkar, *Modern India 1885-1947*, p362.

34 C Markovits, *Indian Business and Nationalist Politics*, p168.

35 For the ILP in this period, see T Cliff and D Gluckstein, *The Labour Party: A Marxist History* (London, 1986).

36 For the Congress Socialist Party see A K Chaudhuri, *Socialist Movement in India 1934-1947* (Calcutta, 1980).

37 D N Panigrahi, *Quit India and the Struggle for Freedom* (New Delhi, 1984), pp13-14.

38 See M Bose, *Raj, Secrets, Revolution*, pp179-189.

39 This was eventually attached to the SS and, apparently quite horrifically, took part in operations against the French Resistance in 1944.

40 The standard account of the Cripps Mission is R J Moore, *Churchill, Cripps and India 1939-1945* (Oxford, 1979). See also N Owen, "The Cripps Mission of 1942: A Reinterpretation", *The Journal of Imperial and Commonwealth History*, 30 (2002).

41 A Sharma, *The Quit India Movement* (Delhi, 1992), p121.

42 The British had already discussed what to do if Gandhi went on hunger strike once he was arrested. Leo Amery, the secretary of state for India, on 3 August had argued that if "he insists on committing suicide, surely he might just as well do it". This he informed Linlithgow was the cabinet position. Linlithgow replied on the day of the arrests that the provincial governors were convinced that if Gandhi died in British custody there would be an "explosion of hatred which will get right down to the villages...we would have few friends left"—from N Massergh (ed), *Constituional Relations Between Britain and India: The Transfer of Power 1942-1947 vol II: Quit India 30 April-21 September 1942* (London, 1971) pp550, 632, 637.

43 Years later Francis Williams asked Attlee about his "ordering the arrest of Gandhi and Nehru" and was told, "Yes. It was necessary... If they chose to set themselves against the government in war they had to answer for it"—from F Williams, *A Prime Minister Remembers* (London, 1961), pp205-206.

44 A C Bhuyan, *The Quit India Movement* (New Delhi, 1975), p67.

45 R Callahan, *Churchill: Retreat From Empire* (Tunbridge Wells, 1984), p199.

46 D N Panigrahi, *Quit India and the Struggle for Freedom*, p25.

47 N Massergh, *Constituional Relations Between Britain and India*, p835.

48 D N Panigrahi, *India's Partition: A Story of Imperialism in Retreat* (London, 2004), pp236-237.

49 N Massergh, *Constituional Relations Between Britain and India*, pp662, 669, 707, 733-734, 853-854.

50 P Woodruff, *The Men Who Ruled India*, 2, (London, 1963), p308.

51 V Damodaran, *Broken Promises: Popular Protest, Indian Nationalism and the Congress Party in Bihar* (Delhi, 1992), p241; S Hanningham, "Quit India in Bihar and Eastern United Provinces: The Dual Revolt", from R Gruha (ed), *Subaltern Studies*, 11 (Delhi, 1983), p158; F Hutchins, *India's Revolution: Gandhi and the Quit India Movement* (Cambridge, Ma, 1973), pp242-243.

52 R H Niblett, *The Congress Rebellion in Azamgarh* (Allahabad, 1957), pp12-17. See also S Chakravarty, *Quit India Movement* (Delhi, 2002), p192.

53 F Hutchins, *India's Revolution*, p232.

54 For the revolutionary or parallel governments see in particular A K Jana, *Quit India Movement in Bengal* (Delhi, 1991); A B Shinde, *The Parellel Government of Satara* (New Delhi, 1990); and G Pandey (ed), *The Indian Nation in 1942* (Calcutta, 1989).

55 N B Bonarjee, *Under Two Masters* (London, 1970), pp190, 193.

56 R H Niblett, *The Congress Rebellion in Azamgarh*, pp26, 40, 41, 47.

57 S R Bakshi, *Congress and Quit India Movement* (New Delhi, 1986), pp276-277, 282.

58 D N Panigrahi, *Quit India and the Struggle for Freedom*, p7.

59 See S Sengupta and G Chatterjee, *Secret Congress Broadcasts and Storming Railway Tracks* (New Delhi, 1988).

60 See P Greenough, "Political Mobilization and the Underground Literature of the Quit India Movement 1942-44", *Modern Asian Studies*, 17 (1983).

61 V Damodaran, *Broken Promises*, p260.

62 J P Narayan, *Towards Struggle: Selected Manifestoes, Speeches and Writings* (Bombay, 1946), p47. See also V Nargolkar, *J P's Crusade For Revolution* (New Delhi, 1975).

63 B M Bhatia, *Famines in India* (Delhi, 1991), p321. See also P Greenough, *Poverty and Misery in Modern Bengal: The Famine of 1943-1944* (Oxford, 1982); and M S Veskataramani, *Bengal Famine of 1943: The American Response* (Delhi, 1973).

64 J Nehru, *Discovery of India* (London, 1947), p429.

65 S Gopal, "Churchill and India", in R Blake and W R Louis (eds), *Churchill* (Oxford, 1993), p465.

66 J Barnes and D Nicholson (eds), *The Empire At Bay: The Leo Amery Diaries 1929-1945* (London, 1988), pp943, 950.

67 P Moon (ed), *Wavell: The Viceroy's Journal* (London, 1973), pp54, 123.

68 S Gopal, "Churchill and India", pp465-466.

69 J Barnes and D Nicholson (eds), *The Empire at Bay*, pp812, 842; W R Louis, *In The Name of God Go! Leo Amery and the British Empire in the Age of Churchill* (New York, 1992), p172.

70 J Colville, *The Fringes of Power: Downing Street Diaries 1939-1955* (London, 1985), p563.

71 The subject is completely ignored in the more recent biographies—G Best, *Churchill: A Study in Greatness* (London, 2001); R Jenkins, *Churchill* (Basingstoke, 2001); P Addison, *Churchill: The Unexpected Hero* (Oxford, 2005). Even Martin Gilbert's massive *Road To Victory: Winston S Churchill 1941-1945* (London, 1986), in over 1,300 pages of text, has no space for the Bengal Famine.

72 N B Bonarjee, *Under Two Masters*, p294. As he points out, by the end of the war the Indian army was 2.5 million strong and during the conflict the Indian armed forces suffered over 30,000 men killed fighting for the British Empire.

73 N Owen, "'Responsibility Without Power': The Attlee governments and the end of British rule in India", in N Tiratsoo, *The Attlee Years* (London, 1991), pp167, 181. See also H V Brasted and C Bridge, "15 August 1947: Labour's Parting Gift To India", in J Masselos, *India: Creating A Modern Nation* (New Delhi, 1990).

74 A I Singh, *The Limits of British Influence: South Asia and the Anglo-American Relationship 1947-1956* (London 1993), p12.

75 R Pearce (ed), *Patrick Gordon Walker: Political Diaries 1932-1971* (London, 1991), pp23-24.

76 W R Louis, *Imperialism At Bay 1941-1945* (Oxford, 1977), p14.

77 B Pimlott, *Hugh Dalton* (London, 1985), p577.

78 A I Singh, *The Origins of Partition in India 1936-1947* (Delhi, 1987), pp146-147.

79 A M Wainwright, *Inheritance of Empire: Britain, India and the Balance of*

Power in Asia (Westport, Ct, 1994),
pp60, 62.

80 G Chattopadhyay, "Bengal Students
in Revolt Against the Raj 1945-46", in
A K Gupta (ed), Myth and Reality: The
Struggle for Freedom in India 1945-47
(New Delhi, 1987), p157.

81 G Chattopadhyay, "The Almost
Revolution: A Case Study of India in
February 1946", in Essays in Honour of
Professor S. C. Sarkar (New Delhi,
1976), pp431, 435.

82 S Sarkar, Modern India 1885-1947, pp423-
425. See also S Mahajan, "British
Policy, Nationalist Strategy and
Popular National Upsurge in 1945-46"
in A K Gupta (ed), Myth and Reality.

83 J Darwin, Britain and Decolonisation
(Basingstoke, 1988), p92.

84 P Moon (ed), Wavell, p399. For the
little-known A V Alexander see J
Tilley, Churchill's Favourite Socialist:
The Life of A V Alexander
(Manchester, 1995).

85 A Bullock, Ernest Bevin: Foreign
Secretary (London, 1983), pp360-361.

86 There has not been space here to deal
with issues of communalism. For
partition, however, see D N
Panigrahi, India's Partition (London,
2004), and A I Singh, The Origins of
Partition in Imdia 1936-1947.

87 A Campbell-Johnson, Mission With
Mountbatten (London, 1972), p221.

**The Suez invasion:
losing the Middle East**

1 E Shuckburgh, Descent to Suez: Diaries
1951-1956 (London, 1986), p187.

2 J Bill, "America, Iran and the politics
of intervention, 1951-1953", in J Bill
and W R Louis (eds), Musaddiq,
Iranian Nationalism and Oil (London,
1988), pp262-263.

3 E Abrahamian, "The 1953 Coup in
Iran", Science and Society, 65
(2001), p186.

4 As above, p193.

5 A Ansari, Modern Iran Since 1921
(London, 2003), p112.

6 E Abrahamian, "The 1953 Coup in
Iran", p189.

7 W R Louis, The British Empire in the
Middle East 1945-1951 (London, 1984),
p673.

8 N Owen, "Britain and decolonisation:
The Labour government and the
Middle East 1945-51", in M Cohen and
M Kolinsky (eds), Decline of the British
Empire in the Middle East (London,
1998), p5.

9 B Donoghue and G W Jones, Herbert
Morrison: Portrait of a Politician
(London, 1973), pp497-498.

10 W R Louis, The British Empire in the
Middle East 1945-1951, p675.

11 The best account of "Operation
Buccaneer" is in J Cable, Intervention
at Abadan: Plan Buccaneer (London,
1991). "This book", Cable wrote,
"relates how, in 1951, Britain planned
to use force in order to retain control
of the world's largest oil refinery...
Units of the British navy, army and air
force were deployed, given their
preparatory orders and, at one point,
brought to three hours'
notice...under strong pressure from
the President of the United States,
British forces were stood down,
British subjects withdrawn from
Abadan and oil-wells, pipelines and
refinery abandoned" (pix).

12 W R Louis, The British Empire in the
Middle East 1945-1951, p688.

13 For the coup see in particular M
Gasiorowski and M Byrne (eds),
Mohammad Mosaddeq and the 1953 Coup
in Iran (New York, 2004). Also S
Dorril, MI6 (London, 2000), and R J
Aldrich, The Hidden Hand: Britain,
America and Cold War Secret Intelligence
(London, 2001). And for its wider
significance see Z Karabell, Architects
of Intervention: The United States, the
Third World and the Cold War 1946-1962
(Baton Rouge, 1999).

14 W R Louis, The British Empire in the
Middle East 1945-1951, pp226, 227.

15 See M Mason, "Killing Time: The

THE BLOOD NEVER DRIED

British Army and its Antagonists in Egypt, 1945-1954", *War and Society*, 12 (1994), and C Tripp, "Egypt 1945-52: the Uses of Disorder", in M Cohen and M Kolinsky (eds), *Decline of the British Empire in the Middle East*.

16 J C Hurewitz, "The Historical Context" in W R Louis and R Owen, *Suez 1956: The Crisis and its Consequences* (Oxford, 1989), pp24-25.

17 M J Cohen, *Fighting World War Three from the Middle East* (London, 1997), pp132-142. In the end some £2 million was spent on developing Abu Sueir for B-29 use. The Egyptian government was, of course, never told of the plan to bomb the Soviet Union from its territory. When the Egyptian prime minister Mustafa Nahas Pasha was told by the British that the bases were necessary to protect Egypt against Russian attack, he quite correctly pointed out that the only reason the Russians had for attacking Egypt was the presence of British bases.

18 Anwar Sadat quoted in D Hopwood, *Egypt: Politics and Society 1945-1990* (London, 1993), p24.

19 P Hahn, *The United States, Great Britain and Egypt 1945-1956* (Chapel Hill, 1991), p133.

20 G Blaxland, *The Regiments Depart* (London, 1971), pp226, 230.

21 M Mason, "'The Decisive Volley': The Battle of Ismailia and the Decline of British Influence in Egypt, January-July 1952", *Journal of Imperial and Commonwealth History*, 19 (1991), p50.

22 D A Farnie, *East and West of Suez: The Suez Canal in History* (Oxford, 1969), p701.

23 D Williamson, *A Most Diplomatic General: The Life of General Lord Robertson of Oakridge* (London, 1996), p163.

24 M J Cohen, "The strategic role of the Middle East after the war", in M Cohen and M Kolinsky (eds), *Decline of The British Empire in the Middle East*, p33.

25 For recent biographies of Nasser see in particular S K Aburish, *Nasser: The Last Arab* (London, 2004), and A Alexander, *Nasser* (London, 2005).

26 M Holland, *America and Egypt: From Roosevelt to Eisenhower* (Westport, Ct, 1996), pp23, 28.

27 W R Louis, "Churchill and Egypt", in R Blake and W R Louis (eds), *Churchill*, (Oxford, 1993), p477.

28 E Shuckburgh, *Descent to Suez*, p75.

29 As above, p76.

30 Churchill hoped for an opportunity to attack the Egyptians right up until the last moment, but in the end the realities of the situation prevailed. The Egyptian bases were costing £56 million a year and the exchequer was demanding cuts in military spending of £180 million. There were just not the resources for another colonial war. Moreover, the army was itself increasingly sceptical of the value of bases that had to be defended against a hostile population. See W R Louis, "The Tragedy of the Anglo-Egyptian Settlement of 1954", in W R Louis and R Owen, *Suez 1956*, 1956.

31 S K Aburish, *Nasser*, p88.

32 A Nutting, *Nasser* (London, 1972), p126.

33 A Nutting, *No End of a Lesson: The Story of Suez* (London, 1967), pp36, 37.

34 E Shuckburgh, *Descent to Suez*, pp340, 341.

35 A Nutting, *No End of a Lesson*, pp35, 36. In the book Nutting uses the word "removal", but he later admitted that Eden had in fact said "murdered". For MI6's attempt to assassinate Nasser see S Dorrill, *MI6*, pp600-651.

36 For Operation Straggle see A Rathmell, *Secret War in the Middle East: The Covert Struggle for Syria 1949-1961* (London, 1995). This was a joint CIA-MI6 operation, but the Syrians involved called it off at the time of the Suez invasion "since any move against the Syrian government would

be regarded as being in league with Israel and the West" (p122).

37 W R Louis, "Harold Macmillan and the Middle East Crisis of 1958", *Proceedings of the British Academy*, 94 (1996), p211.

38 B Brivati, *Hugh Gaitskell* (London, 1997), p252.

39 P Cradock, *Know Your Enemy* (London, 2002), p116.

40 J Campbell, *Nye Bevan and the Mirage of British Socialism* (London, 1987), p319. The *Tribune* editorial line was strongly against the invasion.

41 W S Lucas, "The Missing Link? Patrick Dean, Chairman of the Joint Intelligence Committee", in S Kelly and A Gorst (eds), *Whitehall and the Suez Crisis* (London, 2000), p119.

42 For the Sèvres Protocol see A Shlaim, "The Protocol of Sèvres, 1956: Anatomy of a War Plot", in D Tal (ed), *The 1956 War* (London, 2001). At Sèvres the Israeli prime minister, David Ben Gurion, tried to interest his new allies in a "redivision" of the Middle East. Once Egypt had been dealt with he proposed that Israel should occupy Lebanon up to the Litani River, leaving a rump Christian state as a French protectorate. He also proposed the partition of Jordan, with Israel taking the West Bank, while Iraq, a British client, took the rest. These were too large ambitions for Britain and France.

43 M Dayan, *The Story of My Life* (New York, 1992), p196.

44 Sir H Trevelyan, *The Middle East in Revolution* (London, 1970), p105.

45 R A B Butler, *The Art of the Possible* (London, 1971), p192.

46 Lord Gladwyn, *The Memoirs of Lord Gladwyn* (London, 1972), pp283, 284.

47 M Heikal, *Cutting The Lion's Tail: Suez Through Egyptian Eyes* (London, 1988), p195.

48 S Meers, "The British Connection: How the United States Covered Its Tracks in the 1954 Coup in Guatamala", *Diplomatic History*, 16 (1992). She writes, "When the commander of the bombed ship *Springfiord* returned to London, he told the press that his crew had been silenced by the British diplomats in Guatemala, who also confiscated a roll of film documenting the sinking of the ship... British diplomats in Guatemala spent months deflecting inquiries and making sure that the *Springfiord's* aerial assailants remained unknown" (p426). See also T Petersen, *The Middle East Between The Great Powers: Anglo-American Conflict and Co-operation 1952-7* (Basingstoke, 2000), pp49-53.

49 H Macmillan, *Riding The Storm 1956-1959* (London, 1971), p157.

50 A Nutting, *No End of a Lesson*, p116.

51 J Amery, "The Suez Group: A Retrospective on Suez", in S I Troes and M Shemesh (eds), *The Suez-Sinai Crisis: Retrospective and Reappraisal* (London, 1990), p121. He put American behaviour down to "Washington's determination to break the British predominance in the Middle East". The defeat led to "a collapse of the will to rule" (pp119-120, 124).

52 B Johnson and E Bramall, *The Chiefs* (London, 1992), p301.

53 S Lloyd, *Suez 1956: A Personal Account* (London, 1978), pp78, 93.

54 R Ovendale, *Anglo-American Relations in the Twentieth Century* (Basingstoke, 1998), p120.

55 Lord Kilmuir, *Political Adventure* (London, 1964), p278. As home secretary, Kilmuir had refused clemency for Derek Bentley in the 1952 Croydon police shooting despite the jury's recommendation. Bentley was hanged so as to maintain police morale, See S Chibnall, *Law-And-Order News* (London, 1977), pp56-60.

56 See N J Ashton, *Eisenhower, Macmillan and the Problem of Nasser* (Basingstoke, 1996), pp100-101.

57 There is a growing literature on the Iraqi Revolution of 1958 but see in

particular H Batatu, *The Old Social Classes and the Revolutionary Movements of Iraq* (Princeton, 1978).

58   H Macmillan, *Riding The Storm 1956-1959*, p511.

59   W R Louis, "Harold Macmillan and the Middle East Crisis of 1958", in *Proceedings of the British Academy*, 94 (1996).

Crushing the Mau Mau in Kenya

1   E Huxley, *White Man's Country*, 1 (London 1935), p157.

2   G H Mungeam, *British Rule in Kenya 1895-1912* (Oxford, 1966), pp84, 143, 161, 164. Charles Eliot, a future vice-chancellor of Sheffield University and ambassador to Japan, confessed in his account of the protectorate that he was "not sanguine as to the future of the African race". When discussing white settlement, he wrote with almost prophetic insight that the part of the country "where the land question is likely to present real difficulties is Kikuyu, as here we have the combination of a climate and country suitable for Europeans and a numerous native population". He insisted that "the interior of the Protectorate is a white man's country" but there would be a place for the Africans as labourers on the white men's farms—*The East African Protectorate* (London, 1905), pp103, 104, 304.

3   A Wipper, "The Gusii Rebels", in R I Rotberg, *Rebellion in Black Africa* (Oxford, 1971), pp167-169.

4   G H Mungeam, *British Rule in Kenya 1895-1912*, p195.

5   C G Rosberg and J Nottingham, *The Myth of Mau Mau* (New York, 1966), p15.

6   N Leys, *Kenya* (London, 1924), p350.

7   E Huxley, *The Flame Trees of Thika* (London, 1959), p16.

8   Lord Cranforth, *A Colony In The Making* (London, 1912), pp85, 173.

9   F Furedi, "The Social Composition of the Mau Mau Movement in the White Highlands", *Journal of Peasant Studies*, 4 (1974).

10   D Anderson, *Histories of the Hanged* (London, 2005), p200.

11   See D Barnett and K Njama, *Mau Mau From Within* (London, 1966), pp54-55. See also S Carruthers, *Winning Hearts and Minds: British Governments, the Media and Colonial Counter-Insurgency 1944-1960* (Leicester, 1995), p132. For a recent discussion of the origins of the Mau Mau name see J Lonsdale, "Authority, Gender and Violence: The War Within Mau Mau's Fight for Land and Freedom", in E S Atieno Odhiambo and J Lonsdale (eds), *Mau Mau and Nationhood* (London, 2003), pp59-60.

12   For the role of the trade unions see F D Corfield, *Historical Survey of the Origins and Growth of Mau Mau* (London, 1960), pp255-258. See also S Stichter, "Workers, Trade Unions and the Mau Mau Rebellion", *Canadian Journal of African Studies*, 9 (1975). For the general strike see M Singh, *History of Kenya's Trade Union Movement to 1952* (Nairobi, 1969), pp274-279; and most recently D Hyde, "The Nairobi General Strike 1950: From protest to insurgency", *Azania*, 36-37 (2001-2002).

13   F D Corfield, *Historical Survey of the Origins and Growth of Mau Mau*, p159.

14   A Clayton, *Counter-Insurgency in Kenya 1952-1960* (Nairobi, 1976), p7.

15   For the most recent account of the Lari massacre and of the reprisals, both official and unofficial, that followed it, see D Anderson, *Histories of the Hanged*, pp19-180.

16   The most recent account of the trial is J Lonsdale, "Kenyatta's Trials: Breaking and Making an African Nationalist", in P Coss (ed), *The Moral World of the Law* (Cambridge, 2000); but see also D N Pritt, *The Defence Accuses* (London, 1966), and P Evans, *Law and Disorder* (London, 1956).

17 *Report to the Secretary of State for the Colonies by the Parliamentary Delegation to Kenya 1954* (London, 1954), p7.

18 Sir M Blundell, *So Rough a Wind* (London, 1960), pp170-171.

19 A Clayton and D Savage, *Government and Labour in Kenya* (London 1974), p389. Tom Askwith, the official put in charge of the authorities' rehabilitation programme, actually argued that internment was a form of social welfare. In his memoirs, he wrote, "If my assessment that the Mau Mau constituted a form of Spartacus uprising of the unemployed and landless Kikuyu is accepted then detention enabled them at least to be fed, sheltered and provided with useful and acceptable employment"—from T Askwith, *From Mau Mau to Harambee* (Cambridge, 1995), p112.

20 M Carver, *Out of Step* (London, 1989), p261.

21 For the Kikuyu experience of resettlement see C Elkins, *Britain's Gulag: The Brutal End of Empire in Kenya* (London, 2005).

22 For the counter-gangs see my "A Counter-Insurgency Tale: Kitson in Kenya", *Race and Class*, 31 (1990).

23 R Edgerton, *Mau Mau: An African Crucible* (London, 1990), pp144, 159.

24 C Elkins, *Britian's Gulag*, p87. For an enthusiastic firsthand account of police activity including the torture and murder of prisoners, both men and women, see W Baldwin, *Mau Mau Movement* (New York, 1957).

25 D Anderson, *Histories of the Hanged*, p313.

26 As above, p353.

27 M Gilbert, *New Despair: Winston Churchill 1945-1965* (London, 1988), p834; S Carruthers, *Winning Hearts and Minds*, p176.

28 F Kitson, *Gangs and Counter-Gangs* (London, 1960), p46.

29 D Anderson, *Histories of the Hanged*, pp199-200.

30 P Murphy, *Alan Lennox-Boyd* (London, 1999), p210. Lennox-Boyd had famously turned up to blackleg during the general strike in top hat and tails. He was sympathetic to the British Union of Fascists in the 1930s, and had been one of a number of Conservative MPs who were members of Mosley's January Club, a BUF front intended to maintain links with the Conservatives. His fascist sympathies did not stop him becoming a junior minister in 1938. After his retirement he was to be one of the founders of the Monday Club, a racist organisation conceived very much along the lines of the January Club.

31 C Leys, *Underdevelopment in Kenya* (London, 1976), pp39, 42.

32 C Elkins, *Britain's Gulag*, p355.

33 D Percox, *Britain, Kenya and the Cold War* (London, 2004), pp171, 173-174.

34 P Clarke, *Hope and Glory: Britain 1900-1990* (London, 1996).

35 A Verrier, *The Road To Zimbabwe 1890-1930* (London, 1986), p19.

36 F C Selous, *Sunshine and Storm in Rhodesia* (London, 1896), p46.

37 F Sykes, *With Plumer in Matebeleland* (London, 1897) pp4, 8.

38 R Blake, *A history of Rhodesia* (London 1977), p114. See also R Rotberg, *The Founder: Cecil Rhodes and the Pursuit of Power* (Johannesburg, 1988), pp557-562.

39 R Baden-Powell, *The Matabele Campaign 1896* (London, 1897), p64. Baden-Powell's execution of Chief Unwini caused considerable controversy at the time—see T Jeal, *Baden-Powell* (London 1989), pp180-185.

40 The best account of this episode remains T O Ranger, *Revolt in Southern Rhodesia 1896-7* (London, 1979).

41 P Ziegler, *Wilson* (London, 1993), p276.

42 H Strachan, *The Politics of the British Army* (Oxford, 1997), p178.

THE BLOOD NEVER DRIED

43　See M Bailey, *Oilgate: The Sanctions Scandal* (London, 1979).

44　For the second *Chimurenga* see D Martin and P Johnson, *The Struggle for Zimbabwe* (London, 1981).

Malaya and the Far East

1　W S Churchill, *The Hinge of Fate* (London, 1951), p81.

2　Lord Moran, *Winston Churchill: The Struggle for Survival 1940-1965* (London, 1968), p43.

3　For these developments see S Tonnesson, *The Vietnamese Revolution of 1945* (London, 1991). One British historian has compared the American refusal to support the French in Vietnam at this time with the conduct "of the Russians towards the Warsaw rising the year before"— D C Watt, *Succeeding John Bull* (Cambridge, 1984), p239. See also J Saville, *The Politics of Continuity: British Foreign Policy and the Labour Government 1945-46* (London 1993).

4　P Ziegler, *Mountbatten* (London, 1985), p331.

5　G Rosie, *The British in Vietnam* (London, 1970), p70. For a recent academic discussion see J Springhall, "'Kicking Out The Vietminh': How Britain Allowed France to Re-occupy South Indochina 1946-46", *Journal of Contemporary History*, 40 (2005).

6　P M Dunn, *The First Vietnam War* (New York, 1985), p264.

7　G Rosie, *The British in Vietnam*, p75.

8　E Taylor, *Richer By Asia* (Boston, 1947), p386.

9　R Singh, *Official History of the Indian Armed Forces in the Second World War: Post-War Occupation Forces* (Delhi, 1958), p199.

10　H Isaacs, *No Peace for Asia* (New York, 1947), pp127-128.

11　A J F Doulton, *The Fighting Cock* (Aldershot, 1951), p243.

12　A Roadnight, "Sleeping With the Enemy: Britain, Japanese Troops and the Netherlands East Indies 1945-1946", *History*, 87 (2002), pp254-255.

13　For a reconstruction of Mallaby's death see J G A Parrott, "Who Killed Brigadier Mallaby?", *Indonesia*, 20 (1975), and J Springhall, "'Disaster in Surabaya': The Death of Brigadier Mallaby during the British Occupation of Java 1945-1946", *Journal of Imperial and Commonwealth History*, 24 (1966). See also R McMillan, *The British Occupation of Indonesia 1945-1946* (London, 2005), pp31-58.

14　Sir D Lee, *Eastward* (London, 1984), p49.

15　D Wehl, *The Birth of Indonesia* (London, 1948), p66.

16　C R B Knight, *Historical Records of the Buffs 1919-1948* (London, 1951), pp432-433. A recent academic account of the battle of Surabaya is provided by D Jordan, "'A Particularly Exacting Operation': British Forces and the Battle for Surabaya, November 1946", *Small Wars and Insurgencies*, 11 (2000).

17　P Dennis, *Troubled Days of Peace* (Manchester, 1987), pp133, 246.

18　M C Ricklefs, *A History of Modern Indonesia* (London, 1980), p205.

19　J Smail, *Bandung in the Early Revolution* (New York, 1964), pp151-152.

20　A Reid, *The Blood of the People* (Kuala Lumpur, 1979), p169.

21　P Dennis, *Troubled Days of Peace*, p149.

22　L Allen, *The End of the War in Asia* (London, 1976), p95.

23　Neither Kenneth Morgan's *Labour in Power 1945-1951* (Oxford, 1984) nor Peter Hennessey's *Never Again: Britain 1945-1951* (London, 1972) mention the episode. Nor does Trevor Burridge's *Clement Attlee* (London, 1985) or Francis Beckett's *Clem Attlee* (London, 1997). The silence is deafening.

24　For a British account of life with the Communist guerrillas during the Japanese occupation see S Chapman, *The Jungle is Neutral* (London, 1949).

For the Malayan People's Anti-Japanese Army see C Boon Kheng, *Red Star Over Malaya* (Singapore, 1983).

25 H W Yin, *Clans and Communalism in Malaya* (London, 1983), pp76-85.

26 For Chin Peng see his remarkable memoir, *Alias Chin Peng: My Side of History* (Singapore, 2003), and a series of academic discussions with him— C C Chin and K Hack (eds), *Dialogues With Chin Peng: New Light on the Malaysian Communist Party* (Singapore, 2004).

27 T N Harper, *The End of Empire and the Making of Malaya* (Cambridge, 1999), p138.

28 M Morgan, "The Rise and Fall of Malayan Trade Unionism", in M Amin and M Caldwell (ed), *Malaya: The Making of a Neo-Colony* (Nottingham, 1977), p182. See also M Stenson, *Industrial Conflict in Malaya* (London, 1970).

29 M Morgan, "The Rise and Fall of Malayan Trade Unionism", p157, and R Ovendale, "Britain and the Cold War in Asia", in R Ovendale (ed), *The Foreign Policy of the British Labour Government 1945-51* (Leicester, 1984), p125.

30 N J White, *Business, Government and the End of Empire* (Kuala Lumpur, 1996), p5.

31 Sir R Thompson, *Make For The Hills* (London, 1989), p94.

32 M Caldwell, "From 'Emergency' to 'Independence' 1945-1957", in M Amin and M Caldwell, *Malaya*, pp221-222; A Short, *The Communist Insurrection in Malaya 1948-1960* (London, 1975), pp383-385.

33 Sir R Thompson, *Make For The Hills*, p93.

34 For Batang Kali see B Lapping, *End of Empire* (London, 1985), pp168-169.

35 S Carruthers, *Winning Hearts and Minds: British Governments, the Media and Colonial Counter-Insurgency* (London, 1995), p100.

36 For the Briggs Plan see in particular R Clutterbuck, *The Long War* (London, 1966), and Sir R Thompson, *Defeating Communist Insurgency* (London, 1966). Both books were written very much with the Vietnam War in mind.

37 For Templer's career see J Cloake, *Templer: Tiger of Malaya* (London, 1985). Templer was strongly in favour of invading Iraq in 1958.

38 As above, p260.

39 P F Cecil, *Herbicidal Warfare* (New York, 1986), p17.

40 J Cloake, *Templer*, p254.

41 A Chin, *The Communist Party of Malaya* (Kuala Lumpur, 1995), p50.

42 See I Beckett, "Robert Thompson and the British Advisory Mission to South Vietnam in 1961-1965", *Small Wars and Insurgencies*, 8 (1997), and J P Cross, *In Gurkha Company* (London, 1986), p23.

43 There is a huge literature on the Malayan Emergency but a number of books deserve mention: R Clutterbuck, *The Long Long War* (London, 1966); A Short, *The Communist Insurrection In Malaya 1948-1960* (London, 1977); R Stubbs, *Hearts and Minds in Guerilla Warfare* (London, 1989); and K Hack, *Defence and De-colonisation in Southeast Asia: Britain, Malaya and Singapore 1941-68* (Richmond, 2001).

44 D Easter, *Britain and the Confrontation with Indonesia 1960-66* (London, 2004), p5.

45 See K Conboy, *Feet To The Fire: CIA Covert Operations in Indonesia 1957-1958* (Annapolis, Md, 2000), and M Jones, "'Maximum Disavowable Aid': Britain, the United States and the Indonesian Rebellion 1957-58", *English Historical Review*, 114 (1999).

46 D Healey, *The Time of My Life* (London, 1990), pp287-290.

47 J Wylie, *The Influence of British Arms* (London, 1984), p68.

48 D Easter, "British and Malaysian Covert Support for Rebel Movements in Indonesia during the 'Confrontation' 1963-66", in R J

Aldrich, Gary D Rawnsley and Ming-Yeh T Rawnsley (eds), *The Clandestine Cold War in Asia 1945-65* (London, 2000).

49 G Simons, *Indonesia: The Long Oppression* (Basingstoke, 2000), p181.

50 D Easter, *Britain and the Confontation with Indonesia 1960-1966*, pp167, 170. See also J Subritzky, *Confronting Sukarno* (Basingstoke, 2000), pp175-176.

51 M Curtis, *Web of Deceit* (London, 2003), p193.

Britain and the American Empire

1 P Knightley, *The First Casualty* (London, 2003), pp374-375.

2 C MacDonald, *Korea: The War Before Vietnam* (Basingstoke, 1986), pp84-85.

3 P Knightley, *The First Casualty*, pp377-378, and T Shaw, "The Information Research Department of the British Foreign Office and the Korean War 1950-53", *Journal of Contemporary History*, 34 (1999).

4 For an path-breaking account of the British warfare state see D Edgerton, *Warfare State: Britain 1920-1970* (Cambridge, 2005).

5 P Jones, *America and the British Labour Party* (London, 1997), pp57,59.

6 See L V Scott, *Conscription and the Attlee Government* (Oxford, 1993).

7 S Duke, *US Defence Bases in the United Kingdom* (Basingstoke, 1987), p35.

8 P Lowe, *The Origins of the Korean War* (London, 1986), p177.

9 C MacDonald, *Korea*, p71. As he notes, on 20 November, the US administration did indeed authorise a study on "the use of the bomb against military targets in Korea, Manchuria and China".

10 W Stueck, *Rethinking The Korean War* (Princeton, 2004), p125.

11 Attlee, it is worth remembering, had supported the atom bombing of Hiroshima and Nagasaki—see T Burridge, *Clement Attlee* (London, 1985), p237. What General MacArthur proposed was the use of at least 26 atom bombs (he later said he would have used between 20 and 50) which would, he believed, have won the war—see B Cumings, *Korea's Place In The Sun* (New York, 1997), p291.

12 S Greenwood, "'A War We Don't Want': Another Look at the British Labour Government's Commitment in Korea 1950-51", *Contemporary British History*, 17 (2003), p19.

13 C MacDonald, *Korea*, p258.

14 A R Millett, *Their War for Korea* (Washington DC, 2002), p266.

15 Only two Labour MPs, S O Davies and Emrys Hughes, actually voted against British participation in the Korean War, although a number of others opposed it privately. Supporters of the war included many on the left of the Labour Party, among them Fenner Brockway, Michael Foot and, of course, Aneurin Bevan. See K Morgan, *Labour In Power* (Oxford 1984), pp424-425.

16 R N Rosencrance, *Defense of the Realm* (New York, 1968), pp140-141. See also J Dumbrell, *A Special Relationship: Anglo-American Relations in the Cold War and After* (Basingstoke, 2001), p45.

17 The king, George VI, told Gaitskell that he was right behind him with regard to NHS charges: "I really don't see why people should have false teeth free any more than they should have shoes free." This was, of course, particularly rich coming from someone who did not pay for false teeth, shoes or anything else for that matter. Gaitskell's wife, Dora, assured the King that her husband was "rather right wing", which apparently everyone thought hilarious. See P Hennessy, *Never Again: Britain 1945-1951* (London, 1992), p417.

18 When one strips away Labour's self-serving triumphalism, "the statistical sources show that post-war Britain was a low spender on social services by comparison with European

nations. By contrast British defence expenditures, after the Second World War, were high by Continental European standards." See D Edgerton, *Warfare State*, p68.

19 G W Davies, "Brothers in arms: Anglo-American Defence Cooperation in 1957", in J Gorst, L Johnson and W S Lucas (eds), *Postwar Britain 1945-1964* (London, 1989), pp206-207.

20 I Clark, *Nuclear Diplomacy and the Special Relationship: Britain's Deterrent and America 1957-1962* (Oxford, 1994), p10.

21 J Dumbrell, *A Special Relationship*, p126.

22 R Aldrich, *The Hidden Hand: Britain, America and Cold War Intelligence* (London, 2001), p609.

23 D Reynolds, *Britannia Overruled* (Harlow, 1991), p216.

24 R Hathaway, *Great Britain and the United States: Special Relations since World War II* (Boston 1990), p44. See also J Prados, *Operation Vulture* (New York, 2002), pp221-222. One Democratic senator urging Eisenhower to intervene militarily in Indochina was Lyndon Johnson, no less (p125).

25 See P Busch, "Killing the Vietcong: The British Advisory Mission and the Strategic Hamlet Programme", *Journal of Strategic Studies*, 25 (2002). See also P Busch, *All The Way With JFK: Britain, the US and the Vietnam War* (Oxford, 2003).

26 For the Vietnam Solidarity Campaign see in particular D Widgery, *The Left In Britain 1956-1968* (London, 1976), and T Ali, *Street-Fighting Years* (London, 2005).

27 C Wilson, "Rhetoric, Reality and Dissent: The Vietnam Policy of the British Labour Government 1964-1970", *Social Science Journal*, 23 (1986), p22.

28 J W Young, *The Labour Governments 1964-1970: International Policy* (Manchester, 2003), p75.

29 J Neale, *The American War: Vietnam 1960-1975* (London, 2001), p62.

30 J Dumbrell, *A Special Relationship*, p154. When the Americans attacked Falluja in Iraq in November 2004, somewhat symbolically Tony Blair sent the Black Watch to assist their assault.

31 For the seizure of what became British Guiana, see Chapter 1.

32 S Rabe, *US Intervention in British Guiana* (Chapel Hill, 2005), pp93, 134.

33 J Campbell, *Edward Heath* (London, 1993), pp341-342, 344, 350.

34 C Meyer, *DC Confidential* (London, 2005), p1.

35 The best account of George W Bush is M C Miller's *The Bush Dyslexicon* (New York, 2002). See also his *Cruel and Unusual: Bush/Cheney's New World Order* (New York, 2004). Bush is, of course, in reality merely the mascot for a team of professionals dominated by vice-president Dick Cheney and secretary for defence Donald Rumsfield. For Cheney see J Nichols, *Dick: The Man Who Is President* (New York, 2004).

36 For a recent account see S Lansley, *Rich Britain: The Rise and Rise of the New Super-Wealthy* (London, 2006).

37 For New Labour and business see D Osler, *New Labour PLC* (Edinburgh, 2002). For the privatisation of the NHS see Allyson Pollock, *NHS PLC* (London, 2004).

38 D Coates and J Krieger, *Blair's War* (Cambridge, 2004), pp106-107.

39 Although Clare Short established herself as one of the scourges of New Labour "spin", she conveniently neglects to tell readers of her *An Honourable Deception?* (London, 2004) about her department's sponsorship of privatisation and the lucrative contracts awarded to the Adam Smith Institute. For this relationship see the War On Want study by J Hilary, *Profiting From Poverty* (London, 2004).

THE BLOOD NEVER DRIED

40 For American Imperialism today see in particular A Callinicos, *The New Mandarins of American Power: The Bush Administration's Plans for the World* (Oxford, 2003), and V K Fouskas and B Gokay, *The New American Imperialism* (Westport Cn, 2005).

41 From the right, P Oborne has dissected New Labour mendacity in his *The Rise of Political Lying* (London, 2005), and from the left, see N Fairclough in his *New Labour, New Language?* (London, 2002), which gives a more theoretical approach. See also L Panitch and C Leys (eds), *Socialist Register 2006: Telling The Truth* (London, 2005), for an international perspective.

42 For Campbell see P Oborne and S Walters, *Alistair Campbell* (London, 2004).

43 J Kampfner, *Blair's Wars* (London, 2004), pp16-17, 28.

44 R Fisk, *The Great War for Civilization* (London, 2005), p871.

45 M Curtis, *Web of Deceit: Britain's Role in the World* (London, 2003), pp134-141. See also M Haynes, "Theses on the Balkan War", *International Socialism*, 83 (1999).

46 For America's longstanding relationship with Islamism see R Dreyfuss, *Devil's Game: How The United States Helped Unleash Fundamentalist Islam* (New York, 2005). See also M Mamdani, *Good Muslim, Bad Muslim: America, the Cold War and the Roots of Terror* (New York, 2005).

47 See W Blum, *Killing Hope: US Military and CIA Interventions Since World War II* (London 2003). See also J Risen, *State of War: The Secret History of the CIA and the Bush Administration* (New York, 2006), for more recent developments. For the CIA's long involvement in torture see A McCoy, *A Question of Torture: CIA Interrogation from the Cold War to the War On Terror* (New York, 2006).

48 See M Begg and V Brittain, *Enemy Combatant: A British Muslim's Journey to Guantanamo and Back* (New York, 2006). For the New Labour government's shameful "rendering" of British residents into American hands see G Mickum, "Britain's Shadowy Role in the Guantanamo scandal", in the *Independent*, 16 March 2006.

49 For the Blair government's attempts to create a climate of fear for domestic purposes see P Oborne, *The Use and Abuse of Terror: The Construction of a False Narrative on the Domestic Terror Threat* (London, 2006). For the ricin plot that never was see in particular pp21-25.

50 See T Ali, *Rough Music: Blair, Bombs, Baghdad, London, Terror* (London, 2005), and M Rai, *7/7: The London Bombings, Islam and the Iraq War* (London, 2006).

51 See J Kampfner, *Blair's Wars*, and more recently S Kettel, *Dirty Politics? New Labour, British Democracy and the Invasion of Iraq* (London, 2006).

52 For the Stop the War Coalition and the great 15 February demonstration see A Murray and L German's marvellous *Stop The War: The Story of Britain's Biggest Mass Movement* (London, 2003). For the invasion's illegality see P Sands, *Lawless World* (London, 2006), pp174-204.

53 See R Cook's *The Point of Departure* (London, 2004) for a forensic demolition of the Blair case for war. Wisely perhaps, the book does not deal with his own period at the Foreign Office. He was sacked as foreign secretary by Blair because he would not have been acceptable to the Bush administration, and was replaced by Jack Straw, an inoffensive nonentity, who could be relied on to do what he was told. He was himself sacked in May 2006 for publicly expressing scepticism about the need to attack Iran.

54 For George Galloway see his *I'm Not The Only One* (London, 2005).

55 G Dyke, *Inside Story* (London, 2004), p314. Dyke, a former New Labour supporter, summed up Alistair Campbell, with admirable restraint, as "a deranged, vindictive bastard" (p31). It should be noted here that under Dyke the BBC had maintained a scandalous news blackout with regard to the Stop the War movement. The largest protest movement in British history went virtually unreported by the Corporation.a

56 See in particular R Fisk, *The Great War for Civilization*; P Rogers, *Iraq and the War on Terror: Twelve Months of Insurgency 2004/2005* (London, 2006), and C Parenti, *The Freedom: Shadows and Hallucinations in Occupied Iraq* (New York, 2004).

Index

general strike forces retreat from war with Soviet Union, 101; overextended, 101; Anglo-Irish Treaty (1921) a "victory for Empire", 106; maintains Egypt as client state, 109; India most serious post First World War challenge, 109; ambitions frustrated by Bolsheviks, 118-119; facing challenge from Japan and United States in China, 119; interest in Palestine primarily strategic, 122; and Zionism, 122; establishment of Israel a major blow, 140; Japan deals crushing blows, 151; shaken by Quit India revolt, 157; dominance in Middle East collapses in 1950s, 164; exploits Iran's oil, 165; lacks troops to occupy Iran, 166; shift in relative position with US over oil interests in Iran, 168; unable to reoccupy Egypt, 171; conspires with France and Israel to attack Egypt, 175; Suez a desperate gamble, 176; American hostility to independent action over Suez, 177; Gaullist option, 179-180; alliance with US after Suez, 180; "de-colonisation" in Africa, 182; unprecedented savagery in defeat of Mau Mau, 190; divergence of interests from white settlers in Kenya, 194; loss of Singapore (1942), 198; act of colonial generosity towards French and Dutch, 199; economic importance of Malaya rubber, 207; motives for establishing Malaysia, 211; Second World War leaves Britain dependent on rival US, 215; double threat from Soviet Union and nationalist unrest, 216; "unequal alliance" and creation of warfare state, 216; defence spending higher than US, 219; greatest humiliation in post war period, 220; different trajectory to French state, 221; debate over Europe, 221; no alternative to US alliance, 221; dependency on US bomb, 221-223; reasons for rejection of Gaullist option, 227; US alliance sacrosanct, 237
British Guiana, 24, 225-226
Brittain, V, 267
Brivati, B, 260
Brixton Prison, 103
Brockway, Fenner, 144, 159, 193, 265

Broin, L O, 244
Brown, Gordon, 10, 215, 229
Brown, J M, 250
Bruce, Frederick, 59, 60
Bruce, G, 245
Bruner, K, 245
Buckley, R N, 240
Bullock, A, 258
Burchell, Thomas, 28
Burma, 66, 67, 68, 152, 157, 167, 198, 199, 204, 207, 235, 244
Burnett-Stuart, Major General, 115
Burnham, Forbes, 225, 226
Burr, Sidney, 138
Burridge, Trevor, 263, 265
Busch, P, 266
Bush, B, 239
Bush, George W, 176, 180, 228, 233
Butler, R A B, 176, 260
Butler, William, 94, 248, 249
Byrne, J, 248
Byrne, M, 258
Byrnes (US Secretary of State), 216

Cable, J, 258
Caldwell, M, 264
Callahan, R, 256
Callinicos, A, 267
Cambodia, 224
Cameron, James, 214
Campbell, Alistair, 231, 236, 268
Campbell, Colin, 78
Campbell, John, 226, 227, 260, 266
Campbell, M, 239, 240
Campbell-Johnson, A, 258
Canning, Lord, 71, 80
Carruthers, S, 261, 262, 264
Carthage, 244
Carver, M, 262
Casement, Roger, 252
Castle, Barbara, 193
Castro, Fidel, 222
Catholic Emancipation, 29, 33
Cecil, P F, 264
Ceylon (Sri Lanka), 167, 244
Chakravarty, S, 256
Chamberlain, Joseph, 123
Chamberlain, M E, 248
Chamberlain, N, 137, 139, 140
Chambers, J, 243

INDEX

THE BLOOD NEVER DRIED